UNIFORMS OF
THE CIVIL WAR

UNIFORMS OF THE CIVIL WAR

Ron Field & Robin Smith

The Lyons Press

Guilford, Connecticut

An imprint of The Globe Pequot Press

First Lyons Press edition, 2001

First published in Great Britain in 2001 by Brassey's,
a division of Chrystalis Books plc

Copyright © 2001 by Brassey's

The text for this edition originally appeared in two separate volumes. *American Civil War, Union Army* by Robin Smith; and *American Civil War, Confederate Army* by Ron Field, published by Brassey's in 1996. This edition has been updated with a new introduction by Ron Field and a revised selection of illustrations.

The Lyons Press is an imprint of The Globe Pequot Press

Production by Omnipress, Eastbourne

Printed and bound in Italy

ISBN 1-58574-422-0

10 9 8 7 6 5 4 3 2 1

The Library of Congress Cataloging-in-Publication Data is available on file.

Contents

Introduction   6

Uniforms of the Union Army   21
    U.S. Regulation Infantry   24
    U.S. Cavalry and Artillery   46
    Color Plate Section I   49
    U.S. Generals, Staff, and Special Units   74
    Zouaves and Militia Units   86
    Color Plate Section II   97
    Union State Uniforms   113
    Insignia and Medals   125

Uniforms of the Confederate Army   139
    South Carolina   142
    Color Plate Section III   145
    Mississippi   165
    Florida   174
    Alabama   178
    Georgia   186
    Color Plate Section IV   193
    Louisiana   203
    Texas   210
    Virginia   219
    Arkansas   231
    Tennessee   238
    North Carolina   243
    Missouri   250
    Kentucky   254
    Maryland   257
    Confederate Quartermaster Issue   261

Bibliography   272
Civil War Directory   278
Index   284

Introduction

The Civil War was a turning point in American history. During the campaigns and battles which raged from 1861 to 1865, approximately 620,000 Americans died, representing 4 per cent of the male population. The causes of this 'irrepressible conflict' concerned slavery and Southern nationalism, and spanned decades of debate, compromise, and concession before finally boiling over into secession in 1860. By that time the Democratic Party, which for generations had championed the cause of Southern Rights, had split into rival factions and presented two nominees for the Presidency, while the emerging Republican Party nominated Abraham Lincoln, an avowed opponent of the further expansion of slavery. With the Democratic Party so divided, it became obvious that the schism would result in a Republican victory. Declaring that 'Government cannot endure permanently half slave, half free . . .', Lincoln was elected president of the United States on

Left: A contemporary wood engraving depicts the Confederate guns firing the first shots of the Civil War, at Fort Sumter in Charleston Harbor, South Carolina, on the morning of 12 April 1861. The fallen gunner in the foreground is artistic license. The only casualty resulting from the two-day bombardment was Private Daniel Hough, Company E, 1st U.S. Artillery, who was accidentally killed by the explosion of 'misplaced powder' during the firing of a 100-gun salute prior to the Federal evacuation of the Fort. (Chrysalis Images)

In this Kurz and Allison lithograph, the Confederate 1st Virginia Cavalry, commanded by Colonel J.E.B. Stuart, attack the 11th New York Volunteers, or 1st Fire Zouaves, during the Battle of Bull Run on 21 July 1861. The troops in the left foreground wearing havelocks to protect their heads from the searing heat possibly represent the U.S. Marine battalion commanded by Major John G. Reynolds. The Marines attempted to form a rearguard when the general Union rout began. (Chrysalis Images)

6 November 1860, receiving 180 of 303 electoral votes and just 40 per cent of the popular vote.

Within seven weeks South Carolina had seceded from the Union, and by June 1861 she was joined by 10 other slave states. Meanwhile, the Confederate States of America had been formed at Montgomery, Alabama, on 8 February 1861, with Jefferson Davis as the president. Confrontation between the two sides soon developed. Lincoln was determined to retain possession of all Federal installations and property, while Davis pledged to occupy them, by force if necessary. Several Federal arsenals and forts fell to the Confederates without bloodshed, but at 4.30 a.m. on 12 April 1861 the guns commanded by Southern General P.G.T. Beauregard opened fire on Fort Sumter, a Federal post in Charleston Harbor, and the war had begun.

The Irrepressible Conflict

Union forces commanded by General Irvin McDowell launched the first large-scale attempt to force the seceded states back into the Union during July 1861. Advancing south from the Washington defences in an attempt to capture the new Confederate capital at Richmond, Virginia, they suffered total defeat on the plains of Manassas, or Bull Run, and were chased back over the Potomac River in confusion. The Army of the Potomac, under George B. McClellan, tried to capture the Confederate capital again during the Peninsula Campaign in 1862, and suffered defeat during the Seven Days Battles. General John Pope attempted another advance on Richmond in August 1862, and came to grief at Second Manassas.

Major General George B. McClellan (fourth from right) poses for a photograph at the headquarters of General George W. Morell, at Minor's Hill, Virginia, during the fall of 1861. Known as 'Little Mac', McClellan was appointed commander of the U.S. Army during the following November. He advanced so slowly toward Richmond in the spring of 1862 that his critics dubbed him the 'Virginia Creeper'. General Morell stands third from the left, while at the extreme right are two distinguished foreign observers – the Prince de Joinville, son of King Louis Phillippe of France, and his nephew, the Count de Pais, who wears the uniform of McClellan's staff, on which he served throughout the Peninsula Campaign. (Chrysalis Images)

Commanded next by General Ambrose E. Burnside, the Union army suffered a further costly defeat at Fredericksburg with a loss of 12,653 men after the failure of fourteen frontal assaults on well entrenched Confederate positions on Marye's Heights. The war did not begin well for the North.

Formed in June 1862, the Confederate Army of Northern Virginia, under General Robert E. Lee, went on the offensive for the first time by invading Maryland during the Fall of 1862. The Confederates were stopped by Union forces under McClellan at Antietam, or Sharpsburg, and 26,000 men lay dead, wounded, or were missing, by nightfall on 17 September of that year. Withdrawing back into Virginia, Lee next defeated a much larger Union force led by General 'Fighting Joe' Hooker at Chancellorsville on 1–4 May 1863. Victory was marred by tragedy, when Lee's ablest commander, Thomas 'Stonewall' Jackson, was fatally wounded by 'friendly fire' during the second day of battle. He died eight days later. Lee lamented, 'I have lost my right arm.'

Lee launched his second invasion of the North on 3 June 1863. Marching an army of 75,000 men into Pennsylvania, he stumbled across the Union Army of the Potomac, under George E. Meade, at Gettysburg while looking for shoes for his foot weary soldiers. The 'high tide' of the Confederacy was gained and lost, as the men of General George Pickett's division clashed with Meade's forces on Cemetery Ridge on the third day of battle. 'It's all my fault', confessed Lee as his army retreated South after defeat at Gettysburg.

In the West, an unknown Union general named Ulysses S.

The dress parade of the 1st Rhode Island Cavalry, in camp near Manassas, Virginia, during July 1862. This regiment had been on campaign in the Shenandoah Valley for several months, and were 'resting at camp' when this photograph was taken. Note the regimental band in the foreground, and the garrison flag flying behind the dismounted troopers. During dress parade, the officer of the day read out all general orders, plus charges and findings from courts martial. Uniformity of dress was always expected on such occasions. (Chrysalis Images)

Grant had captured Fort Henry in Tennessee on 6 February 1862. Ten days later he earned the sobriquet 'Unconditional Surrender' Grant when he also took Fort Donelson. Grant next snatched victory from defeat at Shiloh on 6–7 April 1862. In a bitter struggle on the banks of the Tennessee River, 13,000 Union troops were killed or wounded, and 10,000 Confederates – a total of more men than in all the previous American wars combined. Always under criticism, Lincoln was pressured to relieve Grant from command, but resisted stating, 'I can't spare this man; he fights!'

Placed in command of the Army of the West on 29 January 1863, Grant was ordered to capture Vicksburg, the last Confederate stronghold on the Mississippi River. After a six-week siege, Vicksburg fell on the day following Lee's defeat at Gettysburg – a double blow for the South. As a result, the Confederacy was effectively split in two, being unable to receive support and help from the south-west. Southern spirits were

The tedium of camp life is evident in this photograph, possibly taken in a Union encampment near Falmouth, Virginia. Note the wooden winter quarters on the right, and the two mud-coated wooden chimneys behind the man washing clothes. A 'Dog', or Shelter, tent stands at left, while in the distance may be seen three officer's wall tents. (Chrysalis Images)

raised temporarily by a Confederate victory at Chickamauga, after which General Braxton Bragg's Army of Tennessee trapped the Union Army of the Cumberland, under General William S. Rosecrans, at Chattanooga. After enduring a six-week siege, the beleaguered Rosecrans was relieved by Grant. During the battle, Union troops avenged their previous defeat by storming up the face of Missionary Ridge without orders yelling 'Chickamauga! Chickamauga!'

Grant next sent General William Tecumseh Sherman marching through Georgia, with orders to cripple the South's economy and to cut the Confederacy into further segments.

After destroying Atlanta, Sherman's 62,000-strong army left behind a 300 mile-long path of destruction and reached the Georgia coast on 21 December 1864. Telegraphing the news to Washington, he offered President Lincoln Savannah as a Christmas present!

Grant himself was ordered east to seek out and defeat Lee in Northern Virginia. With an army of 120,000, he fought three bloody battles at the Wilderness, Spotsylvania Courthouse, and Cold Harbor. By this time, Lee's army had shrunk to less than 60,000 men, many of whom lacked food, ammunition, and clothing. On 15 June 1864, Union forces missed an opportunity to capture Petersburg and cut off Confederate supply lines to Richmond. As a result, a nine-month siege of Petersburg ensued. On 25 March 1865, Lee went on the offensive for the

Regimental bands provided welcome relief from the tedium of camp life and livened up the step on the march or going into battle. This band of Union musicians hailed from Dudley, Pennsylvania. The instruments they carry appear to be a combination of 'over the shoulder' saxhorns and cornets. They wear a distinctive uniform consisting of a seven-button coat embellished with officer's-style shoulder straps and sleeve loops. Each man also has a sash tied over his shoulder. (Chrysalis Images)

In this painting by Paul Wood, Father William Corby, of the 88th New York Infantry, stands on a boulder to give absolution to kneeling troops of the Irish Brigade about to go into battle at Gettysburg on 2 July 1863. (Chrysalis Images)

last time, ordering an assault on the centre of Grant's siege lines. After four hours of desperate combat, the attack was broken and the exhausted Confederates retreated in disarray. Grant began a general advance and Lee ordered the evacuation of Petersburg. Richmond finally fell on 4 April 1865, and five days later Lee surrendered the remnants of the Confederate army to the Union commander at Appomattox Court House in Virginia. Meeting his troops for the last time, Lee told them: 'Boys I have done the best I could for you. Go home now, and if you make as good citizens as you have soldiers, you will do well, and I shall always

be proud of you.' Grant permitted Confederate officers to retain their sidearms, while enlisted men kept their horses and mules.

On 14 April 1865, four years after the bloodless Confederate victory in Charleston Harbor, the Stars and Stripes was once again ceremoniously raised over Fort Sumter. That same evening, Abraham Lincoln and his wife Mary took their seats in Ford's Theatre in Washington, D.C. to see the play *Our American Cousin*. At precisely 10.13 p.m., and during the third act of the play, John Wilkes Booth shot the President in the head. Lincoln died at 7.22 the next morning. Four days later, Joseph E. Johnston surrendered his forces to Sherman in North Carolina. The last Confederate troops capitulated in Texas during the following May, and on 23–24 of that month a victory parade was held in Washington to help boost the Nation's morale.

Soldier Life

The armies that fought the American Civil War consisted mainly of citizen soldiery recruited, and then conscripted, from all parts of the Union and Confederacy. Although predomi-

nantly composed of native-born Americans, about 20 per cent of the Union army were immigrants, mainly from the United Kingdom, Germany, and Scandinavia. By the end of the conflict, 10 per cent of Union troops were African American. Many of the former and all of the latter served in segregated regiments. In contrast, 95 per cent of all Confederate armies consisted of native-born Americans. While slaves and a few free blacks performed essential non-combat duties, the Confederate army did not officially enlist black troops until the closing days of the war.

Union soldiers in winter camp. The two men seated in the foreground wear four-button sack coats, or fatigue blouses, while the soldier standing towards the rear is dressed in an enlisted men's frock coat, pattern of 1851. The small arms stacked to their left are U.S. Model 1861 Springfield Rifle Muskets. This rugged weapon saw more action from 1862 to 1865 than any other Federal fire arm. (Chrysalis Images)

Lieutenant Colonel Noah Lane Farnham, the second commander of the 11th New York Volunteer Infantry, wears the gray Fire Zouaves officers' uniform. A stripe, which was gold edged red, is just visible on the seam of his trousers and the shoulder straps on his gray double-breasted field officer's frock coat are dark blue with red edging. Farnham's pose for this portrait shot is remarkably casual, especially with his coat left open revealing his shirt. In mourning for Elmer E. Ellsworth, the Fire Zouaves' first commander who was gunned down in an Alexandria Tavern, Farnham wears a black armband. (Brian C. Pohanka)

At the beginning of the conflict, military units in both Union and Confederate armies usually consisted of men who came from the same community or village. Like the British 'Pals' Battalions raised later during the First World War, they shared the experience of change from civilian to army life with friends, relatives, and neighbours. They also fought and sometimes died shoulder to shoulder, leaving whole neighborhoods grieving for the loss of loved ones.

The average age of recruits in both armies was 25, while 80 per cent were between 18 and 30 years old. Musicians, or drummer boys, were often as young as 9, and the youngest boy killed in battle was only 12 years of age. Some soldiers were over 60! The average recruit was 5 feet 8½ inches tall and weighed 143 pounds. Neither Union nor Confederate recruiting officers were concerned about a potential soldier's age, health, or fitness for duty. The medical inspection of the countless volunteers who rushed to the colors at the beginning of the war was a farce; hence scores of women succeeded in passing themselves off as men and joined the army!

After enlistment and muster into a specific military unit, recruits went through basic training that involved marching, drilling, and weapons instruction. Both armies were trained using 'Hardee's Tactics'. Produced by U.S. Regular Army officer William J. Hardee in 1855, this small volume contained the essential elements of soldiering and tactics of the era. Drilling took up most of the waking hours of the soldier. The aim was to produce a disciplined body of men who could be moved into place on the battlefield with speed and efficiency in order to deliver the maximum fire power at the enemy. Men had to be trained to obey orders automatically, even amid the chaos and confusion of battle. Commands were usually relayed via drum or bugle, as an officer's voice would not normally be heard above the din of combat.

A Union enlisted man was paid $11 a month at the beginning of the war. This had increased to $16 by 1865. Although inflation led to depreciation in purchasing power, many men were still able to send money home to support their families. Confederate soldiers also started the war with the promise of $11 a month, but payment was haphazard and hyper-inflation in the South resulted in their money becoming practically worthless.

Right: Well-equipped Union soldiers, wearing Model 1858 Dress, or 'Hardee', hats, and regulation infantry overcoats, form up for inspection in a main street, possibly in Frederick, Maryland. (Chrysalis Images)

The novelty of army life was short-lived for most men, and in its place came homesickness. Besides the constant drill and irksome discipline, soldiers lived under canvas if tents were available, and constantly suffered from the extremes of climate. Infestation from lice and fleas added to the misery. During the winter months they built log huts and makeshift shelters which provided poor protection during sub-zero temperatures. Sanitation was appalling with open latrines and garbage pits, which created an unbearable stench during the long, hot summer months. In camp, and on the march, men searched constantly for diversions to relieve the tedium. Many hours were spent writing letters home to family and friends. Music

Confederate soldiers of the 9th Mississippi Infantry, commanded by Colonel James R. Chalmers, pose for photographer J.D. Edwards, in camp near Fort Barrancas, Florida, during April 1861. This photograph is one of six found in 1972 in a scrapbook of original sketches belonging to artist C.F. Allgower, illustrator for Harper's Weekly. *Most of these men wear a mixture of civilian clothing and hunting shirts, while one man seated in the rear has the numeral '4' on the front of what might have been a fireman's shirt. (Chrysalis Images)*

provided welcome relief, and sustained morale in both armies. Indeed, Robert E. Lee commented, 'I don't believe we can have an army without music.' Many regiments contained bands, particularly at the beginning of the war. Entertainment was provided in camp, while spirits were lifted on the march and sometimes in battle by tunes such as Battle Cry of Freedom, Bonnie Blue Flag, and Dixie. Sports such as wrestling, boxing, and baseball were popular. Abner Doubleday, who became a Union general in the Civil War, is often credited with inventing the latter game in Cooperstown, New York, during 1835. Gambling was also a favourite pastime, especially with dice and playing cards – although the owners usually threw these away prior to battle, for fear of meeting their maker in sin!

The ever-present prospect of death seems to have strengthened faith in God in the ranks of both armies. Most regiments possessed chaplains, and great quantities of bibles and religious tracts were distributed throughout the military camps. The Confederate troops experienced a great evangelical religious upsurge from the fall of 1862 onwards. The military set-backs of the following year may have contributed greatly to the gathering momentum of this Southern revival.

Actual combat took up only a small part of a soldier's time during the Civil War. The campaigning season usually began during the spring or summer and men generally marched and counter-marched for weeks without contacting the enemy or, as the men called it, 'seeing the elephant'. In a large-scale battle an infantry brigade usually approached the enemy in close order and formed into several two-rank lines of perhaps a thousand men in length. Skirmishers were sent out to disconcert the enemy before the main battle began. The infantry tended to stand their ground and traded volleys. Bayonet charges seldom occurred as men on both sides were loath to use the weapon. Muzzle-loading, calibre .69, smoothbore muskets were still the norm at the beginning of the war. Hence attacks were conducted in mass formation. However, since 1855, the rifle-musket had begun to replace the smoothbore. Although rifling was not new, the adoption of the minie ball, invented by French army officer Captain Claude Minie in 1848, enabled the infantryman to fire with greater range and accuracy. Deadly in the hands of a veteran, this weapon devastated close order battle formations, and led to a change in tactics in which men took to cover and 'advanced by rushes' when attacking the enemy. The North mass produced the Springfield rifle-musket, while the South ran thousands of Enfield rifle-muskets through the blockade from England. By 1864, the North was producing breech-loading repeating rifles, such as the Sharps carbine and the Spencer Repeating Carbine. Patented in 1860 by Christopher M. Spencer, about 200,000 Spencer carbines were issued during the war. Used mainly by cavalry, these had a shorter range than the rifle-musket and were prone to malfunction.

Clothing the Armies

The task of clothing and equipping the vast numbers which swelled the ranks of both armies presented phenomenal problems. On the eve of war, the U.S. Quartermaster's Department was only geared to supply the small Regular Army of 16,000 men. It had an authorized staff of 37 officers, including Quartermaster General Montgomery C. Meigs, and seven military storekeepers. The Schuylkill Arsenal in Pennsylvania had been the chief depository for clothing and equipage since the War of 1812. Purchased under contract from manufacturers, cloth was received, cut according to pattern by government cutters, and issued to seamstresses and tailors who returned hand-finished garments to the Arsenal for inspection and acceptance. Though the sewing machine had been invented by Elias Howe in 1845, and improved later by Isaac Merrit Singer, it was not generally used in the production of uniforms during the Civil War. Hand-sewn garments were considered to be more durable, although machines were used for sewing those articles not exposed to so much hard usage, such as caps and chevrons.

The Schuylkill Arsenal was unable to supply the 75,000 militiamen called into service for three months in April 1861, let alone the quarter of a million men who would rush to arms in response to the various presidential calls issued during the next few months. Hence, that facility was quickly expanded until 8000 to 10,000 sewing women were employed. New clothing depots were also established in New York, Cincinnati, and St Louis during the course of the war. Uniforms began to be made in so-called 'government halls' at several branch depots. Such facilities were opened at Quincy, Illinois, and at Steubenville, Ohio, during 1862 and 1863 respectively. During March 1863, Military Storekeeper G. A. Hull established manufacturing operations at the Louisville clothing depot. Clothing was also produced at various times during the war at Boston, Indianapolis, Detroit, Milwaukee, and Springfield, Illinois. The above branch depots did not contract for cloth but obtained the bulk of their supply from the eastern depots – particularly from Philadelphia and New York.

The sudden huge demand for cloth in 1861 placed an impossible burden on the northern textiles industry. Only a small number of mills were set up to produce the coarse and heavy woollens required by the army. In fact, there was a shortage of army textiles of all types, including blankets and tentage. The use of analine or synthetic dyes, discovered in 1856 by Englishman William Henry Perkin, was still in its infancy. Hence cloth of any 'modest color' was purchased by the Quartermaster Department in the desperation of the first few months of war. These factors resulted in volunteer regiments receiving uniforms of all types, cut, and color, including gray or green cloth, as well as blue. Several northern and western states, such as New York, Vermont, and Wisconsin, clothed their early war regiments in gray out of choice. This led to serious confusion on the battlefield, and resulted in Union troops firing on each other, as at Big Bethel and Bull Run in 1861. On 23 September 1861 Thomas A. Scott, Acting Secretary of War, issued a circular to 'the several governors of the states' requesting no more troops to be uniformed in gray, and recommending the blue U.S. uniform as 'readily distinguishable from that of the enemy'.

Much of the early-war cloth procured via contract by the Quartermaster Department was of inferior quality. Too often contractors increased their profits by skimping on the material used. For example, Brooks Brothers, of New York City, produced a low-grade yarn by tearing to shreds refuse woollen rags, which were mixed with a lesser quantity of new wool. Although the finished cloth look like a superior article, it was a worthless fabric which quickly fell apart and became known as 'shoddy'. Many accounts of this cloth survive. One Northern newspaper described it as 'a rusty gray satinet material' composed of cotton with 'a sprinkling of dog's hair and bristles'! The Military Board of New York reported that the greater part of the 7300 gray jackets supplied in 1861 were of 'inferior cloth . . . badly cut, badly sewed and made up and the buttons used upon all the jackets were of a poor quality and not properly sewed upon such garments.'

With the winter of 1861 approaching and production still lagging behind demand, and domestic cloth fetching extortionate prices, the Quartermaster's Department resorted to the foreign market. George P. Smith, a retired merchant of Pittsburgh, was sent to England with a budget of $800,000 to buy 1,200,000 yards of dark and light blue kersey, or the best available equivalent. Reports of Smith's departure caused protest throughout the Northern textiles industry. The Boston Board of Trade registered vigorous objections to foreign cloth

This photograph of a private of the 10th U.S. Infantry taken in the 1850s, shows all the finery of pre-Civil War American soldiers and the French influences in uniforms that continued all the way through the Civil War. The 10th U.S. Infantry was organized in 1855 and the Private wears a regulation frock coat cut in the French Chasseur à pied pattern. The coat has light blue piping and brass shoulder scales. On show beside the private is his full dress hat or shako. These hats were made of felt stretched over a cardboard or paper base, but some were made entirely out of leather. Just visible on the hat is a light blue welt and pompon, which like the trim on the private's coat designates that he is an infantryman. (David Scheinmann)

importation that would surely glut the American market. They were also reluctant to support foreign labour at the expense of the work force of America, or to see specie taken out of the country. The Board expressed confidence that the woollen machinery of the country would soon be producing at a sufficient rate to provide uniforms for 400,000 men, and to repeat this performance every six weeks thereafter.

Quartermaster General Meigs was opposed to any move that might prevent the import of foreign cloth, but guaranteed that if domestic manufacturers could supply the demand at a reasonable price before the goods could be imported, he would gladly purchase it. This approach appears to have succeeded as, by December 1861, domestic prices were no higher than that coming from Europe. Following this, and after only $380,000 had been spent on foreign goods, he called a halt to foreign purchase on 14 February 1862.

By the second year of the war, most Union troops were adequately clothed and equipped, and the Quartermaster's Department had next to concentrate on building up a reserve and maintaining the supply at clothing depots. By the summer of 1862, six months' supply of clothing was on hand throughout the Quartermaster system, while approximately 3,200,000 yards of cloth was in storage at the Schuylkill Arsenal. When, on 2 July 1862, President Lincoln called for 300,000 volunteers for three years' service, followed the next month by a call for 300,000 militia for nine months, the effect was to wipe out the surplus, leaving little for the supply of the army in the field. By agreement with the individual states, Meigs sent cloth and trimmings for coats and trousers either to the U.S. quartermaster stationed within each state or, if such were not available, to the governors of the states.

To replace depleted stocks, the Quartermaster General also ordered the publication of advertisements in numerous newspapers inviting proposals for the lowest bidder at Philadelphia, New York, and Cincinnati. He directed Colonel George H. Crosman to accumulate a surplus stock at Schuylkill sufficient to clothe and equip 100,000 men. Similar instructions were issued to the New York depot. By 1863, with reserve stocks accumulated, the supply of clothing was well in hand and by the end of 1864, Meigs could report that 'the supply was ample, the quality excellent, and the complaints few'.

The supply of uniforms to the Confederate Army was a vastly different story. In each of the 11 states which joined the Confederacy during 1861 (plus the three 'border states') floods of volunteers to the Southern cause donned pre-war militia dress, or had new service uniforms made up by local tailors, or by their own womenfolk. The variety, cut, and color of these early war uniforms was endless. As in the ranks of the Union Army, confusion reigned on the battlefield, as friend mistook foe – often with fatal consequences. With the approach of the first winter of war, and the realization that the Confederate Government was ill-prepared to clothe those troops entering its service, the first 'Great Appeal' for clothing was issued throughout the Southern newspaper press. With the help of countless 'volunteer aid societies', composed mainly of the wives, daughters, and sweethearts of those at the battlefront, many soldiers received a new suit of mainly gray clothes, an overcoat, a blanket, and a pair of socks. Thus they survived the rigours of the first winter of war.

The winter of 1861–62 also saw the beginning of some central issuance of uniforms by the Confederate Quartermaster Department established at Richmond, Virginia. But too little was made available too slowly, and many men were reduced to unnecessary suffering in rags and bare feet. Hence each state began to produce its own, often quite distinctive, pattern of uniform, generally funded by the Confederate commutation system begun in July 1861, which provided that each enlisted man should receive $21 every six months for clothing.

As the war progressed through the years, so did the uniform appearance of the Confederate soldier, at least in the eastern theatre of the conflict. But what the North Carolina 'Tarheel' wore differed greatly from that of his counterpart from Georgia or Mississippi. Although gray, based mainly on C.S. Army Regulations of 1861, became the color of cloth common to all, many different shades and hues were created out of shortage and necessity.

The summer of 1862 came and went with disaster in the West, and victory in the East. General Braxton Bragg's Perryville/Kentucky campaign was disappointing, while Lee held his ground at Antietam, and Fredericksburg. By the Fall of 1862, both armies were again poorly clad. The C.S. Quartermaster Department was embarrassed and assailed. Soldiers were writing home for clothes, and a second 'Great Appeal' was issued from Richmond for warm winter clothing. The states again responded, but this time North Carolina and Georgia shut out the speculators and Quartermaster agents, and declared that they would clothe their own men first, and the Confederate government could have what was left!

By early 1863, Quartermaster Department clothing work-shops had been established in Columbus and Augusta, as well as Richmond, to make uniforms for the exclusive use of its own bureau. The states that wished to clothe their own troops first were left alone for the present. By 1863 an increasing amount of imported clothing was coming through the blockade, while further manufacturing centres had been set up. By the Fall of 1863, Confederates in some battles and campaigns were described as being better dressed than those in the Federal army.

By early 1864, both the Army of Tennessee, and the Army of Northern Virginia, were in plentiful receipt of Quartermaster Depot uniforms of a similar pattern, if not the same kind of cloth. At the end of that year, with Atlanta and Vicksburg taken, and most of Tennessee in Northern hands, it was back to rags and bare feet for many. The Army of Tennessee, destroyed at Franklin and Nashville, were reduced to wearing captured Federal clothing. According to quartermaster reports, those around Petersburg, Virginia, remained well clothed. Elsewhere, the dissolving armies wandered about the country while the factories continued to produce and the storehouses held supplies that could not be moved to the troops. By April 1865 it was all over, although at the surrender of Confederate forces under General Joseph E. Johnston at Durham Station on the 26th of that month, North Carolina alone had on hand 92,000 sets of uniforms, and vast stores of blankets and leather.

Uniforms of the Union Army

by Robin Smith

U.S. Regulation Infantry	24
U.S. Cavalry and Artillery	46
U.S. Generals, Staff, and Special Units	74
Zouaves and Militia Units	86
Union State Uniforms	113
Insignia and Medals	125

U.S. Regulation Infantry

The blue clad infantryman was the mainstay of Union Forces from 1861–1865. His natural successors were the Doughboys of World War I, the GIs of World War II and the Grunts who fought in Vietnam. Orders issued on 13 March 1861, prescribed that the full dress coat for infantrymen should be a dark blue single-breasted frock coat made without pleats with a skirt extending one half the distance from the top of the hip to the bend of the knee. The coats were to have nine buttons placed at equal distances on the chest and a stand up collar which shouldn't be too high and restrict a soldier's neck movement. In practice it seems that many collars proved to be uncomfortable and local tailors were often contracted to lower them.

During the war, the Government purchased no fewer than 1,881,727 dress coats which were also worn by many infantrymen in the field. The collars and cuffs for infantry frock coats were piped with blue cord and each cuff had two small brass buttons; one just below the piping, the other above. The regulations also prescribed brass shoulder scales, but these weren't commonly seen on infantrymen's frock coats on campaign.

In the field, some men in a regiment might be wearing frock coats, while the rest would be wearing dark blue sack coats. Sack coats evolved from loose fitting fashionable civilian coats of the 1840s which were unusual for the day because they didn't have a seam at the waist, the upper and lower halves being the same piece of cloth.

Sack coats were adopted by the United States Army in 1857 and not only were they cheap to manufacture costing $2.10 each as compared with the $5.56 manufacturing cost for a single frock coat, but they were extremely comfortable to wear and very popular with soldiers throughout the war. Sack coats had no braid or decoration and just a simple turnover collar. Such coats were done up with four large uniform buttons and had an inside pocket on the left breast.

Recruits received sack coats lined with coarse flannel and thin muslin in the sleeves while old sweats wore unlined sack coats. The jackets were produced in four regular sizes; 36-inch breast 30½-inch leg, 38-inch breast 31½-inch leg, 40-inch breast 32½-inch leg and 42-inch breast 33½-inch leg.

From 1858 to 1861 the color of regular infantry trousers was dark blue but the color was changed to sky blue on 16 December 1861. Regulation trousers were high in the waist and had full very round legs. Creases in trousers were unknown in those days. Trousers had a modern style button fly and two pockets at the front. Braces attached to buttons on the front and back of the trousers were the universal way of holding them up, belts were not yet much in vogue. Civil War trousers tended to be cut loose and fitted well up over the stomach. A common mistake of many reproduction Civil War trousers worn by re-enactors today is that they hug the hips like modern trousers and the cut, particularly around the crotch, is not baggy enough.

Infantry trousers usually had one-inch slits at the bottom to help in getting the straight bottoms over heavy shoes. For size adjustment, a slit was also cut into the back of the trousers at the top and a piece of twine threaded through which could be tied up or loosened. Manufactured in coarse kersey cloth, infantry trousers could cause the men a lot of discomfort, particularly on the march. These lines from a post-war medical report about enlisted men published in 1868, are equally applicable to hard marching Civil War soldiers. 'The undeviating thickness of heavy trousers is a source of severe complaint throughout the entire warm season.'

Soldiers were issued with three shirts a year, made in the style of working men's shirts out of flannel, or coarse wool. The army had stopped issuing cotton shirts in 1852, but while flannel shirts may have been warm in winter they were extremely uncomfortable to wear and allegedly more verminous than the many cotton civilian shirts the soldiers wore. Soldiers would try and kill off vermin by smoking their shirts over campfires and crushing them in their fingers was also a popular pastime. Shirts had small turnover collars with a row of three buttons leading up to the neck. They were put on over the head similar to a modern T-shirt and were produced in a variety of colors and check designs. Distinctive double-breasted firemen's shirts were also popular, often worn as an outer garment over another shirt. Firemen's shirts had wide necks and broad collars, and they were often decorated with bone or mother of pearl buttons. Firemen who enlisted as soldiers, such as the Zouaves of the 11th New York Volunteer Infantry, had a particular liking for them.

Although only officially authorized for officers, waistcoats,

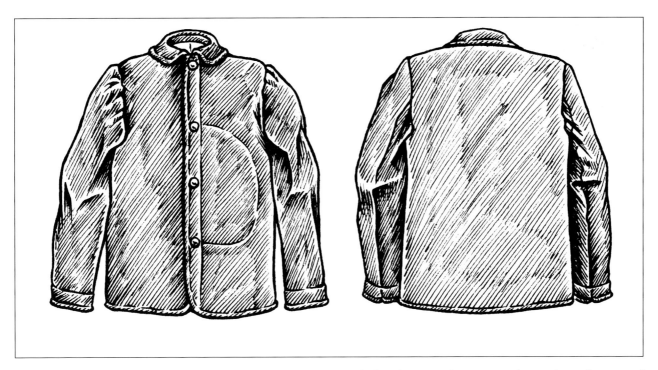

The line drawings of a Union sack coat shows the practical and comfortable nature of the standard issue garment. Most Civil War soldiers would have worn sack coats at some time during their time of service. (Ed Dovey)

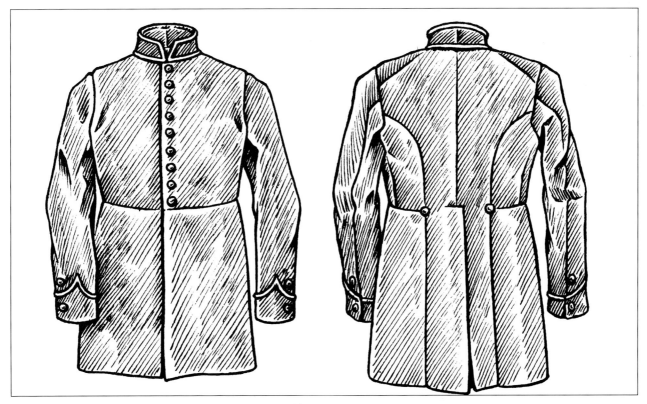

Studying this line drawing of a standard Union issue frock coat, it quickly becomes apparent why many Union soldiers preferred to wear sack coats. Though smart in appearance, frock coats could be uncomfortable to wear, especially with their high collars. (Ed Dovey)

Infantry private poses with his coat open over his shirt but decorum dictated that his coat should still be buttoned at the collar. Note the height of kersey trousers coming up well over his waist. His forage cap is standard issue. (David Scheinmann)

Infantry private wearing a non-regulation vest under his coat and also a non-regulation bow tie or cravat. Such individual touches were far from unusual. (David Scheinmann)

This infantry private wears a dark blue version of the standard infantryman's overcoat which was usually issued in sky blue. This infantryman's coat is particularly long and he also appears to be wearing a special type of cap, but this is misleading. All he's done is to pin the side badge from his full dress hat to his forage cap, giving an unusual appearance. (David Scheinmann)

Private wearing a regulation overcoat and forage cap but underneath he seems to be dressed in a double-breasted fireman's shirt which he's left open at the collar. Such shirts proved to be very popular items of clothing. (David Scheinmann)

because of their comfort and warmth, were worn as a personal choice by all ranks. Usually dark blue in color, waistcoats had up to four slash pockets on the breast. Soldiers were issued underwear, long drawers stretching to the knee and made of flannel. Some soldiers had never worn underwear before and were baffled by the strange garments. One legendary Civil War story claims that soldiers told these raw recruits that their drawers were a special parade uniform.

Socks were issued in vast quantities by the Federal

It was common for soldiers, particularly in the early stages of the war, to take 'extra' weaponry along with them; especially if the armament supply to their company or regiment wasn't all that it should be. This infantry private has a Bowie knife stuffed into the front of his shirt, but hs huge bow tie looks even more formidable. (David Scheinmann)

Photographs showing enlisted men in shirtsleeves are comparatively rare. Note the man's braces and his shirt's baggy sleeves and small collar. This was the most common pattern of shirt found in the Civil War. (David Scheinmann)

government during the Civil War but were not of the highest quality and generally wore out pretty quickly. Many soldiers received pairs of socks as gifts from home and we can easily conjure up a romantic notion of mothers and girlfriends sitting by the fireside, knitting socks for their men far away. Often soldiers used their socks like gaiters and tucked their trousers into them. Gaiters were not a regulation part of the Union uniform and many soldiers found them uncomfortable, but many regiments certainly drew white canvas gaiters from stores, especially Zouave regiments.

Footwear

Ideally infantrymen were supposed to receive four pairs of boots

A Union soldier at the re-enactment of First Bull Run in 1995, at Weston Park, Shropshire, is pictured wearing a havelock over his forage cap. In theory, the cloth covers were meant to deflect the heat, but many soldiers found the cloth flapping around their heads uncomfortable, especially under battlefield conditions. (Ron Field)

a year. The standard issue were ankle boots made of leather usually made with the rougher flesh side of the leather on the outside. Soles were sewn to the uppers or fastened by pegs or nails. It appears that the footwear issued, like so many uniforms, could be of dubious quality. Stories of soldiers wearing boots out with six days of hard marching are not unusual. Army boots were often called brogans and if the sewn soles wore out quickly they were often replaced with pegged soles. For greater comfort, to stop the boots binding round their ankles, soldiers would sometimes cut the tops of their boots down. In the summer some men privately purchased lightweight canvas and leather sporting shoes to wear, which were not unlike modern day bowling shoes.

Overcoats and Ponchos

The U.S. Army had been issuing overcoats to its men since 1851. The regulation overcoat was made of sky-blue kersey cloth and had a cape that buttoned down the front, but in the clothing rush during the early part of the war, it was not unusual to find men dressed in dark blue and even black overcoats. Infantrymen weren't issued with any wet weather clothing until November 1861, when the Secretary of War authorized the issue of waterproof blankets made out of vulcanized rubber, a technique which had recently been invented. Draped around the shoulders or with a slit cut in them so that they could be slipped over the head, gum blankets provided invaluable protection against the weather and laid down under bedding at night would also help to keep soldiers dry. Soldiers would frequently draw checker boards and other designs on the insides of their blankets making a mobile 'games table'.

Headgear

Infantrymen were issued with two types of headgear; a full dress hat and a forage cap. The elaborate full dress hat was adopted in 1858 and named ironically after two future Confederates who had sat on the selection board before the war. The hat was most popularly known as a Hardee hat after Major William J. Hardee, who later became a Confederate general, and sometimes as a Jeff David hat, after future Confederate president Jefferson Davis. The origins of the Hardee hat date back to the Mexican War when Colonel Timothy P. Andrews commanding the regiment of Voltigeurs ordered a brimmed hat for his regiment. The war ended before the hats could be worn and they were put in storage until they were discovered by a dragoon captain who issued them to his men.

The 1858 hats were made out of black felt and the 3-inch brim was looped against the side of the hat and held by a brass 'eagle' fastened to the brim of the crown. The crown of the hat was 6 inches high and featured the insignia of the particular regiment who were wearing the hats on the front. The most spectacular feature of the hats were the three ostrich feathers fastened to the side and a cord with acorn or tassel designs on the end that encircled the hat. At first the cords were black and yellow and later of various colors. Infantrymen were originally ordered to wear their Hardee hats looped up on the left, but in February 1861 infantrymen were ordered to loop their hats up on the right. The hat cords were originally worn with their tassels on the side opposite the feathers but early in the war there was a vogue for wearing them on the front of the hats.

Despite their pedigree, Hardee hats proved to be unpopular with many infantrymen because they were so stiff and heavy. But some soldiers modified their hats by taking off the elaborate

Non-commissioned officers were authorized to wear dark blue stripes down the seams of their trousers, 1½ inches wide. In practice many sergeants and corporals didn't bother, possibly because their trousers didn't come ready made with the stripes and sewing them on was too much trouble. This corporal though, is proud to show off his stripes and he is also wearing a fine looking waistcoat. (David Scheinmann)

decorations and battering in the crown to make them more comfortable. The most popular headwear of the entire war was the forage cap. The government made thousands in its factories and purchased many more from contractors. The typical forage cap was made out of dark blue wool backed by an oval sheet of pasteboard to stiffen and shape the top. Forage caps were lined with cotton and the peaks were leather. A number of soldiers had the habit of pushing the peaks up, presumably because they came too far down over their eyes. Brass buttons held a chin strap in place at the back of the top of the peak but in practice it seems that chin straps weren't often used. Every four years, soldiers were scheduled to receive a black oil cloth forage cap cover as protection in bad weather. Often these cap covers didn't fit properly so men would make their own covers out of their gum blankets.

A popular forage cap accessory in the early part of the Civil War was the havelock, a piece of cloth fitted over the top of the forage cap and sometimes over the peak as well, that draped down over a soldier's neck for protection against the sun. Havelocks were named after British general Sir Henry Havelock and first worn by British troops in the scorching heat

during the Indian Mutiny. Havelocks for the entire 69th New York were provided by a group of patriotic New York ladies at the beginning of the war but later their fascination waned and many were used as bandages or for straining coffee. By the later war period no havelocks were in use.

The 42nd Pennsylvania Volunteer Infantry Regiment, largely lumbermen from the tough wild cat regions of Pennsylvania, had a unique way of decorating their forage caps. Each soldier

14th Brooklyn re-enactors relaxing in camp display the type of stiff knapsacks that were a favourite with militia units in the early war years. The 14th kept their smart red blankets rolled on top and the regimental numerals are stencilled on the backs of their knapsacks, a common practice with many Civil War regiments. (Robert C. Duffy)

Veterans of the 7th Illinois Infantry all wore frock coats to pose for this picture, except for the sergeant on the far left. They are all armed with formidable Henry repeating rifles, the forerunner of the Winchester; and it's a rarity to find Civil War infantrymen so well equipped. It could be that the soldiers privately purchased the weapons they so proudly hold. (Peter Newark's Military Pictures)

of the regiment sported a strip of deerhide on his forage cap and the regiment became known as the Bucktails. Tradition has it that James Landregan of Company I was the first to put a bucktail in his cap and the rest of the regiment quickly followed suit. Bucktails were eventually adopted by an entire Bucktail Brigade formed in 1862 from the 149th and 150th Pennsylvania Infantry. The Pennsylvania originators of the Bucktail tradition sneered at these upstarts, calling them 'bogus Bucktails'.

Although never as popular as standard issue forage caps, McClellan caps were also worn by Union soldiers. These caps were of the French Chasseur pattern and with lower sides than typical forage caps, they were more of a French kepi style. The McClellan caps were popular with several Zouave regiments, such as the 72nd Pennsylvania who wore McClellan caps with red piping around the crowns. High-crowned forage caps were popular with some men because they could slip a sponge, handkerchief or leaves underneath as protection against the sun. Some enterprising sutlers also sold the men forage cap ventilators; pieces of brass gauze which could be pushed into the top of a forage cap to help the air circulate over the wearer's head.

Broad-brimmed slough hats were sometimes worn by the soldiers in Eastern regiments but slouch hats were more popular with Western regiments, who effected more of a rugged appearance than their Eastern counterparts. Private Rice Bull of the 123rd New York Infantry wrote: 'Western troops looked quite unlike our men. They all wore large hats instead of caps.' Straw hats were also popular in certain regiments and must have provided much relief against the sun, but they had their

disadvantages. Straw hats were issued to the entire 16th New York in 1862, but the men found their unusual headgear made them easy targets and they were quickly discarded in favour of forage caps.

Union Infantry Equipment

Since the days of the American Revolution, American soldiers liked to travel light. This may have had a lot to do with the shortages of supply that dogged America during the struggle for independence, but also with the American volunteers' attitude to authority. An American soldier believed he was fighting for a cause and prided himself on his individuality. He considered excess equipment unnecessary and this was reflected in the design of the accoutrements issued to him and the way he would discard anything he found uncomfortable; although in

Typical Union haversack in which soldiers kept their food and other essential requirements. The haversacks had a detachable inner lining shown on the right which could be taken out and washed. If the soldier was carrying salted pork or other forms of meat as part of his rations in hot weather, this was very necessary, although as plenty of accounts of the time reveal, many soldiers didn't bother to be so fastidious with their haversacks. (Ed Dovey)

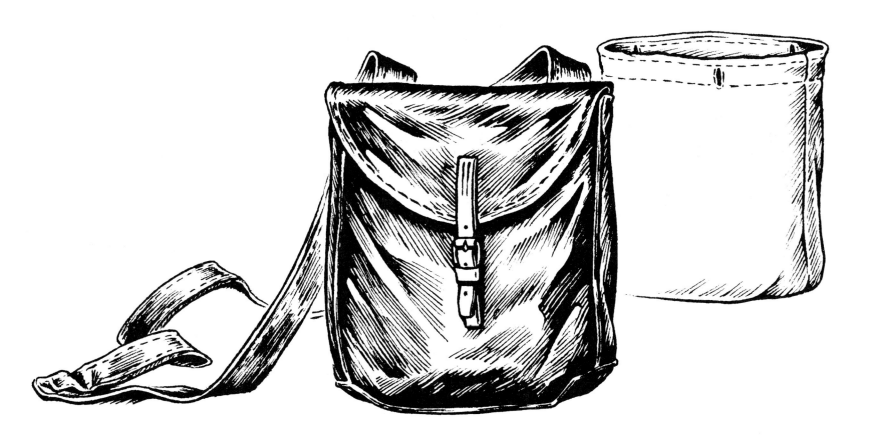

this respect the Union soldier was not as undisciplined as his Confederate foes.

The basic equipment issued to all Union infantry soldiers included a knapsack worn on the back and a cartridge box which was either suspended on a belt over the left shoulder or carried on a waistbelt which also carried the soldier's bayonet and cap pouch. Waistbelts were 1.9 inches wide and 38.5 inches long and they were usually buckled with a brass waistbelt plate with US on the front. Variations included the popular SNY plates standing for State of New York favoured by many New York volunteers. Confederates joked that SNY stood for 'snotty nosed Yank'. Other variations in waist belt plates worn by troops from various states included NHSM plates sported by men of the New Hampshire State Militia. Infantry shoulder belt plates were 2½ inches in diameter. Completing his basic equipment, the Union infantryman carried a haversack and canteen slung over his right shoulder.

Knapsacks

There were two main types of knapsacks; rigid and non-rigid. Rigid knapsacks were particularly favoured by militia units in the early stages of the war and had a square wooden frame covered with waterproof cloth or canvas with two small straps on top to secure a blanket. These rigid knapsacks looked full whether anything was in them or not, adding to a regiment's neat appearance on the parade ground. In the Mexican War, American infantry had worn a rigid knapsack with a waterproofed cover. Though looking smart, rigid knapsacks could be uncomfortable to wear.

In 1853 a non-rigid model knapsack was introduced, but it seems the majority of militia units were content to remain with the old rigid model. Knapsacks covered in animal hide which were favoured in Europe were quite rare in America. But they had been part of the consignment of Chasseur uniforms ordered by the United States Government and Berdan's Sharpshooters were also issued with them.

Regulations regarding facial hair during the American Civil War stated that beards should be kept trim and neat, but these rules were often ignored, which accounts for the spectacular beards sported by many officers and men. Goatees and moustaches were generally favoured by officers, although this officer has gone to extremes. He wears a regulation frock coat with a single row of nine buttons down the front, marking him out as a company officer. (David Scheinmann)

A good view of the regulation waist sash worn by first sergeants. They were made out of red worsted material, with bullion fringed ends, meant to hang down no more than 18 inches from where the sash was tied on the left hip. Regulations stated that sashes were to be worn on all occasions apart from fatigue duties, but they were rarely seen on campaign. (David Scheinmann)

Infantry officer in full dress complete with epaulettes and white gauntlets. It's likely that ostentatious officers may have worn epaulettes on campaign, but in the majority of cases they were replaced by ordinary shoulder straps. (David Scheinmann)

'Soft' knapsacks of waterproofed cotton or canvas were the knapsacks most often carried by infantry soldiers in the Civil War. In 1857 army regulations ordered that all knapsacks should be painted black. Infantry knapsacks were to carry their owner's regimental number in the center and officially this number was to be 1½ inches in length and painted in white paint. Knapsacks were also to be marked on the inside with the letter of the company the soldier belonged to.

Many soldiers dispensed with the knapsacks or lost them on campaign. The 5th New York, whose original knapsacks had been manufactured by the Gutta Percha Company of New York, lost many of theirs after the battle of Malvern Hill. No rules seem to have been enforced about knapsacks and for comfort, many soldiers, particularly infantrymen in the Western campaigns, tossed their knapsacks aside, preferring instead to keep their belongings in a blanket roll tied around the shoulders. This romantic image of soldiers with their possessions bundled up in a blanket is usually associated with Confederates, but it was a common practice with Union soldiers as well. A knapsack crammed full of blankets and personal items could easily become unbearable on the march, especially with the sun heating up the waterproofed canvas. A blanket roll draped around the body was much easier to march with.

Cartridge Boxes and Cap Pouches

The standard infantry cartridge box was made out of black leather and contained two tin inserts each with an upper and lower section where infantrymen kept 40 black powder cartridges. Many infantrymen kept extra cartridges in their coat pockets, transferring them to their cartridge boxes, especially when the supply in the cartridge box containers ran out. Cartridge boxes could be suspended on a soldier's waist belt, but a well stocked cartridge box weighs over 3 pounds, so it made more sense to carry the box on a shoulder belt and distribute the weight more easily. Regulation cap pouches were of black leather and were lined with sheepskin. The corners of the outer flaps fitted tightly over a brass stud and were rounded at the edges.

Haversacks and Canteens

Haversacks and canteens were the fundamental items of equipment which kept the Union soldier alive. In his haversack he stored his food and eating utensils. Rations included salt

pork, sugar, coffee, salt and the staple diet of all Civil War soldiers, hardtack, a biscuit made out of flour mixed with water which was then baked. It was so hard it never rotted and it was not unknown for hardtack to be issued to soldiers long after the Civil War had ended. Eating utensils would usually comprise a knife, fork, spoon and tin plate, but some soldiers even carried non-regulation fancy mess tins. All soldiers had a tin cup which they sometimes carried on the outside of their haversacks looped through the strap.

The regulation haversack was made out of waterproofed cotton cloth. It had a single strap with a buckle, and inside there was a removable cotton bag held in place by three buttons. On a hot day one can imagine what the effect on the contents of this bag would be. Heat exhaustion and not battle was often the cause of many soldiers dying. The sides of roads where the troops passed, would often be lined with soldiers who simply had become victims of the blazing weather conditions and the excessive humidity which characterized the Civil War campaigning season throughout the United States.

At Gettysburg, soldiers from both sides are said to have shared water from the same course of supply at Spangler's Spring. The regulation canteen 1858 pattern held almost 3 pints of water and was made out of two convex pieces of tin soldered together. It had a cork stopper and was covered in blue or brownish woollen cloth.

It is usually accepted that blue was the standard color for canteen covers, but it actually seems likely that brown was the most common color. In theory the covers kept the contents cool and helped to stop the canteens making a noise on the march, but many soldiers had canteens without covers.

After 1861, rings were pressed into both sides of metal canteens and this 'bullseye' type of canteen became the classic canteen of the Civil War, but there were many varieties of canteen including cylindrical wooden canteens and even

Right: The elaborate details of a privately purchased Zouave officer's uniform are shown here in a line drawing of the dress worn by Captain Felix Agnus of the 165th New York Volunteer Infantry. The trousers were a rust red color trimmed in gold, and the dark blue jacket featured yet more elaborate ornamentation. The false vest sewn into the jacket and held in place with flaps and buttons over the left shoulder, was decorated with ornate tombeaux designs, not visible in this picture. The Z in the regulation bugle horn motif worn on the front of Agnus's kepi was a common feature of Zouave officers' headgear. (Ed Dovey)

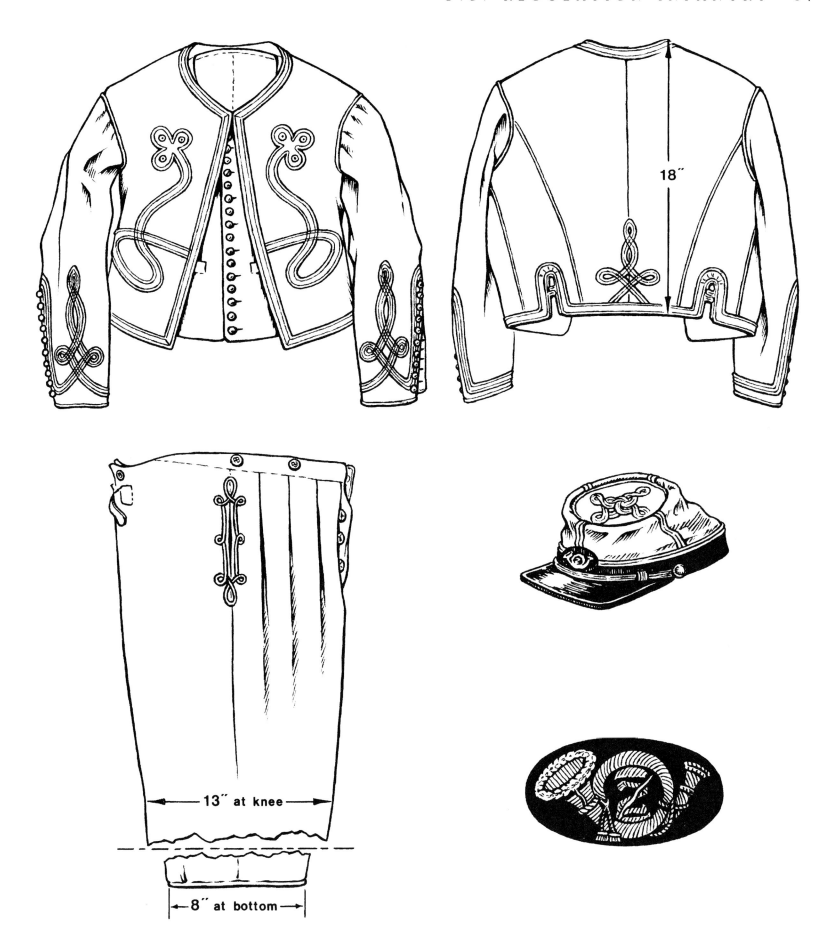

Bandsmen were important for morale and usually wore a more ornate version of standard infantry dress. These are men of the 12th Indiana Volunteer Infantry wearing the semi Zouave dress of the regiment. In battle, bandsmen acted as stretcher bearers. (Michael J. McAfee)

canteens made out of leather. Soldiers often personalized their canteens by painting their name and company number on the cloth cover or by carving their initials and company number on wooden canteens.

Infantry Weapons

The basic arm of the Union infantry soldier during the American Civil War was a muzzle-loading rifle musket and troops were armed with a bewildering variety of these weapons. Not only was there a scramble to get troops uniformed at the beginning of the war, there was also a panic to get recruits armed. The situation wasn't helped by the fact that the Confederates had captured Federal arsenals in South Carolina, Louisiana, and Texas, and at Harper's Ferry, Virginia. The total number of muskets available to Union soldiers looked fine on paper and numbered over 437,000, but less than 40,000 of these pieces were serviceable modern weapons. The majority were

A lieutenant of the 18th United States Colored Troops wears a broad-brimmed slouch hat and a waistcoat under his frock coat. (David Scheinmann)

Thomas Callan was a lieutenant in the 128th United States Colored Troops whose officers and men took a particular pride in their appearance. Not only did they have to face the enemy, but also prejudice about the worth of colored troops from their own side. All officers of colored troops were white and most were staunch abolitionists. Many black troops serving under officers like Callan preferred wearing frock coats in the field and their clothing was standard infantry issue. Some black troops were outfitted in red trousers but these were later rejected because the men didn't want to be set apart from white troops. (David Scheinmann)

antique pieces that had been altered from flintlock to the percussion system.

The first 'modern' weapon used by Union troops was the 1855 rifle musket designed to take a Minie ball of the type invented in France to make loading rifled weapons easier. The rifle also used the Maynard percussion system which worked rather like a child's toy cap gun. Instead of placing a metal percussion cap on the nipple of the gun to fire the charge in the barrel, a mechanism rolled out a line of paper percussion caps each time the weapon was cocked.

The Springfield rifle musket, developed from the 1855 rifle musket which was expensive to produce, is the weapon most closely associated with American infantrymen and these weapons became the workhorse of Union forces in the Civil War. The Springfield Armoury in Massachusetts began turning out massive quantities of the rifles in 1861.

Both the Union and the Confederacy despatched agents to Europe to produce arms to supplement domestically produced weapons. Many rifles were imported from Germany and France but the most serviceable and popular imported rifle muskets were British Enfield rifle muskets. By the middle of the war it was estimated that half of the Union troops were armed with Enfields, and what made this weapon particularly popular was that its calibre was almost identical to the domestically produced Springfield rifle musket. The same ammunition could be used for both weapons.

The method of loading a weapon had changed dramatically since Napoleonic times. Soldiers still tore open cartridges and rammed home the charge; but unlike old flintlocks there were no priming pans on their rifles, the percussion system was much

Far right: Neatly turned out Union infantryman with a watch chain hanging from his non-regulation waistcoat. The majority of Union soldiers liked to adapt uniforms to suit themselves. (David Scheinmann)

Right: This company officer wears regulation dress. Despite the habit of many officers of wearing various forms of clothing, this is what a typical officer, perhaps without his waist sash, would have looked like in the field. (David Scheinmann)

The officer in this picture holds a kepi decorated with gold braid and it's likely that he is a Zouave or Chasseur officer. Despite the gaudy dress of their men, many of these officers wore standard frock coats and one of the loops to support the waist belt can be seen on this officer's coat. (David Scheinmann)

more efficient, particularly in wet weather. In many regiments soldiers found themselves with different weapons. In one company of a Pennsylvania regiment the majority had Enfield and Springfield muskets mixed with soldiers who carried Belgian and Austrian rifle muskets.

When it was mustered in, the 5th New York was armed with a mixture of weapons including Harper's Ferry muskets and muskets converted to the percussion system with locks dated 1844 and 1845. The regiment didn't exchange all its smooth-bores for Springfield rifles until May 1862.

Thomas Meagher, who raised the Irish Zouaves, Company K 69th New York, and who later commanded the Irish Brigade in the Union Army, wanted all his men to be armed with model 1842 smoothbore muskets. In theory, rifle muskets could be used at longer ranges because they were more accurate, but Meagher thought that having his men armed with less accurate smoothbore muskets would suit the close quarters fighting at which he wanted his men to excel and emulate their ancestors. But the truth is that although rifle muskets were more accurate than smoothbores their increased range was often negated by the tremendous amount of black powder smoke. In general soldiers could only see for short distances through this smoke, so the advantages of a rifled musket were often literally blotted out.

The effects can be appreciated by spectators at modern day Civil War re-enactments where even comparatively small amounts of men firing muzzle-loading weapons quickly become shrouded in black powder smoke.

Breech-loading weapons were available in the Civil War, but were mainly confined to use by the cavalry. It was thought that if breech-loading weapons were used by standard infantrymen then they would waste ammunition. However breech-loading weapons did see use with the infantry, notably with the 42nd Pennsylvania and Berdan's Sharpshooters who used Sharps carbines. The Sharps carbine had a sliding breechlock which was opened by pulling the trigger guard down. A linen cartridge was inserted in the breech and when the breechlock was closed the back of the cartridge was sheered off. Sharps carbines had a percussion lock but a magazine held a number of detonating pellets which were ejected on to the nipple. An interesting feature of Sharps carbines was that some models incorporated a small coffee mill with a detachable handle in the butt.

Colt who were chiefly renowned for pistols, produced a rifle with a revolving chamber. It was the first repeating rifle adopted by the United States Government and early models had been

Some soldiers, like the man in this picture, had the curious habit of tilting their kepis up. It wasn't merely fashionable, but a practical way of keeping sweat out of a soldier's eyes. (David Scheinmann)

used in the Seminole War in 1838, but there was a considerable sideflash when the weapon was fired and also the danger that all six cylinders would go off at once. The rifle saw limited use in the war; Berdan's Sharpshooters used them while they were waiting to be armed with Sharps rifles. In their formidable armoury, Berdan's Sharpshooters also had a variety of specialist sniper rifles many of which had been privately purchased.

The most sought after breech-loading weapon of the Civil War was the Spencer carbine. A tube in the stock fed copper cased bullets into the breech. Southern soldiers said that Northerners could load up their Spencers on Sundays and fire them all week. Captured Spencers were highly prized, but the South lacked the capability of making ammunition for them. When stocks of captured ammunition were exhausted, they couldn't be used.

Bayonets

Socket bayonets were used with both Enfield and Springfield rifle muskets. Eighteen inches long and with 3-inch sockets they fitted snugly over the top of the musket barrel latched on to the top sight. Bayonet scabbards wee made out of leather and capped in brass. A black buff leather frog sewn and rivetted together was attached to the scabbard and suspended from the waist belt at an angle. Bayonet scabbards were worn under the soldier's haversack and canteen.

Union Infantry Officers' Dress

Officially all infantry officers in regulation dress were to wear frock coats of dark blue cloth. These coats had a standing collar usually about 1½ inches in height and reached down two thirds to three fourths of the distance from the top of the hip to the bottom of the knee. Coats were double breasted for colonels and single breasted for captains and lieutenants. Colonels' coats had two rows of seven buttons on the chest, while captains' and lieutenants' coats had one row of nine buttons on the chest, placed at equal distances. Since 1851 the sleeves of officers' frockcoats had been getting fuller. Sleeves were generally 17 inches wide in 1861 and some officers wore them 20 inches wide before the war ended.

For full dress, officers wore gilt epaulettes with a sky-blue disc set on the crescent with the regimental number embroidered on the disc in gold. Rank badges were displayed on the epaulette

This is what the typical Union soldier during the Civil War looked like. The private poses against a studio backdrop and not outdoors in camp, wears the standard issue four button sack coat, and an ordinary forage cap. His cartridge box is suspended from a shoulder belt and his belt buckle is the ubiquitous standard 'U.S.' oval model. The only distinguishing points about this soldier are that he hasn't taken care in aligning his belt buckle in the middle of his stomach to look smart for his photo, and the fact that he's turned up the collar on his sack coat. (David Scheinmann)

strap. Colonels had a silver eagle, captains had two silver bars while lieutenants had one silver bar. On campaign, officers wore shoulder straps, embroidered in gold around the edges with rank insignia displayed on each end.

Like their frock coats, infantry officers' trousers were made of a finer material than those of enlisted men. Regulations of 1861 stated that they should be of dark blue cloth with a sky-blue belt, ⅛ inch in diameter, let into the outer seam. Officers were authorized to wear ties or cravats, but regulations stated that the tie was not to be visible at the opening of the collar.

Custom dictated that an officer should not show his shirt front, waist coats worn under the frock coat were extremely useful for covering up the officer's shirt when he opened his frock coat for comfort in the hot weather.

Commissioned officers wore a cloak coat of dark blue cloth closed by four frog buttons made out of black silk and loops of black silk cord. Rank was indicated on both sleeves by a knot of black silk braid. A colonel's coat had five braids in a single knot and a captain's had two braids in a single knot.

Union officers, like officers in all armies, enjoyed considerable freedom of dress. In the field they often discarded their frock coats in favour of short jackets and loose fitting sack coats, which were longer and shouldn't be confused with enlisted men's sack coats. Some officers even left off the authorized shoulder straps on their sack coats so that they would be less conspicuous in the field, but this was not common practice. Since they were not regulation, officer's sack coats came in a variety of styles. The most common was a four-button coat made out of flannel, while a style favoured with New York officers was of dark blue cloth with five buttons and pockets on either side in the front. These pockets, together with the fronts, collars and bottom edges of the coats, were edged with ½-inch black mohair braid. Some officers' sack coats were even made with comfortable velvet collars, to provide maximum comfort to the wearer on campaign.

The dress of officers commanding the many militia regiments in the Union forces, provided variations on the regulation officers' uniforms. In 1861 officers of the 11th New York Volunteer Infantry wore gray double-breasted frock coats with two rows of seven buttons on the chest and four small buttons set on gold braid loops on the cuff slashes. Shoulder straps were dark blue with red edging and the officer's trousers were also gray with gold stripes down the seams edged in red. Captain J. Blake of the 69th New York State Militia wore a short jacket

edged in gold and black braid. The jacket also had gold shoulder knots. Completing the uniform, Blake's trousers were dark blue edged with gold stripes down the seams. Not only did Thomas Francis Meagher wear a gold trimmed Zouave uniform when he formed company K of the 69th New York, at Fredericksburg in December 1862, he was reported to have worn a frock coat made out of green velvet. Colonel Robert Nugent of the 69th, was renowned for wearing a checked shirt under his jacket and an officer's black and gold hat cord as a neck tie.

As might be expected, the uniforms worn by Union Zouave officers were extremely colorful. Minutes of a meeting held by 5th New York officers on 27 April 1861 prescribed that the trousers should be 'red and large no stripe'. Officers also wore smart dark blue frock coats for full dress, but their fatigue uniforms were a matter of personal choice. One officer, Captain Cleveland Winslow, was particularly spectacular in his mode of dress. Zouave Thomas Southwick wrote: 'Instead of a military frock coat which was part of the uniform worn by other officers, he wore a fancy Zouave jacket gaudily decorated. His military cap he jauntily wore to one side of his head. Altogether he was half Italian bandit and half English highwayman, a romantic looking fellow.'

The uniform of Felix Agnus who commanded the 165th New York, Second Battalion Duryée Zouaves, was equally as spectacular. Tailored by Brooks Brothers of New York, the jacket was decorated with red tape and cord offset with gilt cord. The jacket sleeves had galloons of two intertwined strips of gold braid and each sleeve opening from cuff to shoulder was decorated with 10 brass ball buttons.

Officer's Headwear

Many officers wore kepis which were similar in style to forage caps but were lower and had a straight visor. The tops of the kepis were also countersunk and had a rim. Tops of the kepis worn by Zouave and Chasseur officers would usually feature much gold trimming. McClellan style kepis favoured by many officers featured a square ducktail brim. Officers also wore forage caps, and the distinctive Mcdowell style of forage cap was particularly high in the crown. Some officers' kepis and forage caps were lined with silk. Hardee hats were regulation headwear for both officers and men; but like the soldiers, many officers found them uncomfortable to wear preferring wide-brimmed slouch hats in the field.

Officer's Weapons

All officers carried swords, but they were rarely used in combat and were worn more as a badge of rank. The regulation staff and field officers' swords were the 1850 pattern, carrying the initials US in the floral designs on the brass guard. Many variations of these swords were made abroad particularly in Klingenthal, Germany. The 1860 pattern sword had a graceful thin blade but failed to carry much favour with officers, who preferred the sturdier 1858 pattern. Swords, mainly the 1840 non-commissioned officer's sword were also carried by sergeants throughout the Civil War and were in service with the American army as late as 1910.

Pistols

Surprisingly, handguns were not part of the official arms issue to infantry officers. Sidearms carried by infantry officers and indeed the many infantrymen who began the war with a brace of pistols stuck into their belts, were privately purchased. The most common sidearm was the famous Colt six shot single action revolver. Each cylinder in the revolver was loaded using a paper or linen cartridge containing powder and ball rammed home with a rammer under the barrel. A percussion cap was then placed on the nipple at the other end of the chamber and each time the hammer was cocked, the cylinder was rotated and fired when the trigger was pulled and the hammer hit the cap.

U.S. Cavalry and Artillery

On the eve of the Civil War, the cavalry arm of the Union forces, like the infantry, was woefully understrength. There were only five regiments of regular cavalry and they were out protecting settlers on the plains. The 1st Regiment of dragoons had been recruited in 1836 while the 2nd regiment had originally been raised as a mounted rifle regiment in 1844. The 1st and 2nd Cavalry, the newest of these regiments, had been raised in 1855. A third cavalry regiment was raised in June 1861 and later all the regular mounted units were redesigned as the 1st, 2nd, 3rd, 4th and 5th cavalry regiments in order of seniority.

The army could also draw on the small number of mounted militia units in the North, but these were never as many as the infantry militia units. Maintaining horses and equipment was expensive in the North which unlike the rural South did not have such fine traditions of horsemanship. Nevertheless some militia cavalry units had flourished in the North. The 3rd Regiment, Hussars, of the New York State Militia, wore dark blue cloth jackets and fur busbies but it was said that their horses were delivery wagon horses, used by many of the regiment's personnel in their ordinary jobs. As a whole, the regiment didn't see action during the Civil War but one troop was in service with the Army.

The National Lancers of Boston whose lineage dated back to 1836 and who became Troop A of the 1st Battalion of Light Dragoons, Massachusetts Volunteer Militia wore smart red jackets and elaborate czapkas as part of their full dress uniform. Men from the National Lancers, minus their lances, saw service with the 1st Massachusetts Volunteer Cavalry and anybody experienced on a horse was a boon to the struggling Union cavalry.

General Winfield Scott, the ageing War of 1812 and Mexican War hero, who commanded the United States Army at the outbreak of the Civil War, had cantankerously spurned the use of cavalry for the coming struggle and many offers from established militia regiments or offers to raise fresh regiments were rejected by the War Department. A diehard artilleryman, Scott maintained that the war would be decided by cannon and that Northern cavalrymen would not be able to operate properly in the South. Volunteer cavalry was accepted on the basis that individual states provided mounts and equipment.

The North was slow in recruiting cavalry. A request to raise a serious number of 40,000 cavalry was not made until February 1862, when each state was asked to supply cavalry units. Equipment shortages which had also plagued the infantry were prevalent. At the beginning of the war the government had barely 5000 sets of horse equipment to issue. Outfitting a cavalry regiment was also very expensive, costing in excess of $400,000. However there were advantages to recruiting a cavalry regiment.

Cavalry had always been the most glamorous arm of military service as they swept passed lowly infantrymen, so recruiting usually went well among men who wanted to be something more than a foot soldier. The trouble was that the men who knew horses well, such as farmers, also knew the amount of work in caring for a horse and enlisted elsewhere. Quite often, eager recruits were city boys with no real knowledge of the animals; but they soon learned. Even before he was taught the most basic drill moves, the cavalryman was taught how to look after his mount.

Despite the government's extra investment in equipping the cavalry, it was not used as decisively as Confederate cavalry in the early stages of the war. Union cavalry was largely confined to picket duty resulting in the frequent infantryman's jibe 'Whoever saw a dead cavalryman?' Eventually the cavalry gained its independence and, grouped into brigades and divisions, became equal to Southern horsemen.

Cavalry Dress

Officially, cavalrymen were to wear a short jacket, usually called a shell jacket, made out of dark blue cloth, with one row of 12 small eagle buttons on the chest placed at equal distances.

(Continued on page 58)

Right: Charles H. Masland of the 6th Pennsylvania Cavalry, the famous Rush's Lancers, draws his sword for a patriotic pose. Note the shoulder scales on Masland's uniform, which the Lancers favoured more than other cavalry regiments. (U.S. Army Military History Institute/Jim Enos)

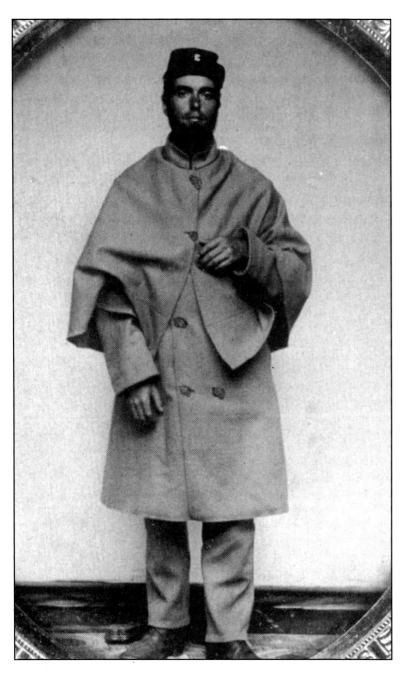

Private pictured wearing the regulation double-breasted overcoat for mounted men, but the coat has far fewer buttons on the cape than are normally seen. Wearing coats like these when mounted could be warm but cumbersome. (David Scheinmann)

Right: Union cavalryman in shell jacket with shoulder scales. He's also wearing dark blue trousers undoubtedly reinforced on the insides of the legs to cope with the rigours of being on horseback. (David Scheinmann)

State national color purchased by officers of the 50th Pennsylvania Volunteer Infantry at their own expense to replace their flag lost at the Battle of Second Manassas (Second Bull Run), 29–30 August 1862. This flag was carried by the regiment during the Battle of Fredericksburg, and was later sent to Philadelphia to have battle honours painted on, so was not carried at Gettysburg. A new state color was issued to the regiment in Fall 1863, and Colonel Hoffman, the regimental commander, had this flag sent home. (Courtesy of the Civil War Library and Museum, Philadelphia, Pa.)

Previous page: Comprising regiments from Wisconsin, Indiana and Michigan, the Iron Brigade was one of the most famous units of the American Civil War. During its time of service, the Wisconsin, who started the war in gray uniforms at First Ball Run, had the greatest number of deaths in battle of any regiment in the Union Army. One out of every five of its men never returned home.

The hatless private kneeling down is wearing an ordinary sack coat, the last resort of soldiers in many 'specialist' regiments whose uniforms were worn out or lost on campaign. The figures next to him wear the typical frock coats of the Iron Brigade and Hardee hats. These hats were ornamented with feather plumes, worn on either side, but under campaign conditions, many didn't last very long and were thrown away when they became dilapidated. However, based on evidence in contemporary photographs of Iron Brigade soldiers with plumes in their hats some months after their uniforms were issued, the soldiers illustrated in this plate have them. Many Iron Brigade soldiers, like the two privates pictured here, wore brass eagle badges to secure the turned up sides of their hats. Most hats featured the infantry's distinctive horn insignia worn on the front.

The 2nd Wisconsin lieutenant wears regulation officer's dress but instead of the Hardee also favoured by many officers of the Iron Brigade, he wears a forage cap. The lieutenant carries a .44 Colt army revolver and brandishes an imported German sword, the same pattern as an English rifle officer's sword of 1827 with a gothic hilt. (Painting by Chris Collingwood)

State Regimental Color presented to the 138th Pennsylvania Volunteer Infantry by the citizens of Bridgeport and Morristown, Pennsylvania, during *Christmas 1864 while the regiment was involved in the siege of Petersburg. (Courtesy of the Civil War Library and Museum, Philadelphia, Pa.)*

Union zouave uniforms and equipment. (far left) Fez, pantaloons, jacket, leggings and gaiters worn by Corporal Walter H. Mallorie, Co. B, 76th Pennsylvania Volunteers ('Keystone Zouaves'); (center) jacket worn by Private Edward A. Fulton, 72nd Pennsylvania Volunteers, when wounded at Antietam. Note the corps badge pinned to the breast; (right) jacket, pantaloons, and fez worn by Private Thaddeus Paxon, Co. F, 114th Pennsylvania Volunteers ('Collis' Zouaves'); (bottom right) fez which belonged to Private Latham Avery Fish, Co. C, 9th New York Volunteers ('Hawkin's Zouaves'), worn at Antietam. (Artifacts courtesy of Don Troini, military artist)

Union camp artifacts: (top left) patent coffee boiler and tin mugs stood around a Sibley stove. Spread out on the rubber blanket are various personal items, including (left to right) a soldier's 'housewife', a handkerchief, a folding candle stick; a chess set; a pipe and tobacco; a tintype; a diary and pocket bible. The haversack at bottom right contains a straight razor and case; military manuals; playing cards, and a folding eating utensil. (Courtesy of The Museum of the Confederacy)

Left: A typical Union infantryman, July 1863. His forage cap is regulation and has a stamped brass infantry bugle insignia attached to the top, plus 5th Corps badge. He wears a standard four-button sack coat and sky-blue regulation trousers. He carries a non-rigid knapsack with his blanket neatly stowed on top. His accoutrements consist of a M1855 cartridge box attached to a shoulder belt with 'eagle' plate, both of which are made of black bridle leather. The box contained two tin inserts designed to hold 40 rounds of cal. 58 Minie ball paper cartridges. The oval U.S. plate on its flap was designed to weigh the flap down when open, thus keeping out the elements. Attached to his waist belt, fastened by a U.S. oval buckle, is a regulation Model 1845 cap pouch. He has a black, painted haversack, and plain faced tin canteen covered with brown wool, suspended from his right shoulder. His tin mug is attached to the chain of his canteen, a practice with some infantrymen. Many canteen and haversack straps were too long, which caused the canteen or haversack to bang on the wearer's side. Hence soldiers tended to shorten the offending straps by tying a knot in them. His shoes are regulation-issue brogans. He holds a Springfield rifle musket. The details at right consist of (top) a McDowell-pattern forage cap with distinctive high crown; rigid box-pattern militia knapsack with army blanket attached; pair of brogans, showing hobnailed sole; wool-covered plain canteen, Model 1855 cartridge box, and triangular socket bayonet in scabbard. (Painting by Chris Collingwood)

Right: Union Hardee Hat and Branch Service Insignia: (top row left to right) Pattern 1858 hat insignia for regiment of mounted men; Pattern 1851 hat insignia for regiment of mounted men; Pattern 1851 ordnance enlisted man's stamped brass insignia, underneath which is an engineer enlisted man's stamped brass 'castle' insignia; Pattern 1851 cavalry enlisted man's stamped brass

insignia. (second row left to right) Pattern 1851 infantry enlisted man's stamped brass hat insignia; Pattern 1851 artillery officer's stamped brass insignia; Cavalry officer's stamped brass insignia. (third row left to right) Pattern 1851 infantry officer's stamped brass insignia; Pattern 1851 artillery enlisted man's stamped brass insignia; unofficial badge of the Cavalry Corps, Army of the Potomac, of stamped brass. (bottom left to right) Pattern 1851 infantry officer's embroidered hat insignia. The numeral inside the bugle indicates the regiment; Pattern 1851 officer's embroidered eagle – all service insignia; Pattern 1851 cavalry officer's embroidered hat insignia. (Artifacts courtesy of West Point Museum, West Point, New York)

Personal effects and decorations of Major General Galusha Pennypacker: The youngest general in American history, Galusha Pennypacker was wounded five times during the Civil War, and was awarded the Medal of Honor for conspicuous bravery during the Union action at Fort Fisher. He was appointed general at the age of 20, before he was old enough to vote! (left) US Army Model 1904 Medal of Honor complete with case, awarded to General Pennypacker. (centre) General officer's frock coat with velvet collar and cuffs, as worn by Pennypacker, placed over which is his Model 1850 presentation sword and scabbard. The sword is an import, having been made in Germany by Clauberg of Soligen (a town near the Rhine). (right) US Army Model 1896 Medal of Honor, formally in the possession of General Pennypacker. (Artifacts courtesy of Chester County Historical Society, West Chester, Pa.)

Sporting a revolver tucked into his waistbelt, and trousers tucked into his boots, this cavalryman wears an unusual dark blue overcoat. The regulation overcoat color was sky blue, but in the haste to get men adequately uniformed, dark blue overcoats were also sometimes issued. (David Scheinmann)

Left: A typical cavalry private poses to have his image made. Note the high collar of his shell jacket and the sword knot just visible dangling down from his sword. In combat, this would be wound around his wrist to stop him dropping his sabre. (David Scheinmann)

The stand up collar was cut away at an angle of 30 degrees and had two blind buttonholes on each side in yellow worsted ⅛ inch wide, each with one small button. The top buttonhole was 4 inches long, the lower 3½ long. The bottom and front ends of the collar were edged in the same braids, as were the front edge, bottom and two back seams of the coat. Yellow was the facing cover for cavalry, but the 1st and 2nd cavalry who had been mustered into service as the 1st and 2nd dragoons before the Civil War, were proud of their heritage and some of their jackets were lined in orange, the dragoons' traditional facing color.

To hold his waist belt in place, the cavalryman had two small bolsters stitched to the back of his jacket. Shorter and more stylish than the infantryman's standard sack coat, the tight fitting shell jackets which extended only as far as the cavalryman's waist gave him greater ease when moving in the saddle, but nevertheless cavalrymen would wear sack coats or fatigue blouses in the field. These fatigue blouses reached halfway down the thigh and were made out of dark blue flannel.

Shots showing cavalrymen mounted for campaign are comparatively rare but here we see what a cavalryman would have looked like in the field. Note the blanket tied up behind his saddle, the manageable way the cavalryman's sabre is hooked to his belt and the yellow stripe denoting his branch of service, running down his trouser seam. (David Scheinmann)

A Cavalry sergeant and private pose for the camera and show the disparity of dress you could expect to see in any cavalry regiment. The figure on the right favours a forage cap. (David Scheinmann)

The distinctive yellow facings of this cavalryman's uniform mark him out to be a bugler. Note the double seams of yellow on his trousers and the fancy stitching on the top of his boots. The bottom of his pistol holster can also be seen poking out from underneath his elbow. (David Scheinmann)

They fastened with four brass buttons and like a sack coat had an inside pocket over the left breast. Like infantrymen's trousers, cavalry trousers were standard issue blue kerseys but they were reinforced around the crotch and inside legs to prevent wear.

Cavalrymen were issued with sky-blue cloth overcoats similar to those of the infantry. They had a stand up collar 5 inches high and were double breasted with two rows of buttons. The coats fell to 6 to 8 inches below the knee and for practical purposes had a slit up the back which when the rider was dismounted could be done up with a concealed flap and buttons. Cavalrymen's coats had a cape attached which was lined with yellow and could be buttoned up as an added protection against the cold. In foul weather cavalrymen also wore a waterproof cape called a talma which had sleeves and reached to the knees.

While many cavalrymen were proud of their yellow-trimmed shell jackets, some preferred single-breasted plainer jackets without trim that were made to their own specifications. One Wisconsin cavalryman complained that his regulation jacket was 'oh so yellow that it made me sick'. Some states manufactured cavalry shell jackets which were close approximations of the official issue varying in the design of the piping, number of buttons and height of the collar.

The uniform of the 15th Pennsylvania Cavalry featured jackets slightly longer than issue shell jackets and they had red piping on the collar, sleeves and front. The piping was also formed into two rectangular shapes on either side of the jacket front. The shell jackets of the 2nd Missouri Volunteer Cavalry, though trimmed in regulation yellow, featured a curious diamond design on the jacket fronts, unique in the Union cavalry. 'All additions to or alterations of this uniform as prescribed are positively prohibited,' ordered the regiment's commander, Captain Lewis Merrill.

The men of Wilder's Mounted Brigade, Indiana and Illinois infantrymen who were 'galvanized' into cavalrymen to help fight Confederate cavalry and bushwackers harassing supply lines, took no pride at all in the regulation yellow-trimmed shell jackets they were issued with. 'We drew cavalry uniforms but cut off the yellow stripes from the seam of the pants and jackets, so that we might not be taken for cavalry,' wrote B. F. McGee, regimental historian of the 72nd Indiana Volunteer Infantry, an outfit not at all enamoured of their new uniforms.

The regular troopers of the 2nd Cavalry, who before the war had been the 2nd Dragoons, did not want to give up their orange facings at any price. 'Alas for the cherished orange it must give place to the gaudy yellow,' recalled by Theo F. Rodenborough in his book *From Everglade to Canyon with the Second Dragoons* (New York 1875). But orders permitted the former dragoons to wear their shell jackets with orange facings until they wore out and some men continued to wear them until well into the war.

Cavalry Headwear and Footwear

Like the infantry, cavalrymen were issued with a full dress Hardee hat, but the cavalry found it equally as uncomfortable,

The straps attaching the officer's sword to his waistbelt are well shown in this picture. Civil War officers carried their swords hooked to the waistbelt with the hilts to the rear so that they hung parallel to the left leg. With his trousers tucked into his boots this man looks every inch a cavalry officer, but surprisingly he doesn't wear shoulder straps. (David Scheinmann)

especially with the added stress of wearing the unwieldy hats while riding a horse. Like the infantry, cavalrymen would sometimes manipulate their hats into more comfortable shapes, but for the most part cavalrymen wore forage caps. Shoes were regulation bootees, but many cavalrymen were issued with or privately purchased knee-length leather boots. Even more individualistic than the infantry, many cavalrymen were notorious for wearing civilian dress especially in the later stages of the war. In 1864, orders were issued to the men of the 2nd Iowa cavalry that they had to destroy all their civilian clothes and get back into regulation attire.

Amazingly some men even had to be ordered not to wear Confederate clothing. Some cavalrymen found that Confederate uniforms made out of jean cloth were cooler to wear than the standard issue Federal woollen uniforms.

Cavalry Equipment

Basic cavalry equipment was the sword belt with two slings on the left side from which the cavalryman's sabre was suspended and a pistol holster and cap pouch worn on the left side. Up until the mid-1850s the sabre had been suspended on a shoulder strap fitted with two sabre slings to support the weight of the heavy dragoon sabre. But when the light cavalry sabre was introduced and support pads were added to the back of cavalry jackets, there was no need for the shoulder strap which had proved to be unpopular. In August 1859 James Ewell Brown Stuart, then a lieutenant in the 1st cavalry before he found fame as a Confederate cavalry commander, had invented a brass device for attaching the sabre to the waistbelt and took a patent out on his invention, but only a few of the attachments ever saw service.

Ammunition for the cavalryman's pistol was kept in a pouch behind his holster. Belt holsters were a comparatively new innovation, single shot pistols had been carried in saddle holsters, but in 1850 the Colt firearms company began manufacturing leather belts with holsters and in 1855 the War Department began ordering them for the cavalry. The most common way to wear a holster on the belt was on the right side with the butt of the holster pointing to the front.

Cavalry officer Colonel Max Friedman wears a regulation field grade officer's coat underneath his overcoat. (David Scheinmann)

The cavalryman's carbine was suspended from a sling worn over the left shoulder. Carbine slings were made out of black leather and were 56 inches long by 2½ inches wide. Slings were adjusted with a brass buckle and a hook on the sling snapped into a ring on the carbine buckle. Cavalrymen wore their carbine slings mounted or dismounted. Carbine ammunition was usually carried in a box on the carbine belt. Cavalrymen either slung their canteens over their shoulders or looped them around the saddle. Haversacks were carried the same way and contained the same items as an infantryman's haversack. Other equipment carried by cavalrymen would include saddle bags, a length of rope and the horse's feed bag. Strapped over the pommel at the front of the saddle the horse soldier carried his rolled overcoat or talma. On the cantle behind the rider was a rolled blanket and tarpaulin.

Cavalry Horses

Early on, cavalrymen learned that their horses were their most valuable items of equipment. The credo of most cavalrymen was that they took care of their horses before they took care of themselves and while an infantryman might be able to relax at the end of a day, cavalrymen spent hours grooming, feeding and watering their mounts.

In the winter of 1861 the 1st Maine Cavalry built stables for their horses while the men themselves slept out in the snow. But all the attention lavished on horses couldn't alter the effects of battle, and supplying enough mounts was a problem until the Union War Department established the Cavalry Bureau in 1863. The bureau was given the responsibility of mounting and equipping all Union cavalrymen and in 1864 it supplied over 150,000 mounts to troopers.

Cavalry Saddles

The McClellan saddle became the Union cavalry's most widely used saddle during the Civil War and was still being issued to mounted troops in the American army as late as World War II. The saddle was named after General George B. McClellan. McClellan saddles were extremely serviceable and were largely based on the saddles McClellan had seen being used by Cossacks when he had been an observer in the Crimea. McClellan saddles were light and strong and easy on a horse's back.

They were also comfortable for the rider, apart from the early

Derided at the beginning of the war, Union cavalry turned into an effective arm and this cavalryman has the air of a true veteran. Unlike many cavalrymen he's retained his cumbersome Hardee hat. (David Scheinmann)

Right: Colonel Richard H. Rush, the founder of the famed Lancer regiment that came to bear his name, wears a version of the stiff high-crowned patented whipple hat. It was one of the more unusual items of headgear worn in the Civil War and incorporated a rear flap to protect the wearer's neck. (U.S. Army Military History Institute/Jim Enos)

models covered in rawhide which often split. McClellan saddles were fitted with wooden stirrups with leather hoods. Under the saddle, a regulation blanket was folded like a pad. These blankets were usually dark blue wool with an orange border stripe and US in orange letters in the centre. Gray blankets with yellow trim were also issued.

Officers used McClellan saddles but favoured English saddles as well. Over the saddle, officers were supposed to drape a dark blue shabraque edged with gold lace.

Suitably saddled and equipped, all cavalry regiments should have been imposing sights, but the reality of a newly recruited cavalry regiment was often far from imposing, as remembered by Captain Vanderbilt in his History of the 10th New York Cavalry: 'Such a rattling, jerking, scrabbling cursing. I never heard before. Green horses some of them had never been ridden turned round and round, backed against each other, jumped up or stood up like trained circus horses. Some of the boys had never ridden anything since they galloped on a hobby horse and they clasped their legs close together, thus unconsciously sticking the spurs into their horses' sides.'

Sabres

Cavalrymen were usually either armed with the model 1840 heavy cavalry dragoon sabre or the 1856 light cavalry sabre. The heavy cavalry sabre had a curved blade and a half basket guard, with a wooden grip covered with leather and wound with twisted brass wire. The light cavalry sabre which gradually replaced the 1840 pattern was similar except that the blade was lighter and shorter.

Although many cavalry actions in the war were fought by troopers shooting at each other from comfortable distances with revolvers, the shock of an attack by sabre swinging cavalry could still have important effects in the war. Both types of U.S. cavalry sabre were based on French patterns, and had sword knots attached to the guard which was worn around the wrist to stop the sabre being dropped in action. Like many infantrymen, some cavalrymen thought their appearance was not complete without at lease one knife tucked into their belts as well as carrying a sabre. Most popular were hunting knives or the famous Bowie knife, the deadly looking broad-bladed knife originated by Rezin Bowie the brother of the Alamo hero, Jim Bowie. Some of these Bowie knives even had large hilts and also made first-class knuckle dusters.

Pistols

The standard revolvers carried by Union cavalrymen were Colts. Other models included pistols manufactured by the Starr arms company and Remington, but the Colt revolver was the mainstay of the Union cavalry. The standard issue was the Colt 'Army' pistol which was .44 calibre, but the .36 calibre 'Navy' model was also popular because of its lighter weight.

Carbines

Carbines saw limited use with the infantry but they were the standard arm of the cavalryman. A muzzle-loading rifle used on horseback is cumbersome and impractical, the best way to arm a cavalryman was with a breech-loading carbine. The Sharps carbine was very popular and the similarly designed Starr carbine was also widely used, but it was not as hard wearing and was particularly susceptible to getting clogged with black powder residue after the weapon was fired several times.

The Smith carbine was unique in that it used rubber cartridges which sealed the gap in the carbine breech, but the drawback was that these unusual cartridges could be difficult to remove. Other weapons included Gibbs carbines, but these had to be broken apart at the breech to insert a linen cartridge and the weapon was later officially condemned as being unserviceable.

Merrill carbines had a top-loading mechanism but they were not popular and neither were Burnside carbines, where cartridges again had a habit of jamming. The Spencer was the most serviceable weapon. The army bought 95,000 of them and they became the most popular cavalry carbine. Henry rifles, usually privately purchased, were also used but as they were longer than carbines they were often unwieldy on horseback and lacked a ring attachment to fit on to the cavalryman's shoulder belt.

Union Cavalry Officers' Dress

Regulation dress for officers comprised a dark blue frock coat single breasted for captains and lieutenants and double breasted for all other officers. Trousers were sky-blue with a one eighth yellow welt on the seam, except for general officers whose trousers were left plain. Many officers didn't wear the frock coat in favour of shell jackets and many modified the standard

Officers of the 27th New York Light Artillery wear special fatigue jackets with Russian shoulder knots, as prescribed in 1860 regulations. (David Scheinmann)

uniform or even designed their own. An officer of the 1st Rhode Island Cavalry added gold tape to the collar and sleeves of his regulation frock coat, while Colonel Alfred Duffie of the same regiment created his own uniform which had a double-breasted shell jacket, an embroidered chasseur cap and baggy chasseur trousers.

Colonel Israel Garrard of the 7th Ohio Cavalry also wore Chasseur trousers and his shell jacket was laden with gold loops. Alfred Torbert who began his Civil War career as colonel of the 1st New Jersey Infantry later became a cavalry commander and in 1864 wore a blue jacket with a wide collar and two rows of buttons. His black felt hat was creased down the centre with a single star in a wreath on the front. Crossed sabres were pinned on the right side. Sartorial style in cavalry officers varied from the elegant to the bizarre. It was not unusual to find officers wearing straw hats and battered Hardee hats with the brims coming down over their eyes. One officer of the 4th Pennsylvania Cavalry wore a coat even longer than a regulation frock coat, which he left unbuttoned to show off his fancy striped shirt and white collar.

Lancers and Hussars

Lancers and Hussars had been a military tradition in Europe for many years and their influence eventually filtered through to America. The Union army never fielded large numbers of lancers or hussars, but a number of specialist units were recruited and saw good service. It is a little surprising that in the romantic notions of soldiering that persisted throughout the Civil War more of these type of units were not raised.

Two troops of regular cavalry were armed with lances as an experiment in the 1840s, but the idea didn't catch on. During the Mexican War, some members of the Mexican Spy Company, irregulars who provided scouts and guides for the American army, carried lances, and a few lancer militia units flourished before the Civil War, but although the Union bought over 4000 lances from contractors at the start of the Civil War, most of them ended up surplus to requirements, only a handful of lancer regiments was raised and few saw active service. One unit, the 1st Michigan Cavalry, who grandly called themselves the 1st United States Lancers, appear to have modelled themselves on the British 16th Lancers who had scattered the enemy with a charge at the Battle of Aliwal during Britain's Indian campaigns in the 1840s.

The Michigan Lancers wore a light colored shell jacket and trousers and also sported jaunty pillbox forage caps, similar to the pillbox caps of the undress headwear of lancers in the British army. The men were fully equipped with lances as well as standard issue pistols, carbines and equipment; but they were later disbanded and never saw service. It was thought that the many Canadians in the ranks could cause trouble, particularly if their mother country Britain became embroiled in the Civil War, taking sides with the South against the Union. The thought of Britain recognizing the Confederacy and moving her troops stationed in Canada across the border to invade the North was always a Union fear.

The most famous Union Lancer regiment was Rush's Lancers, the 6th Pennsylvania Cavalry. Very much an elite regiment it was raised in Philadelphia by Colonel H. Rush between August and October 1861, with financial aide from prominent citizens in the city. Rush's Lancers, who at first were just armed with sabres and colt revolvers, adopted the lance at the suggestion of General McClellan who had seen lancers in action during his time as a war observer in the Crimea. Rush's Lancers wore the regulation cavalry uniform with a few minor variations. The jacket collar had only one loop of braid and one button, instead of the regulation two. Made out of Norwegian fir, their lances were 9 feet long and tipped with a blade 11 inches long.

A soldier wounded by such a blade could face a particularly unpleasant time. The lance points produced a narrow slit wound in the skin, which would heal on the surface, but debris carried in on the blade would fester underneath. A scarlet swallow-tailed pennon decorated each line and a leather sling was also attached to each lance so that lancers could carry them comfortably over their right shoulders. Each company of Rush's Lancers was also armed with 12 Sharps carbines for picket and scout duty.

As recorded in a sketch drawn by Winslow Homer of the regiment embarking at Alexandria Virginia for Old Point Comfort, the men were still wearing brass shoulder scales on their shell jackets in 1862. The men wore three variations of boots, the first were of soft leather which reached above the knee, the second were stiff leather boots with a protector for the knees in front and the third were a lower version of these boots reaching just up to the knees.

Some of Rush's lancers also seem to have done without boots, preferring shoes instead. Trousers worn this way would have been held down by straps under the instep. For full dress, Rush's lancers wore a high-crowned hat with a flap that could be folded down over the neck like a havelock. Officers had black ostrich feathers attached to the sides of their hats and crossed sabres insignia. Enlisted men's fatigue caps had horizontal leather visors, sometimes with the brass letters RL, regimental number 6 and crossed sabres on the top of the crowns.

Some historians have dismissed Lances used in the Civil War as novelty weapons that had little effect in combat, but Rush's Lancers saw some good service with theirs. Rush's Lancers first saw action shortly before the Battle of Hanover Courthouse in May 1862, when they charged an advance body of enemy cavalry and drove them away at lance-point. At Gaines's Mill, later in 1862, Rush's lancers were one of the units attacking an Alabama brigade and before South Mountain Rush's Lancers scattered a body of dismounted enemy cavalry in a wood. But one of their finest moments came at Antietam in September

Right: A member of the 1st U.S. Hussars poses for the camera in the unit's distinctive uniform which attracted many recruits, even in the weary days of the latter stages of the war. (U.S. Army Military History Institute/Jim Enos)

1862 when a well timed charge scattered enemy artillery.

It seems that the psychological effect of a charging line of cavalrymen armed with lances had a tremendous effect on the enemy, but Union authorities deemed that lances were no longer suitable for mid-19th century combat. In the summer of 1863 Rush's lancers reluctantly put their lances into storage and would never use them again. From then on, they fought like ordinary cavalrymen.

Hussars

After the Battle of Gettysburg, the Union began to get increasingly war weary. In October 1863 President Lincoln issued a call for new regiments and the New Jersey authorities hit upon a brilliant idea to speedily attract recruits into one of the State's new cavalry regiments. The 3rd New Jersey Cavalry was called the 1st United States Hussars and recruits were promised a special hussar uniform, unlike any others worn in the Union army. Originally recruited by European armies, the attitude of devil-may-care hussar units with their colorful uniforms had won them an even greater reputation than lancers and recruits anxious to be dashing hussars were not slow to fill the ranks of the 3rd New Jersey Cavalry.

The uniform of the 1st United States Hussars was based on those worn by Austrian Hussars and the 3rd New Jersey quickly became known as the Butterflies because of their exotic dress. Their jackets were cut in the regulation Union cavalry style and trimmed in yellow but they were fastened with 12 large buttons and two rows of 12 buttons formed a plastron at the side. Buttons were connected by double rows of yellow cord and cuffs were ornamented with yellow cord knots. Collars were edged with yellow tape and on each side featured an orange patch on which were set two yellow cords.

Lieutenant William Starks, adjutant of the 1st U.S. Hussars, wore this elaborate blue hip length pelisse edged in black astrakhan. His dark blue trousers look as if they have a single gold stripe running down the seams. (U.S. Army Military History Institute/Jim Enos)

Right: Dashing Colonel George E. Waring of the Fremont Hussars wears an unusual style kepi and double-breasted jacket under his cape. His unit was also known as the 1st Regiment Western Cavalry. (Massachusetts Commandery Military Order of the Loyal Legion & the U.S. Army Military History Institute/Jim Enos)

Hussars were issued with talmas which were made out of sky-blue material with yellow braid and tassel, and often worn flung back over the shoulders. Trousers appear to have been standard issue, but had broad yellow stripes on the seams. One of the most distinctive parts of the uniform was the pill box hat worn by the men, which was worn cocked at an angle or like an ordinary forage cap. The hussars' caps had a chin strap and were trimmed yellow. Crossed sabre insignia and the company letter was worn on top of the cap and hussars wore a brass 3 in a wreath on the fronts of their caps. Officers' uniforms were even more spectacular with gold rather than yellow cord.

Cavalry veterans sneered at the Hussars who were at first confined to courier duties. But in the Shenandoah Valley in the latter stages of the war the regiment developed plenty of fighting skills including capturing an entire enemy regiment. They may have been called Butterflies but the 1st United States Hussars also had a wasp-like sting.

Michigan Cavalrymen

The most famous Cavalry brigade of the American Civil War was Brigadier General George Armstrong Custer's Michigan Cavalry Brigade. Most enlisted men wore exact copies of the regulation cavalry shell jacket with its yellow braid, but one photograph of an enlisted man in Company G shows him wearing an unusual zouave-style jacket. What really marked the Michigan Brigade out was its exceptional *esprit de corps* reflected in the uniform accessories it was issued with by its commander Brigadier General George Armstrong Custer.

Although best remembered for his defeat at the Little Big Horn 11 years after the war, Custer had an exemplary Civil War career which catapulted him from serving on the staff of Major General George B. McClellan to command of the Michigan Cavalry Brigade and then command of the Army of the Potomac's third cavalry division. Custer took command of the Michigan cavalry Brigade in the summer of 1863 just days before the Battle of Gettysburg when Custer led the Wolverines, as his brigade became known, in a decisive action against Confederate cavalry. In admiration of their leader, some of Custer's men began to sport red neckties like the one he wore and before long it became fashionable in the entire brigade.

In the way they kept their uniforms and polished their equipment, Custer's men were a cut above most standard cavalry regiments. Custer selected the most smartly dressed companies of the brigade to act as his escort and smartly dressed individual troopers were chosen to act as orderlies at Brigade headquarters.

Custer also instituted his own 'awards system' for officers of his brigade who had performed particularly well. At his own expense, he commissioned Custer Badges from the New York jewellers Tiffany and Co., which were proudly worn on the chest by recipients. Each Custer badge was a solid gold Maltese Cross surmounted by a single Brigadier's star. Custer's name was also inscribed on the cross and the award could only be given on his direct orders. One Custer badge recipient was Colonel James H. Kidd who was wounded at Falling Waters and Winchester. Kidd eventually succeeded Custer as commander of the Michigan Cavalry Brigade.

Union Artillery

Many distinguished Civil War commanders served their military apprenticeships with the artillery during the Mexican War, a conflict which became a golden age for this branch of the service. One company from each of the four American artillery regiments was designated as a light battery and with each member of the battery mounted could manoeuvre as fast as the cavalry. One commander, Sam Ringgold, even had special uniforms issued to his command that included dark blue jackets, faced red, sky blue trousers, and a shako with red cords that became known as the Ringgold cap.

After the Mexican War, the artillery started going into decline. For the sake of economy many of the light batteries were dismounted and at the start of the Civil War there were only five regular artillery regiments. Each regiment had 12 companies, but only two of these companies in each regiment were equipped as field artillery with guns and horses. The rest of the companies served as infantry or heavy artillery manning the cumbersome heavy guns on the coast.

Artillery Uniforms

Broadly speaking, there were two types of uniforms worn by the Union artillery. Heavy artillery who manned coastal defences or

Right: Looking like a regular in the German army, this picture is of an unidentified United States Hussar taken in about 1860. Note the ornate trappings and Death's head motif on the busby. (Michael J. McAfee)

the fortifications around Washington wore the infantry regulation dress of frock coats and Hardee hats. Light artillery who served in the field officially wore shell jackets like the cavalry but artillery jackets were trimmed with scarlet braid, marking the artillery's branch of service. Unique to the light artillery was the dragoon style Ringgold cap with its high peak and red horsehair plumes.

In 1858, light artillerymen were ordered to wear hardee hats like the rest of the army, but they were unwilling to part with their Ringgold caps and in early 1859 they were authorized to wear scarlet cap cords and tassels on the hats and to place crossed

cannon and regimental numerals on the fronts. In practice it seems that the elaborate headgear saw little field service being replaced by kepis or forage caps.

In practice a field battery would wear a variety of uniform styles and infantry sack coats were common. In 1860 the government authorized a special jacket for light artillery

These men of company I Rush's lancers were photographed on the Virginia Peninsula in 1862. The company guidon visible in this picture still survives and is in the collection of the War Library and Museum, Loyal Legion of the United States, Philadelphia. (U.S. Army Military History Institute/Jim Enos)

officers, which had Russian shoulder knots of gilt cord, but many officers also wore the regulation nine button frock coat in the field, or like infantry and cavalry officers adapted dress to suit their fancy.

Northern artillery units never quite boasted the same individuality in their uniforms as some artillery units in Confederate service such as the Washington Artillery of New Orleans or the Richmond Howitzers, but they performed admirably. At Gettysburg, the 9th Massachusetts Artillery who had previously seen precious little action manning the defences of Washington found themselves in the thick of the action when almost single handedly they delayed the charge of a Confederate brigade and bought precious time for Union troops to entrench on Cemetery Ridge.

Manpower shortages late in the war meant that many Union heavy artillery regiments who had little service posted in the defences around Washington, were ordered to go to the front. Their smart frock coats and Hardee hats set them apart from the other soldiers and they became objects of derision, but the 'bandbox soldiers' proved they could fight. In May 1864 the 1st Maine Heavy Artillery lost 476 men at the Battle of Harris Farm and would also sustain heavy casualties at Petersburg.

Cannon

The muzzle-loading field piece was the standard workhorse of the artillery of the Civil War and usually six guns were grouped into a battery. The field artillery piece that saw the most use in the Civil War was the 12-pounder Napoleon 1857 model. A smooth-bore weapon, it was ideal at close ranges against enemy infantry. Parrott guns had breeches reinforced by a thick metal jacket and were accurate up to a range of 2 miles. Other deadly weapons in the North's artillery arsenal included 3-inch ordnance rifles which were cast in wrought iron. Columbiad guns, manned by the heavy artillery on the coast, saw little service.

Lieutenant Adam J. Slemmer of Company G. 1st United States Artillery, wears a frock coat and has a scholarly air of authority that typified many artillery officers during the American Civil War. (David Scheinmann)

U.S. Generals, Staff, and Special Units

Union Generals were authorized to wear double-breasted frock coats with dark blue velvet collars and cuffs. Major-generals had nine buttons placed in threes in two rows and brigadier generals had eight buttons in each row placed in pairs. Generals wore white shirts under their coats, black ties and usually a dark blue waistcoat with nine buttons. Dark blue trousers completed a typical general's clothing. The truly extravagant part of a Union general's uniform was the French-style *chapeau de bras* he was authorized to wear. The

chapeau de bras had been cancelled in the dress regulations of 1851 but was re-authorized in the regulations of 1859. In practice though most generals preferred to wear smart black felt Hardee hats pinned up on the right side with an embroidered gold eagle badge and with three black ostrich feathers on the left. Around their waists, generals wore a silk sash over a sword belt. The sashes were tied over the left hip.

General's overcoats were dark blue with four silk buttons at the front and a cape, a double silk knot on each sleeve indicated rank. Away from official work many generals preferred to wear officers' sack coats in the field, but some Union army generals were lacking in sartorial style. Surrendering at Appomattox Court House in 1865 General Lee wore a bright new uniform and a jewelled dress sword, but General Grant who had finally been able to wear Lee's army down, turned up to the surrender ceremony dressed very shabbily. 'Grant covered with mud in an old faded uniform looked like a fly on a shoulder of beef,' recalled one of Grant's staff, Colonel Amos Webster.

Staff officers wore basically the same basic uniforms but their cuffs and collars were dark blue. Field grade officers had two rows of seven buttons down the fronts of their frock coats, while company grade officers had a row of nine buttons. Epaulettes carried their corps and rank insignia, and rank insignia was also worn on dark blue shoulder straps. Colonels had a silver eagle, lieutenant colonels had two silver oak leaves, captains had two gold bars at each end of their shoulder straps while second lieutenants had a single gold bar at each end. First lieutenants' shoulder straps were plain. Staff officers' trousers had gold braid cord down the seams, their hats were decorated with black and gold cords and their waist sashes were crimson.

Major General Nathaniel Prentiss Banks in full dress, including an ornate chapeau. (David Scheinmann)

Right: This portrait of Brigadier General Dan Sickles details the velvet standing collar of his frock coat, and the single silver star that designates his rank can be seen on his epaulette. (David Scheinmann)

U.S. Marines

The U.S. Marine Corps in the American Civil War didn't have the same prominence in the Army that the Marines occupy today. The corps numbered under 5000 men and despite the bad performance of a detachment of Marines at First Bull Run, who together with the Fire Zouaves of the 11th New York broke and ran during a heavy artillery bombardment, the Marines performed well in many coastal operations. For full dress, Marines wore dark blue frock coats with yellow braid and scarlet trim. For campaign dress, they wore single-breasted frock coats trimmed in red on the collars and white linen trousers which were very suited to the humid conditions on the coast which they often fought in. Officers commonly wore double-breasted frock coats with Russian knots to indicate rank. Caps were Chasseur pattern kepis with a brass infantry horn and M on the front. Marines also had white buff equipment belts with brass rectangular belt plates and NCOs wore their yellow silk chevrons the tips up, not down like the army.

Marines carried unusual knapsacks which had two carrying straps, an adjustable breast strap and was marked USM on the back. Marines were originally armed with 1855 rifle muskets and officers carried infantry officers' sabres. Additional arms for Marine officers would include revolvers of the same type carried by infantry officers.

Berdan's Sharpshooters

The green forage caps and uniforms of Hiram Berdan's two regiments of sharpshooters made them unique in the Union forces during the American Civil War. They were elite regiments and the selection process to join as described by Lieutenant Colonel William M. Ripley in his book *Vermont Riflemen in the War for the Union*, was a tough one: 'it was required that a recruit should possess a good moral character, a sound physical development and in other respects come within the usual requirements of the army regulations. It was required of them that before enlistment they should just clarify to be called "sharp shooters" by such a public exhibition of their skill as should fairly entitle them to the name and warrant a reasonable expectation of usefulness in the field. The recruit should in effect be able to place ten bullets in succession within a ten-inch ring at a distance of two hundred yards.'

Brigadier General George Brinton McClellan and his wife. The two separate rows of eight buttons designating his rank can clearly be seen on McClellan's regulation frock coat. (David Scheinmann)

Right: This Berdan's Sharpshooters enlisted man wears the unit's distinctive frock coat and characteristically his trousers are tucked into tan-colored gaiters. (Michael J. McAfee)

One of the better photographs of Major General Ulysees S. Grant who cared little for smart dress, but who habitually wore a bow tie. (David Scheinmann)

Right: Hospital steward wearing the distinctive green armband of medical orderlies. (David Scheinmann)

Two engineer privates pose with the distinctive turreted insignia of the unit clearly visible on their forage caps. (David Scheinmann)

Right: This sergeant of the Veteran Reserve Corps wears the unit's light blue uniform. (David Scheinmann)

Colonel Berdan was virtually given a free hand in the choice of sharpshooters' uniforms, but strangely enough his first choice for the sharpshooters' clothing was not green, but blue. Originally, Berdan wanted his men to wear loose fitting heavy dark blue sack coats with metal buttons. The sack coats would have a black fringe around the collar and bottom. The men would wear soft felt hats ornamented with black feathers. Possibly influenced by the green uniforms of the German Jaeger units who had served with the British during the American Revolution, Berdan later changed his mind thinking that blue would be too conspicuous in the field, writing that 'The green-ness would better correspond in the leafy season with the colors of the foliage'.

The men wore forest-green double-breasted frock coats piped light green and their trousers were described as being of an Austrian blue-gray color. By 1862, these were exchanged for dark green trousers, although some of the men still wore the lighter colored pants. Berdan's Sharpshooters historian Captain C. A. Stevens wrote that the men's clothing presented a striking contrast to the regulation blue of the infantry and a correspondent for the *New York Post* picturesquely said that the green clad sharpshooters reminded him of Robin Hood's outlaws.

The original overcoats issued to Berdan's Sharpshooters were made of gray felt and many if not all were trimmed light green like the men's frock coats. It was a poorly conceived garment not only because in wet weather the material went very stiff, but because the men could be confused with the enemy. Lieutenant Colonel Ripley of the Sharpshooters wrote: 'Certain gray overcoats and soft hats of the same rebellious hue were promptly exchanged for others of a color in which they were less apt to be shot by mistake by their own friends. The fighting taught them the lesson that the gray overcoats and soft hats had to go, lest they be shot by their own friends.'

Some period photos of Berdan's Sharpshooters show individual men wearing sack coats rather than frock coats. These might be ordinary issue infantry sack coats issued because of clothing shortages or they may be special sack coats of green material like the Sharpshooters' standard issue frock coats. It's almost impossible to tell, from old black-and-white photographs. Berdan's Sharpshooters' forage caps were made out of heavy wool and were forest-green in color. Visors differed from the standard enlisted man's cap and resemble the pattern of a McDowell forage cap visor. The men

In the early days of the war, men of the 5th New York Volunteer Infantry used to wear havelocks under their fezzes and sometimes even tucked them up around their chins. (Brian C. Pohanka)

originally sported ostrich plumes in their kepis, but it seems that with rigorous combat in the field these would have quickly worn out.

Apart from their green forage caps, the 1st regiment of Berdan's Sharpshooters and possibly the 2nd regiment, were also issued with another type of headgear. It was described as 'a gray round hat with a leather visor, a flap to cover the neck and holes for ventilation.' These unwieldy hats were discarded in the spring of 1862, not least because men wearing them could again be mistaken for Confederates.

Berdan's Sharpshooters often wore a distinctive brass badge on their forage caps, which had the initials U.S.S.S. surrounded by a wreath. Soldiers joked that the letters stood for Unfortunate Soldiers Sadly Sold and not United States Sharpshooters. Another unique feature of the Sharpshooters' uniforms were the black non-reflective hard rubber buttons on their uniforms. No other unit in the Union army is reported to have worn them. Knapsacks carried by the sharpshooters were of a Prussian design and were made of tanned leather with the hair on the outside. They were heavier than regulation knapsacks but apparently fitted the men's backs well and were very roomy inside. It appears that Berdan's Sharpshooters were a particularly fine looking unit, who revelled in the distinctiveness of their uniforms. 'By our dress we were known far and wide and the appellation of "green coats" was soon acquired,' wrote Captain C. A. Stevens, the regimental historian.

Engineers

Building roads and bridges the Corps of Engineers had an unglamorous but necessary job. Sometimes they were also called to fight. The regular Union army's small engineer corps was bolstered by volunteer engineer regiments including the 50th New York Engineers and the 1st Michigan. Engineers wore infantry frock coats trimmed in yellow, with nine buttons down the front and two on each cuff. A distinctive badge worn by engineers on their forage was a brass turreted castle. Strangely the men of Elmer Ellsworth's United States Zouave cadets also wore this insignia on the collars of their Chasseur dress; possibly because Ellsworth planned to form an engineer battalion in the Cadets, or because he simply liked the design.

Engineer officers wore standard dress, but their trousers featured a gold seam stripe down each leg. Topographical engineers who were responsible for making maps, wore special buttons on their coats marked TE and even when they were merged into the Corps of Engineers they jealously guarded the privilege of wearing their unusual buttons.

In the field, engineers were issued with overalls to protect

Soldiers battered their hats into a variety of shapes to personalize them. This cavalry or artillery private, favoured a stovepipe effect with his hat. (David Scheinmann)

their uniforms from mud and a special pioneer corps made up of men drawn from other regiments was created in the Union Army of the Cumberland. On their left shoulders, the men wore a special cloth badge with a crossed hatchet motif.

The Signal Corps

The Signal Corps was another small but useful part of the Union Army. Strangely, they appear to have been dressed in cavalrymen's jackets and trousers and although not seeing active combat were well armed with revolvers.

Enlisted signalmen wore badges with crossed signal flags motifs on their sleeves. During the Peninsular Campaign when there was a brief craze for using manned balloons to look down on enemy positions, a special unit of signalmen was created who wore badges with BC, standing for Balloon Corps, motifs on their sleeves.

Veteran Reserve Corps and Medics

The Veteran Reserve Corps was created in 1863 as the Invalid Reserve Corps, but this name proved unpopular so it was changed. The Corps was composed of invalid soldiers performing light work or garrison duties freeing able soldiers for the field. Some companies of the Reserve Corps actually saw some combat themselves at Fort Stevens in the Washington defences when they helped to repel a raid by Jubal Early's Confederate cavalry. During the skirmish, the Corps lost five men.

Men of the Invalid Corps wore sky-blue cavalry-style jackets, but with shoulder straps. The color of these jackets was reminiscent of the jackets worn by soldiers in the Mexican War. Ordinary sack coats were worn for fatigue duties and trousers and forage caps were regulation. Officers of the Veteran Reserve Corps wore sky-blue frock coats, with dark blue velvet collars, cuffs and shoulder straps. Their sky-blue trousers had double stripes of dark blue cloth down the seams.

The first proper ambulance corps was established in the Army of the Potomac in 1862. Before that the only people

Bucktails were not the only soldiers to personalize their headgear. The infantry private wears an unusually shaped hat with a sprig of greenery or a feather stuck in it. (David Scheinmann)

Left: The way Union soldiers wore their uniform differed greatly. Some looked immaculate while others, like this soldier wearing his sack coat open, favoured a devil-may-care approach. This soldier has an oilskin cover on his forage cap. (David Scheinmann)

taking immediate care of wounded soldiers were bandsmen acting as stretcher bearers and about 10 soldiers relieved from normal duties by each regiment, but these men were usually misfits. In the Army of the Potomac each infantry regiment was eventually provided with three ambulances, each cavalry regiment had two ambulances and each artillery regiment had one. Privates in the Ambulance Corp were to wear 2-inch wide bands around their caps and a green half chevron 2 inches broad on each arm.

Army surgeons wore majors' uniforms and assistant surgeon wore captains' uniforms. Their dark blue trousers had gold cord running down each leg seam and their sashes were usually emerald green. Though medical care was far from perfect, soldiers could expect far better treatment if they were wounded than their forbears in previous wars. Assisting surgeons in the army was a team of medical cadets, dressed as second lieutenants and recruited from unqualified doctors in training.

Hospital stewards helped doctors and they wore a frock coat trimmed with crimson. On each sleeve they wore distinctive green sashes and their trousers had crimson stripes down the seams of each leg. For formal occasions, stewards were authorized to wear brass shoulder scales on each shoulder.

Personalising Uniforms

During the Civil War, many regiments were renowned for the individual touches they made to their uniforms. The Bucktails who sported strips of deer hide in their kepis have already been mentioned, but they were far from being the only Union regiment who stood out even though they wore regulation army dress. Some members of the 124th New York Volunteer Infantry, who were mainly recruited from Orange County New York State, wore orange ribbons looped in their buttonholes when they left to join up with the rest of the army and at the Battle of Chancellorsville in May 1863, where the regiment lost two fifths of its men the 124th's commander Augustus Van Horne Ellis urged his men forward using their nickname. The craze for men of the 124th pinning orange ribbons to their coats was noted by Private Henry Howard in his diary: 'One of the late (General Amiel) Whipple's aides came through the ward and saw the red tape on one of the men's buttonholes. He said "there is an orange blossom" and put his hand in his pocket and gave him a dollar.'

Already a fine unit, the ribbons gave the 124th New York an even greater sense of identity and purpose as they showed at the Battle of Gettysburg in July 1863, two months after they had been nicknamed Orange Blossoms at Chancellorsville. During the Battle of Gettysburg the 124th was stationed near Devil's Den and lost many more men trying to force back a Confederate attack that ultimately overwhelmed them.

A frock coat worn by Major John H. Thompson of the 124th New York still survives and has an orange ribbon still tied around the fifth buttonhole. The ribbon is 9 inches long and ⅝ inch wide.

Civil War soldiers wore a wide variety of unofficial insignia. Some members of Rush's Lancers wore badges with crossed lances and the men of the 11th New York Volunteer Infantry, the Fire Zouaves, were very fond of wearing the badges of the various hose, hook and ladder companies of the firefighting crews they had belonged to before the war.

Identity discs

Modern soldiers are issued with dog tags, but during the American Civil war there was no way of identifying soldiers killed in battle. Many soldiers before going into combat would pin slips of paper with their name and regiment to the backs of the coats in the hope that if they were killed they could be identified. Sometimes they also scratched their names into their waistbelts, or stencilled them on their haversacks, canteens or knapsacks. Many soldiers bought identity discs which were advertised by jewellers in popular magazines of the day such as *Harper's Weekly*.

Identity discs usually came in two types. The first was a badge made out of gold or silver engraved with the soldier's name and unit. The second was made out of brass or lead, and similar to the modern dog tag, was bored with a hole through which a length of string could be threaded for the disc to be worn around the wearer's neck. These tags usually had a patriotic motto on one side, with the owner's name and regiment on the other. Some soldiers even had their discs stamped with the names of the battles they had fought in. Civilian manufacturers sometimes set up shop on roadsides to supply passing troops with discs. In 1864 the entire 14th New Hampshire Infantry was supplied with discs stamped out by a dealer as the regiment marched through West Virginia, heading for the Shenandoah Valley.

Right: Major General Ambrose Burnside wears a nine-buttoned frock coat. His style of beard was much imitated and called a Burnside. (David Scheinmann)

Zouaves and Militia Units

By the mid-19th century, the French Army had a tremendous influence on military dress worldwide, especially in America. The traditional bond with the United States forged during the American Revolution, when France supported the fledging country in its fight for independence, and later the glowing reputation of French troops in the Crimea, was particularly noticeable in the many exotic French-style uniforms worn by Northern volunteers. The most famous of these volunteer units were the many Northern Zouave regiments and companies, based on the famed Zouaves of the French Army whose reckless exploits during the Crimean War had won them much fame.

The original Zouaves were natives of the Zouaoua tribe of North Africa, particularly noted for their bravery who together with some French settlers were formed into two battalions and served with the French Army during France's North African campaigns in the 1830s. By the time of the Crimean War the ranks of the Zouaves were filled entirely by French men. Three Zouave regiments of the line had been created and a regiment of Imperial Guard Zouaves was raised in 1855. Union General George B. McClellan, who as a captain had been an American observer in the Crimea, called Zouaves the 'beau ideal of a soldier'.

On the eve of the American Civil War, a Zouave craze swept America started by Elmer E. Ellsworth, a penniless law student and military enthusiast who was so enthralled by the stories of Zouave exploits told to him by Charles A. DeVilliers, a former French Army surgeon who had served with a Zouave regiment in the Crimea, that he decided to form his own Zouave unit from a company of the Illinois State Militia. Several Zouave companies, such as the company found in the Gardes Lafeyette, a militia unit largely composed of French immigrants in New York, already existed in America; but Ellsworth and his men,

This photograph of a 5th New Yorker was taken early in the war. Note the private's rolled blanket kept on top of his knapsack, and the badge, possibly his company's letter, on the front of his fez. There also appears to be another badge or piece of insignia attached to the front of his jacket. This man is completely uniformed and equipped ready for campaign, an enviable state for many soldiers as the war progressed. (Brian C. Pohanka)

A company of the 5th New York photographed at their camp near Fortress Monroe, Virginia, in the summer of 1861. When British War correspondent, William Howard Russell, saw the 5th on parade he claimed that many of them were not wearing fezzes, but just turbans that looked like discolored napkins wrapped around their heads, giving them a less than soldierly appearance. (Brian C. Pohanka)

who grandly called themselves the United States Zouave Cadets, enthralled the public during a drill display tour of East Coast cities in 1860.

Ellsworth later raised the 11th new York Volunteer Infantry, a unit of tough New York firemen who proudly called themselves Fire Zouaves, but Ellsworth and his men were destined not to see much glory. In Alexandria, Virginia, Ellsworth was gunned down and killed when he tried to remove a Confederate flag from a tavern and his dispirited men broke and ran when they came under heavy artillery fire at First Bull Run.

The classic French Zouave uniform was an adaptation of native North African dress comprising a fez, outlandish baggy trousers, and a short jacket worn over a shirt vest. The jacket was ornamented with trefoil designs called tombeaux on each side of the chest. The uniforms of American Zouaves varied from almost exact copies of French Zouave uniforms to wide interpretations of the Zouave style.

Ellsworth's first unit, the United States Zouave Cadets, wore no less than three styles of uniforms, but they were loosely based on French Chasseur uniforms and bore little resemblance to true Zouave uniforms, a point noted at the time in a report about the United States Zouave Cadets in the French newspaper *Courier des Etats Units*: 'These Zouaves are, however, three quarters contraband. Their uniform has nothing, or rather very little of the uniform of the French corps whose name they have adopted.'

The same can be said of the New York Fire Zouaves, the second unit raised by Ellsworth, who were originally outfitted in gray jackets of a Chasseur pattern and blue trousers. The jackets quickly wore out but the men kept their blue trousers and were issued with fezzes and blue waist sashes. A distinctive feature of the Fire Zouaves' uniforms was the red fireman's shirt they proudly wore. The men also shaved their heads like the French Zouaves.

Nearly every Northern State or town boasted Zouaves, even out west in Indiana, where the most famous Zouave regiment

James E. Taylor served with the 10th New York Volunteer Infantry, National Zouaves, until 1863. The 10th had quite a bewildering variety of uniforms during its existence, and in this photograph Taylor wears the distinctive dark blue jacket and light blue trousers of the 10th's last issued uniform. His trousers are tucked into white gaiters. (Michael J. McAfee)

Right: Reconstruction of a 5th New York, Duryée's Zouaves, on campaign 1862. This uniform with the distinctive red tombeaux on the chest separate from the red trim, is the third uniform issued to the regiment in February 1862 and the one most closely associated with the unit. The baggy trousers of the first uniform issued to Duryée's Zouaves featured blue trim around the pockets. Trousers issued later, like the ones worn in this picture, were plain. (Paul Smith)

The men of 14th Regiment New York State Militia, the famous Red-legged Devils from Brooklyn, wore these distinctive kepis with red tops from the beginning of the war to the end. Many soldiers fixed brass numerals to the front, although judging from many contemporary photographs this practice doesn't seem to have been as widespread as previously thought. This kepi was worn during the war and the red dot in the center of the top, is the badge of the 1st Corps in which the 14th Brooklyn served. (Martin L. Schoenfeld)

was Wallace's Zouaves founded by Colonel Lew Wallace, who was later to find fame as the author of the novel *Ben Hur*. Wallace was greatly impressed with the Zouave ideal, but as a devout Christian he didn't want his men dressed in Moslem clothing as represented by the true Zouave uniform, so his men were originally dressed in gray Chasseur pattern uniforms.

According to James Hennessey, the most authentically dressed Union Zouave regiment was the famed 5th New York, Duryée's Zouaves. War observer General Prim of the Spanish Army said they looked exactly like the French 2nd Regiment of Zouaves after he inspected them.

The regiment was commanded by Colonel Abram Duryée, a big name in New York militia affairs. It was said that the 5th decided to adopt a full Zouave uniform when Felix Agnus a veteran of the French 2nd Regiment of Zouaves who had emigrated to America, wore his Zouave uniform when he enlisted with the Advance Guard, as Duryée's Zouaves were first known.

Regimental historian, Alfred Davenport, left this account of the 5th uniform: 'A more picturesquely unique and fantastical

costume could scarcely be conceived. The breeches were wide flowing Zouave pants of a bright red, narrow and pleated at the top, wide at the bottom and baggy at the rear. These were topped with a broad sash of the same color edged with blue tape and falling nearly to the knee on the left side. The jacket was of a coarse blue material, trimmed with red tape, short, loose, low-necked and collarless and running in front. The shirts were of the same material with a broad stripe of red down the bosom. The leggings were heavy white canvas, buttoned to the knee and the shoes were clumsy, buttoned to the knee and the shoes were clumsy, square toed scows. The caps were close-fitting red fezzes turned back from the top of the head, to which was attached a cord with a blue tassel that dangled down in the middle of the back.'

Some 5th New Yorkers complained that the first issue of uniforms was not of the best quality and poorly made, especially the baggy trousers which were cut too high in the calf, but the tailoring firm who made the uniforms said that some Zouaves were wearing ordinary trousers under the baggy pants which affected the drape. However, they did agree to lengthen the last 125 pairs they delivered by 2 inches.

The 5th New York's fezzes were manufactured by the Seamless Clothing Company and were of red felt with a blue tassel. For ordinary wear the tassel was left to fall to the shoulder, but in action the cord could be drawn up through the fez to stop it getting in the way. For parade or as a matter of choice in the field, Zouaves wore white turbans around their fezzes. Despite its colorful uniforms, there were times when the 5th New York which served from 1861 to 1863, looked shabby. Indeed stories that Union soldiers were invariably better dressed than their Southern foes are a myth. As the experiences of the 5th New York show, hard campaigning took its toll on both armies.

The 5th was mustered into the United States service on 9 May 1861 and its uniforms were in a sorry state by the time the regiment arrived for a period of garrison duty in Baltimore,

Right: Lorenzo Clark poses in the uniform worn by the Zouave company of the 74th New York Volunteer Infantry. Like Company K of the 69th New York, or Company B of the 13th Regiment New York State Militia, it was not unusual for a single company in a volunteer unit to wear Zouave dress. But not only did the 74th's Zouave company have ornate tombeaux designs on its jackets, they had tombeaux designs on either side of their vests, visible in this photo. (Michael J. McAfee)

Maryland in July 1861. Regimental historian Alfred Davenport wrote: 'Our men looked shabby, some of the uniforms being absolutely worthless.' In a letter to the Secretary of War dated 27 July 1861 the regiment's commander Abram Duryée pleaded for something to be done about his men's clothing, writing: 'The uniforms furnished to us are nearly worn out and in a ruined condition.'

New uniforms for the regiment eventually arrived in September 1861, but they were not of good quality. Lieutenant Colonel Gouverneur Kemble Warren of the 5th bitterly complained that the linings of the jackets were made out of a material that shrank and pulled the jackets out of shape if they became wet. New uniforms were issued in September 1861, but the following year the Zouaves were in a bad way again. Alfred Davenport left this description in a letter: 'Our regiment is ragged and ununiformed, wearing all kinds of clothes, they might either dress us up in our regular Zouave suit or give us the regulation uniform, the latter is much better for service, warmer and neater, but they seem disposed to give us neither, therefore we should have been naked long ago had we not bought pants from the regulars and other regiments who have plenty to spare.'

Despite these deprivations, the 5th New York and its successor regiments the 5th New York Veteran Battalion and the 165th New York, Second Battalion Duryée Zouaves, had admirable service records. Civil War Zouave regiments have sometimes been dismissed as nine day wonders, but they were active throughout the conflict. The uniform of the 9th New York Volunteer Infantry, Hawkins' Zouaves, with its dark blue trousers and dark blue jacket became the United States Quartermaster Department standard issue Zouave uniform worn by other regiments including the 164th New York. Surplus 9th New York Hawkins' Zouaves uniforms were also worn by some post war Militia units.

A regiment was even raised to honour Elmer Ellsworth, the man who had done so much to popularize Zouaves in America before his untimely death. Patriotic citizens of the Ellsworth

Distinctive 'flower' tombeaux were a feature of the Zouave uniforms worn by many Zouave regiments from Indiana and other parts of the West. Private A. G. Garrett of the 34th Indiana Veteran Volunteer Infantry, wears a jacket which has a 'false vest' sewn into it. His sleeves carry diagonal veteran's stripes, showing that Garrett signed up again after his original time of service expired. (Michael J. McAfee)

Association nominated candidates for the 44th new York Volunteer Infantry, who were known as the People's Ellsworth Regiment or by the more spectacular title, Ellsworth's Avengers. Soldiers in the regiment had to be under 30 and stand not less than 5 feet 8 inches tall.

Their Zouave uniform comprising dark blue jackets and trousers and a red shirt trimmed blue was heavily influenced by the clothing worn by another unit the Albany Zouave Cadets. The men also received the standard regulation New York fatigue uniform of short dark blue jacket and sky-blue trousers, but photos of enlisted men taken in Alexandria, Virginia in 1864 show them still wearing their popular Zouave dress.

Pennsylvania provided some fine Zouave regiments, notably the 114th Pennsylvania, the Collis Zouaves. In August 1861 Captain H. T. Collis raised a company of Zouaves called the zouaves d'Afrique to act as bodyguard for General Nathaniel Banks and then he was commissioned to raise a full regiment of Zouaves, the 114th Pennsylvania. Collis Zouave musician Frank Rauscher described the uniform in his book *Music On The March*: 'The uniform adopted for the regiment was precisely like that of the original company – red pants, Zouave jacket, white leggings, blue sash around the waist and white turbans, which pricked up the pride of the new recruits and gave the regiment an imposing and warlike appearance. The material for these uniforms was all imported from France, and special arrangements were made to secure a sufficient supply of the same to replenish the uniforms during the whole term of service.' It seems though that late in the war the men were forced to wear ordinary sky-blue kersey trousers because supplies of scarlet cloth imported from France had run out.

During 1863 and 1864, the Union Army decided to transform three regiments who had been clad in ordinary army dress into Zouaves as a reward for their proficiency at drill and to maintain a Zouave *esprit de corps*. The regiments receiving these uniforms were the 146th New York in June 1863 and the 140th and 155th Pennsylvania who were issued with Zouave uniforms in the early part of 1864. 'The cloth is by far better material than any clothes issued before' wrote a private of the 140th New York. 'It is of

Private Lee Matthews of the 76th Ohio Volunteer Infantry wears a particularly elaborate Zouave jacket, a style which was also worn by the 53rd Ohio. This curious tombeaux design was one of the most elaborate of the Civil War. (Michael J. McAfee)

good quality – the dark blue trimmed with red.'

The new uniforms were particularly welcome to the men of the 155th Pennsylvania who had begun their service in 1862 wearing shapeless long blue coats. 'The exchange to the Zouave uniform from the plain blue infantry uniform was enjoyed immensely,' wrote the 155th's regimental historian. Although they now proudly called themselves Zouaves, the men of the 146th New York were issued with a light blue uniform of the style worn by the *Tirailleurs Algériens* or Turcos of the French army, native North African troops whose record equalled that of the Zouaves. The 146th's trousers lacked quite the same bagginess as Zouave trousers, but the men were happy with their dashing uniforms, which had been manufactured under the personal supervision of their commander, Colonel Kenner Garrard.

Frequently mistaken for Zouaves because of their red trousers, the 14th Regiment New York State Militia, better known by their spectacular title the Red Legged Devils from Brooklyn, were one of a number of Union militia units whose uniform was inspired by the dress of the *Chasseurs à pied* of the French Army. This smart, comfortable uniform, was adopted by a regimental board of officers in 1860, replacing the 14th's old uniforms that had included blue frock coats.

Some of the 14th's distinctive dark blue jackets had 'false vests' sewn into them. The buttons down the front of the jackets were ornamental and only the vests could be buttoned up, drawing the edges of the jacket closer together. Other types of jacket worn by the 14th didn't have the false vest sewn in at all, but a waistcoat-like garment worn under the jacket that fastened at the side and had a line of decorative buttons along the front. Red Austrian knots worn on the shoulders were a prominent feature of 14th Brooklyn jackets early in the war, but many were removed later, possibly because they got in the way and were impractical.

It looked as if the entire Union Army might be dressed in Chasseur uniforms if an experiment outfitting selected infantry regiments in Chasseur dress worked out. In August

Left: This sergeant of the 9th New York Volunteer Infantry, Hawkins' Zouaves, wears the uniform that became the standard issue Zouave uniform issued by the Army. The jackets were dark blue trimmed red and the matching dark blue trousers had ornamental red designs around the pockets. Either black or white gaiters were worn. (Michael J. McAfee)

1861, Montgomery Meigs the Quartermaster General of the United States Army, sent a letter to the United States Embassy in Paris, requesting that the Ambassador order 10,000 complete sets of Chasseur uniforms and equipment for Union soldiers. The firm of M. Alexis Godillot was contracted to supply the uniforms and accoutrements including French regulation knapsacks and the entire consignment was shipped to New York within four months of the order being placed.

The best regiments in a brigade drill competition held in Fitz John Porter's Division in the Army of the Potomac, were selected to receive the uniforms and the winners were the 62nd Pennsylvania in the 1st Brigade, the 18th Massachusetts in the 2nd Brigade and the 83rd Pennsylvania in the 3rd Brigade. 'Our boys are overjoyed at their good fortune and the colonel says we will have to work hard to keep up our reputation,' wrote one of the uniform recipients in 1861. The Chasseur uniform was the regulation 1860 French light infantry uniform, with a dark blue coat trimmed yellow and ornamented with dark green epaulettes. The full dress cap was leather and a French forage cap was also supplied. Other items included a fatigue jacket, a hooded jacket known as a *talma*, and white gloves.

The uniform looked spectacular but overall proved to be a disappointment. The average sized Frenchman being smaller than the average American, many of the uniforms proved to be too small, but this problem was alleviated in some cases by putting gussets in the seams. It's debatable whether any complete uniforms were worn in combat, but a soldier of the 83rd at the siege of Yorktown in the summer of 1862 is reported to have had the tassel shot off his cap. Although the 83rd was ordered to puts its uniforms into storage in March 1862, it seems some soldiers may have kept 'souvenirs' to wear in the field. Many of the Chasseur uniforms were later 'cannibalized' to provide some of the Zouave uniforms for the 155th Pennsylvania. The capes supplied with the uniforms were converted into Zouave jackets and some of the trousers were even converted into Voluminous Zouave pantaloons.

When he originally ordered the uniforms, Quartermaster Meigs wrote that he hoped that they would 'serve as models and will doubtless introduce many improvements in our service,' but he was to be proved wrong. The following year there was a further upsurge in interest in Chasseur uniforms, when it was proposed by a military board that the whole army should be outfitted in them, but the proposal was dropped. It was solely volunteer regiments that brought exotic touches to the Union army.

During the American Civil War, the ethnic background of soldiers was often reflected in the uniforms they wore. Cities teeming with immigrants were full of first or second generation Americans determined to prove their loyalty to their new country, but also anxious not to forget the ties with the military heritage of the places they came from. The 39th New York Volunteers, who were known as the Garibaldi Guard, were named after the famous Italian patriot and modelled their uniforms on those worn by the famed Italian Light Infantry, the Bersaglieri. The men adopted the famous Bersaglieri hats with a plume of cock feathers and they proudly fixed the initials GG on the front.

The 79th Regiment, New York State Militia was composed largely of men of Scottish ancestry who specifically requested that they be designated the 79th Regiment to establish ties with the British 79th Regiment, the Cameron Highlanders. In the 79th New York's regimental history it was recorded that in October 1860 the men were wearing: 'handsome State jackets with red facings, blue fatigue caps and Cameron tartan pants.'

The men were also later outfitted in kilts for their full dress uniforms. The regiment was mustered into service in early 1861 and had a fine pipe band. But despite being nicknamed the 'Cameron Highlanders' 'Highland Guard' and 'Bannock-burn Battalion', it's unlikely that many if any of the 79th wore their kilts or trews at First Bull Run. For some inexplicable reason the men were ordered to lay aside their kilts and trews before the regiment marched into Virginia. Photos later in the war though, do show some members of the 79th in trews and it can be assumed that they were worn on later campaigns.

New York's huge Irish community was represented in the 69th New York State Militia, but romantic tales of the regiment wearing jackets with emerald-green cuffs and collars, although mentioned in many accounts about the Civil War, are myth. In 1851 the regiment adopted a green tail coat with a shako but in 1858 when they were designated as an artillery regiment serving as light infantry they wore a New York regulation single-breasted dark blue coat.

At First Bull Run many members of the regiment fought in their shirtsleeves and some following Gaelic warrior customs even fought in bare feet. The only really distinctive uniforms worn in the 69th were those worn by Company K who were called the Irish Zouaves or Meagher's Zouaves after their

This 14th Brooklyn private wears the 15 button version of the regiment's jacket which unlike other jackets didn't incorporate a sewn-in false vest. Underneath his jacket this man would wear a Zouave style vest which buttoned up at the side. The buttons down the front of the vest are purely decorative. (Martin L. Schoenfeld)

founder, Thomas Francis Meagher, an Irish dissident. Meagher's men wore dark blue jackets and vests trimmed red but their caps and trousers were the same pattern as the rest of the regiment.

(Continued on page 105)

Previous page: Union cavalry at Five Forks, April 1865. The figure in the foreground represents General George Armstrong Custer shortly after his promotion to major general in the Fall of 1864. He wears a broad-brimmed hat, a sailor's shirt with white stars and trim on the collar, over which is a cut down double-breasted officer's frock coat. He also wears dark blue trousers with gold stripes. Completing this ensemble was Custer's trademark – his red necktie. The two troopers at rear wear regulation shell jackets with distinctive yellow trim on the collar, front, and cuffs. All three men are wielding sabres. (Painting by Chris Collingwood)

Union cavalry artifacts: At left, resting against the Regulation U.S. Army, Model 1859, McClellan saddle, with blanket roll, is a Model 1860 Spencer breech-loading, repeating carbine. To the right is a selection of cavalry uniform clothing, including a double-breasted overcoat for mounted troops, a trooper's shell jacket, and a musician's shell jacket, complete with braid across the chest.

Draped across all is a 9-foot-long lance with pennant, of the type used by the 6th Pennsylvania Cavalry ('Rush's Lancers') between 1861 and 1863. The edged weapon is a Model 1860 sabre which was standard issue to Union cavalrymen. (Artifacts from the J. Craig Nannos Collection, & the Civil War Library and Museum, Philadelphia, Pa.)

Union artillery clothing: (left to right) Light artillery shako hat complete with artillery insignia; musician's shell jacket; overcoat for mounted troops; enlisted men's shell jacket; Hardee hat complete with stamped brass ornament; frock coat with artillery branch service trim; and service trousers. From left to right, the weapons consist of a Model Colt Army revolver complete with holster; Model 1840 Light Artillery sabre with scabbard and waist belt; Model 1833 Foot Artillery short sword and scabbard. (Artifacts from the J. Craig Nannos Collection, & the Civil War Library and Museum, Philadelphia, Pa.)

Right: Massed Union artillery at Malvern Hill, July 1862: the artillerists depicted wear standard-issue uniforms consisting of forage caps bearing Pattern 1851 artillery enlisted man's stamped brass crossed cannon insignia, and shell jackets complete with red worsted trim. One of the men at rear wears brass shoulder scales, normally reserved for full dress. These were originally designed to fend off enemy sword thrusts. The officer on horseback wears a regulation frock coat and buff gauntlets. The man at left is ramming home a charge in the Napoleon cannon. (Painting by Chris Collingwood)

Union general officer's uniforms and equipment: (left to right) Frock coat of Major General G. K. Warren – note the corps badge pinned to the breast; General Warren's forage cap; General William Tecumseh Sherman's frock coat, complete with sash; frock coat of Brigadier General C. P. Herring; slouch hat worn by Major General John Sedgewick; frock coat of Major General R. B. Potter. Below right is the dress chapeau and box of Major General George H. Meade. (Artifacts from the Civil War Library and Museum, Philadelphia, Pa.; West Point Museum, West Point, N.Y., and the Bob Walter Collection)

Union officer's corps badges, medallions, & insignia: (left hand pic) (top left) 1st Division, 6th Corps badge of Brevet Major James W. Latta; (top right) Identification badge of Colonel P. J. Yorke; (bottom left) 1st Division, 4th Corps badge; (bottom right) Identification badge of Colonel C.P. Herring. (right hand pic) (top left) 3rd Brigade, 1st Division, 5th Corps, watch fob of Colonel C.P. Herring; (middle) 1st Division, 5th Corps pin of Captain N. Bayne; (top right) Identification pin; (bottom left) Devin's 1st Division, Sheridan's Cavalry Medallion; (bottom right) Badge worn by Lieutenant Daniel Layton. (Artifacts from the Civil War Library and Museum, Philadelphia, Pa.)

The letters on the forage cap worn by this proud American Chasseur are difficult to make out, but undoubtedly they are the numbers of one of the regiments who was awarded the prize of wearing Chasseur à pied uniforms especially imported from France, because of their prowess at drill.It's often claimed that many of the imported uniforms were too small for strapping American volunteers to wear, but this private fills his uniform comfortably. (David Scheinmann)

The only distinctly Irish part of the uniform was a green waist sash. Company K only wore their colorful uniforms at Bull Run, for the rest of the war they wore standard infantry clothing like their comrades. At Fredericksburg in 1862, Meagher, who now commanded the Irish Brigade of which the 69th became a part, ordered his men to put green sprigs of boxwood in their forage caps to distinguish them from the other Union troops.

There was a bewildering variety of dress in many other militia units on the eve of the war. The Putman Phalanx who were organized in Connecticut in 1858 modelled their uniforms on those worn by the George Washington's Bodyguard during the American Revolution and their dress included tricorne hats. A similar costume was adopted by Ruggles 51st New York State Militia who formed the basis of the 12th New York Infantry, but it's doubtful that such antiquarian dress ever saw combat. The Boston Light Infantry who were known as the Tiger Regiment wore black bearskin busbies with a blue plume and gold tassel. Bearskin busbies were a popular feature of many militia units including the Chicago Light Guard, the New York City Guard and the Connecticut Governor's Footguard whose bearskins featured a peak and a resplendent brass cap badge. Many Irish militia regiments criticized the units who wore them, saying that as British Guards units were outfitted with them they were a sign of British oppression. They must have forgotten that the British Army had copied its bearskin busbies from those worn by Grenadiers in the French Garde Imperiale.

One of the best known American militia units was the Albany Burgesses Corps, formed when leading citizens in Albany petitioned the governor of New York State to form an independent artillery company. The dress coat of the Albany Burgesses Corps was a magnificent scarlet double-breasted tailcoat which had two rows of buttons bearing the letters ABC. Coat tails were turned back and lined white and had a four button pocket flap. Officers wore gold-fringed epaulettes with the ABC monogram on the crescent, but apparently the men in the ranks had ones of white worsted.

Line officers and enlisted men wore their black bearskin caps for full dress and each bearskin had a gold tassel on the front. Staff officers wore a black full dress chapeau with a black leather plume and gold lace cockade. As an undress uniform the chapeau was replaced with a dark blue cap which had a red and black pompom, held by an elaborate brass ornament bearing the state coat of arms of an embroidered NY within a wreath. In the summer, white linen trousers were worn for parades, otherwise

the men wore woollen trousers. The equipment of the Albany Burgesses Corps was equally as sumptuous. Their waistbelts carried a buckle with the initials ABC picked out and their black bayonet scabbards and cartridge boxes were of the finest leather. The Burgesses Corps also had a fatigue uniform which was similar to the regulation United States Army frock coat except the frock coats of the Albany Burgesses Corps were indigo in color.

The Cincinatti Rover Guards who became part of the 2nd Ohio Volunteer Infantry had an entire dress uniform made out of scarlet cloth. The coats were trimmed light buff and the trousers had a broad buff stripe on the seam trimmed with gold lace. Caps were regulation but they had a special visor made out of burnished and lacquered leather, richly decorated with a gold embroidered bugle, a star and eagle and the initials CRG. Plumes on the helmets were red tipped white. Cross belts were white and the belt plate for the cross belts was of burnished gilt brass and featured a five-pointed star motif. Waistbelts were lacquered, with the initials CRG in burnished metal. The Cincinatti Rover Guards didn't wear its magnificent uniforms all the time. For fatigues, the men wore a less spectacular uniform which had a dark blue jacket, a cap trimmed with red cord and black trousers.

Left: The popular Chasseur pattern of dress is again reflected in the uniform worn by this young private of the 12th New York State Militia, although the bagginess of his trousers is almost Zouave style. This man wears russet or tan colored gaiters and his regiment's numbers are visible on the front of his light blue kepi. Mustered in for three months at the beginning of the war, the 12th New York never saw much active service. (David Scheinmann)

Far left: The 34th Ohio Volunteer Infantry, the Piatt Zouaves were renowned for wearing 18th-century-style tricorne hats as part of their Zouave uniform but this ungainly looking duo prefer to wear fezzes. The jackets, which appear to be dark blue trimmed red, seem to be of a Chasseur style cut. (Michael J. McAfee)

The 39th New York Volunteers, the famed Garibaldi Guard, parade past President Lincoln. Their authentic copies of the dress worn by the italian Bersaglieri were some of the most striking uniforms of the war, but on campaign many of the men wore forage caps and red shirts. As shown in this picture, the 39th carried no less than three colors. They not only had the usual national and regimental colors, but carried additional unofficial colors based on the red, white and green design of the Italian National flag. (Peter Newark's Military Pictures)

Right: The 155th Pennsylvania Volunteer Infantry wore a dark blue uniform with distinctive yellow tombeaux designs that show up well in this photograph of a private clutching his fez as he rests his hand on a studio prop. The arm wound this private received, might have been as a result of the terrible fight the 155th Pennsylvania took part in during the Wilderness Campaign. (Michael J. McAfee)

The 22nd Regiment, New York State Militia, was funded by banking and insurance companies in the city who were worried about the departure of so many of New York's militia units who were being posted away to defend Washington. The 22nd New York State Militia wore a gray single-breasted frock coat edged with a red collar and cuffs trimmed with white piping. Trousers which were tucked into yellow leather leggings were also gray with a red stripe edged with white piping down the seams. Kepis were gray with a red band and top, which was again edged with white piping. Because of their gaudy trimming the men became known as the Strawberry Grays. For the first year of the war, the 22nd was stationed in New York City but inevitably it was ordered south and was stationed for a time at Harper's Ferry. By this time, though, the regiment had sent home its distinctive

The tombeaux designs of the 146th New York Volunteer Infantry show up well in this photograph but like yellow embroidery in most period photographs, they've registered black. This private wears a checked skirt under his jacket. Checked shirts were popular in the Civil War. (Martin L. Schoenfeld)

The 75th New York Volunteers had a curious almost nautical style of piping around the cuffs of their jackets, as shown on the jacket of this private. (Martin L. Schoenfeld)

This private of the 79th new York Volunteer Infantry wears the Scottish full dress of his regiment, including a kilt made out of Cameron of Erracht tartan. For undress, tartan trews were also worn, but trying to find supplies of enough tartan to outfit the entire regiment proved to be a problem. On 2 June 1861, when the regiment paraded in Baltimore, one journalist reported that the crowd who had come out to see the 79th in their Scottish uniforms was disappointed because only a third of the regiment were outfitted in Scottish dress. (Michael J. McAfee)

1st Lieutenant Thomas Cartwright wears the regulation uniform of Duryée's Zouaves, the 5th New York Volunteer Infantry. Cartwright died of wounds received at Gaines' Mill in 1862. (New York Division of Military and Naval Affairs)

gray coats and wore standard regulation army sack coats.

The 1st Regiment Rhode Island Detached Militia wore unusual long blue blouses ending just above the knee, which were not unlike British 18th- and 19th-century farmers' smocks. The most distinctive part of the regiment's uniforms were the rolled red blankets that every man carried. Ambrose E. Burnside, who had organized the regiment and went on to have a particularly disastrous career as a general later in the war, designed the uniforms and according to observers in Washington 'the absence of smart trappings made the unit look ready for business'. Burnside, who seems to have been infinitely better as a tailor than a general, also modified the men's blankets. Each blanket had a hole cut in the centre so that the men could wear them as ponchos and this was particularly welcome in cold weather.

The men of the Second Regiment, New Hampshire Volunteer Militia, began the war wearing 'claw hammer' or 'spiketail' coatees which were almost Napoleonic in style and gave the regiment a particularly distinctive look. Their trousers had a broad red stripe down the seams.

The 71st Regiment New York State Militia elected to wear smart frock coats of the 'national color' dark blue. The regiment's personnel were native born Americans who saw the increasing number of militia regiments formed from immigrants as a threat. New York's most esteemed militia regiment, the 7th New York State Militia, which dated back to 1806, wore a full dress and fatigue uniform both of gray and was known as the 'Old Graybacks'. The fatigue jacket comprised a shorter jacket with black cuffs. The 7th had for a time been commanded by Abram Duryée's Zouaves. Although never seeing combat itself, many of the 7th's officers went on to distinguished careers with other regiments. In Philadelphia the Scott Legion formed from veterans of the Mexican War who had last seen service from 1846 to 1848, wore the regulation Mexican war uniform including sky-blue shell jackets and dark blue forage caps.

A company of the 164th New York Volunteer Infantry relaxing in camp with their arms stacked. It is claimed that the 164th had green tassels on their fezzes to show off their proud Irish heritage. Uniforms like these worn by the 164th, saw services with many National Guard Units in the years after the war had ended. (Michael J. McAfee)

Union State Uniforms

Although the Union Army had developed a regulation uniform, many states jealously guarded the right to equip their own volunteers. Most states had drawn up their own uniform regulations and many men joining units in these states started the war in uniforms that not only were locally prescribed, but in many cases were manufactured in the state concerned. Some of these states followed the U.S. Army regulations almost exactly, but before 1861 states didn't draw uniforms from army stocks. Regulations in other states varied the design and color of local volunteer uniforms, but some volunteer units, such as the many Zouave and Chasseur regiments already described, chose to ignore state regulations completely and designed their own fanciful uniforms; but thousands of volunteers went to war in regulation state uniforms.

New York infantry privates in camp wearing state regulation jackets rounded at the front. (David Scheinmann)

After 1851 there was a growing trend, notably in Northern cities, to provide volunteer regiments with a standardized uniform, particularly with regiments where each different company designed its own uniforms and could have a motley appearance on parade. Wealthy cities such as New York seem to have been particularly successful in getting many of their volunteer regiments neatly uniformed in standard dress. In 1859, the 69th New York State Militia changed its green tail coats for blue uniforms in keeping with the 1858 New York militia regulations and was a typical volunteer regiment that began the war wearing state regulation dress. A report in October 1859 noted: 'The uniform of this regiment is all new and according to the regulation as adopted. The change in the uniform of this regiment is highly creditable to them as the one they have discarded was good and they could have retained it; but, desirous of conforming to the regulation color, they sacrificed their prejudice for a color that was cherished by them and adopted blue.'

The 69th received coats based on U.S. Army regulations which were described as: 'A single breasted frock coat of dark blue cloth with a skirt extending to within four inches of the bed of the knee. One row of nine buttons on the breast, placed at equal distances; stand-up collar to rise no higher than to permit the chin to turn freely over it, to hook in front of the bottom, and slope thence up and backward at an angle of thirty degrees on each side; cuffs pointed according to pattern, and to button with two small buttons at the outer seam. Collar and cuffs edged with a welt of scarlet cloth. Narrow lining for skirt of the coat of same material and color of the coat; pockets in the folds of skirts with one button at the hip to range with the lowest buttons on the breast; no buttons at the ends of the pockets.'

It appears that the regulation coats were often longer than specified, extending as far as the knee. The 69th added narrow red shoulder straps to their coats secured by a small button, and on top of these for full dress they wore scarlet worsted epaulettes.

New York regulation trousers on the eve of the American Civil War, were based on regulation army trousers worn before 1854 and they were sky blue with a ⅛-inch scarlet welt on the seams. Full dress caps were based on the army regulation cap of 1851 and were made out of dark blue cloth on a felt body, but varied a little in dimensions. The crowns were about 6 inches in diameter and were designed to tilt forwards slightly and had a black leather band around the bottom. The caps had visors and a black leather chinstrap attached to the helmet by two buttons.

Officers' dress conformed to the 1858 pattern New York regulations which was a close approximation of U.S. standard army pattern, except that the skirts of coats were longer. Regulations stated: 'All officers shall wear a frock coat of dark blue cloth, the waist to extend to the top of the hip and the skirt to within one inch of the bend of the knee.' The coats were lined black and the epaulettes and shoulder straps were of the standard New York regular army pattern. Coats were worn with sky-blue trousers which had scarlet welts down each side bordered with gold lace. New York regulation officers' caps were to be made out of dark blue cloth but the crowns were meant to lie flat without any stiffening inside.

Regulations adopted in April 1861, prescribed dark blue jackets for New York troops, which were meant to have eight buttons on the front and reach down 4 inches from a man's waistbelt. Trousers were described as being light blue with a full cut in the legs. New York State issued overcoats were to be of a similar pattern as the regular army.

The New York issue regulation forage caps were very unusual. They were supposed to incorporate a waterproof cover similar to a havelock, which fell to the shoulder. This complicated accessory was designed to be buttoned on the kepi visor and it was also fitted with strings so that it could be tied at the chin. Regulations also stated that each enlisted man should be provided with two cotton flannel shirts, two pairs of stout woollen socks, a pair of stout shoes and a waterproofed blanket.

The most usual jacket issued to New York Volunteers was dark blue with a low standing collar. These jackets had light blue trim, although some jackets had piping of a blue green color. New York jackets had shoulder straps, similar to the straps found on many Confederate jackets, but the New York jacket shoulder straps were trimmed light blue. Eight large brass buttons with the state insignia were worn down the front of the jacket, featuring the coat of arms of the City of New York and the motto 'Excelsior'.

Jackets were lined with cotton and a narrow pocket, called a slash pocket, was often a feature over the left breast. Jacket sleeves had two small buttons on each cuff, but these were for decorative purposes only: the cuffs could not be opened. New York State jackets were issued to more than 100 regiments from

Right: This corporal is also a New Hampshire Volunteer. (David Scheinmann)

New York and New York State and the majority were good, hard wearing garments.

In 1863 New York wanted to clothe all its many militia units the same way, with dark blue jackets which had pointed white cuffs. Two styles of uniform were available; the first was the ever popular Chasseur pattern with a long Chasseur jacket, a piped cap of dark blue and full sky-blue trousers. The second comprised a dark blue polka jacket trimmed with white piping. This uniform had the same cape as the Chasseur uniform and sky-blue trousers.

Trousers were a light indigo color and had tape edging around the pockets for militiamen who wore Chasseur jackets. Dark blue kepis were provided with the state coat of arms worn on the front. Mounted units of the militia wore regular cavalry style jackets with forage caps or brimmed hats. Buttons again featured the state coat of arms and officers and non commissioned officers had handsome rectangular sword belts with an NY motif raised in silver. Enlisted men wore standard SNY beltplates.

It generally looks as if New York's enlisted men armed and equipped by the state were well catered for. In 1862 the Quartermaster General of the State of New York issued the 143rd New York Volunteer Infantry, another typical regiment with this bonanza of items; 1160 infantry jackets, 1000 infantry trousers, 1000 infantry great coats, 1600 great coat straps, 1000 caps, 1016 letters, 3043 numbers, 1105 blankets, 2000 shirts, 2100 drawers, 2100 pairs of socks and 1000 pairs of shoes.

Connecticut's militia system dated back to the 17th century and boasted the longest established militia units in the Union. Indeed, two of its present National Guard regiments can claim direct descendancy from units formed in the state over 300 years ago. The state was proud of its volunteer forces but on the eve of the Civil War many units were lacking adequate uniforms. The *Military Gazette*, published in New York, claimed that Connecticut's eight state regiments were 'in a most sickly and ephemeral condition' and such comments prompted the Connecticut authorities to improve the quality and design of state issued uniforms. A state uniform had originally been adopted by Connecticut in 1847 which with minor exceptions was similar to the uniform worn by the U.S. Army.

In 1851 Connecticut based its State uniforms on the new pattern uniforms being introduced into the regular army, the Governor of Connecticut felt that these uniforms would combine 'the essential requisites of neatness, cheapness,

comfort and utility'. The new uniforms cost less than 15 dollars and all militia units were ordered to wear them when their existing uniforms wore out.

The new uniform for officers and men was a dark blue frock coat and trousers. Buttons were arranged the same as the regular army. Dark blue cloth caps were part of the uniform which had distinctively colored pompons. Officers' overcoats were double breasted, while those for enlisted men were single breasted. Strangely response was slow from the militia units to equip themselves with these state issued uniforms. The Adjutant General said that units not conforming to the new uniform pattern should be fined and even planned to circulate a series of colored prints depicting the uniform so there could be no excuse in volunteers not knowing about them.

Eventually four fifths of the Connecticut militia were outfitted in state uniforms which, because of their accessories, were some of the most colorful of the American Civil War. Two companies of each Connecticut regiment were usually classed as rifle companies and wore green pompons on their caps, green piping on their coats and green trouser stripes.

An independent rifle regiment was raised in 1861 and all the men had green facings. But although their uniforms were smart, the armaments issued to some of the men, as recalled by one militiaman, were less than adequate. 'They brought out a lot of old Springfield smooth-bore muskets for us, the same as they had already given to some of the other companies of our regiment. We just informed them that we were not going to carry them guns – we preferred Sharps rifles. We were a rifle company; hadn't we got green stripes sewed on our pants?'

Connecticut artillerymen wore scarlet pompons and had scarlet piping and trouser stripes. Cavalrymen had orange facings and many wore felt hats and plumes instead of dress caps. Volunteers were usually uniformed and equipped by the towns from which they came. The blue cloth for the uniforms was cut up by teams of local ladies and made into uniforms. Until proper forage caps could be obtained many men took the stiffening out of their formal dress caps and wore them with the crowns flat.

Right: This well armed volunteer wears a typical state issued jacket with shoulder straps. He's also wearing a state buckle, but it's almost impossible to make out the full design. (David Scheinmann)

In early 1861 supplies of blue cloth ran out so that one Connecticut volunteer infantry regiment had to be uniformed in gray. Their uniforms were based on the famous gray uniforms worn by the 7th Regiment New York State Militia, the Old Graybacks. The men were also issued with a light gray cap.

Connecticut regiments were renowned for the formality of their dress and they were especially noted for the time they took polishing their brasswork, but Connecticut regiments like regiments in general suffered from uniforms made of poor quality cloth, some of which didn't last beyond the first months of the war. Four Connecticut infantry regiments were issued with trousers and jackets made out of a cheap blend of wool and cotton that quickly fell apart during the rigours of the Bull Run campaign. It's said that when the men returned home many of them paraded in trousers made up out of old blankets and some even wore items of captured Confederate clothing.

Connecticut full dress shakos, some of which saw service during the War bore the state coat of arms; vines with grapes over the motto *Qui transtulit sustinet*. Officers wore the letters CM as their badge. Buttons on state issued uniforms also bore the same motto as the shakos. Despite the previous comments of the rifleman bemoaning the fact that his unit was not well equipped with weapons, it seems that Connecticut volunteers issued weapons by the state were generally better off than the volunteers from many other states.

Connecticut was a heavily industrialized state and was able to buy its weapons from a variety of local manufacturers, including the Colt Firearms Company. Samuel Colt even planned to raise, arm and equip a regiment at his own expense. Colt wanted to raise a regiment composed of tall men of good character and insisted on the right of being able to select all the officers personally, but authorities deemed that the regiment would be elitist and Colt's request to raise a body of troops for the Union was eventually turned down.

Connecticut troops were issued with several unusual items of equipment by the state, including a unique canteen and ration box combined. Many of the issued knapsacks seem to have been particularly uncomfortable because the carrying straps meant the whole weight was concentrated on a man's lung area. The

Left: This New Hampshire volunteer holds his forage cap which bears the initial E for his company, the number of his regiment, and NHV for his state initials. (David Sheinmann)

rubber knapsacks also had an appalling smell. The *New Haven Daily Register* wrote: 'They are the meanest specimens of equipment that you can smell about as far as they can be seen.'

The State of Maine issued many of its volunteer forces with uniforms which came in a bewildering variety of shades of gray. In 1861 troops received frock coats with eight buttons stamped with the Maine coat of arms down the front, gray trousers and gray forage caps. These could be in Canada gray or were issued in light gray, cadet gray, and a bluish cadet gray color. Blue uniforms were also issued to some regiments in the state which unlike the regulation army uniforms had dark blue trousers, instead of light blue kerseys. Indeed, for some reason Maine troops always preferred wearing dark blue to light blue trousers.

Soldiers from Maine had Mexican war style waistbelt plates marked with VMM, which stood for Volunteer Militia of Maine. These waistbelts were smaller than the regulation size, but the men's cartridge box plates also marked VMM came in the same size as regulation army cartridge box plates. Maine soldiers were armed with 1855 rifle muskets and 1858 pattern Enfields from state stores.

It seems that Maine State issued uniforms, unlike some uniforms issued by other states, were not worn long into the war. The majority of men replaced the state dress with regulation army dress after they marched to Washington in the summer of 1861. Doubtless some Maine items did stay in service, including the state's waist belt plates and cartridge box plates.

A poor frontier state, Minnesota could not afford to outfit its troops in the smart uniforms many of the smart Eastern states supplied. The uniform issued to Minnesota troops reflected their background and comprised rugged thick shirts which in the main seem to have been red or checkered, black trousers, and wide-brimmed black hats. Parts of the uniform seem to have been extremely serviceable and certainly the men of Minnesota were renowned for their famous check or red shirts throughout the war. Some accounts about Minnesota troops as late as 1863 mention their broad hats and shirts. Officially the regular army had long taken over supplying the Minnesota troops with uniforms by this time, but it seems that many men still treasured and maintained their early war uniforms.

At the outbreak of the Civil War Michigan's state authorities ordered that uniforms should immediately be made up of blue flannel or some other suitable material blue in color. Many Michigan soldiers ended up wearing dark blue trousers and dark blue jackets which had standing collars like army regulation frock coats. The Michigan jackets had nine buttons down the front and shoulder straps. The men were also supplied with shirts, drawers, forage caps, socks, shoes, haversacks, canteens and cooking utensils, and the state also armed some of its soldiers with limited quantities of 1855 rifle muskets. The rest were largely armed with imported weapons.

On 9 May 1861, New Jersey's State Board of Commissioners prescribed the uniform for the state's three month regiments as a 'dark blue frock coat, light blue pants and army cockade hat'. It appears that the dress the majority of New Jersey State troops wore would have differed very little from that of the regulars, except that their sack coats had five buttons down the front instead of four, but a feature of many officers' coats is that they were trimmed light blue down the front and on the cuffs. Unusually the state equipped two Zouave regiments, with their uniforms, and these had dark blue jackets, with dark blue waistcoats and trousers, a blue sash edged in light blue and blue and red forage caps.

Elite militia units in New Jersey could become part of the New Jersey Rifle Corps and wear either Chasseur pattern jackets or fatigue jackets. They could choose to wear either gray or blue Chasseur or fatigue jackets.

State issued buttons for New Jersey troops featured the New Jersey coat of arms although some buttons just had NJ stamped on them. New Jersey's arsenal at Trenton supplied many New Jersey troops with weapons, notably copies of the 1861 rifle musket.

Before the Civil War, Vermont hadn't provided any uniform regulations for its state troops and the rush to get volunteers into uniforms saw stocks of gray cloth being hastily ordered. The 1st Regiment Vermont Volunteers wore a dated looking gray uniform with tailed coats, but other regiments were outfitted in frock coats made out of brownish gray material trimmed in blue. The coats had nine buttons down the front and the trousers and forage caps issued to Vermont's volunteers early in the war were also distinctively trimmed in blue. State buttons bore the state coat of arms and Vermont underneath, and the 13th Vermont Regiment had special cap badges which featured the regimental number in a wreath. Arms issued to Vermont troops were a mixture of 1855 rifle muskets and smoothbore 1842 muskets.

The regular army eventually took over clothing supplies for Vermont regiments but it seems that instead of wearing comfortable sack coats Vermont troops preferred instead to

Odd looking Whipple caps, like the one worn by this soldier were widely issued to troops from New York and New Hampshire. Despite their ungainly appearance, the hats proved to be popular. (David Sheinmann)

wear regulation frock coats throughout the war as many pictures of Vermont troops show.

It seems that several states were lacking the means to outfit and equip their forces for the war. The worst offender was Ohio where the State Arsenal contained little more than a few boxes of rusty smoothbore weapons, some of them more than 20 years old. It was even rumoured that some of these muskets dated as far back as the war of 1812. It would be a nightmare getting Ohio troops ready for war because the arsenal contained no accoutrements, not even basic items like belts or cartridge boxes.

It was a daunting task to make proper preparations but Ohio's Jacob D. Cox was determined that Ohio troops should be outfitted and armed properly. At the beginning of the Civil War, Ohio wanted to clothe her troops in uniforms that were so close to army regulations that little change would be required when the troops went into U.S. service. However, the state wanted some part of the soldiers' uniforms to be distinctive, so it was recommended that the state coat of arms should be stamped on buttons and cap plates; but it seems that many of the troops just had regulation buttons on their clothing.

Before 1862, when the Federal authorities took over the task of uniforming Ohio's soldiers, Ohio arranged to outfit its troops by issuing clothing contracts to a number of firms both inside and outside the state. It was stressed that uniforms should be: 'thoroughly well made and trimmed and in all respects to conform to Regulations'. Ohio even contracted for a supply of 8000 regulation infantry frock coats with brass shoulder scales, but supplies of blue cloth ran out and fresh stocks were difficult to procure.

Ohio infantry regiments had to be clad in less elaborate uniforms comprising blue flannel blouses, and sky-blue kersey trousers. Blue fatigue caps with havelocks or glazed covers were given to troops and black felt hats were also issued, but these quickly lost their shape. Shirts were made out of red or gray flannel. Ohio's artillery and cavalrymen were issued with dark blue cloth shell jackets and dark blue reinforced trousers. Overcoats were of sky-blue kersey.

Like many states, Ohio had troubles in getting enough supplies of blue wool, so uniforms were often made out of gray cloth instead and at least 10 Ohio regiments were uniformed in gray and more than 5000 jackets made out of cadet gray cloth were issued. Late in the war, the Ohio State Militia was formed, a unit that wore uniforms identical to the regular army but which had state distinctions on waistbelts and cartridge box plates. Cartridge box plates and waistbelt plates were similar to regulation plates, but bore the initials OVM. Circular shoulder belt plates bearing the OVM initials were also worn.

Ohio regiments were armed with a bewildering array of weapons including 1842 smoothbore muskets converted from flintlock, Prussian muskets converted from flintlock, and Enfield rifle muskets.

It was planned that all Pennsylvania regiments should be uniformly dressed in blue, but again sufficient quantities of blue material were impossible to obtain so gray uniforms were widely worn. Colors varied from cadet gray to tan or light gray and very dark gray. Some jackets which were made out of 'mixed forest cloth' were light gray on one side and dark gray on the other, making a very strange appearance.

Most Pennsylvania troops in the early days of the war would have worn gray forage caps, gray jackets and trousers. Jackets usually had 9 or 12 buttons down the front and were looped at the bottom like many New York State jackets to keep waistbelts in place. Some troops also wore trousers of a linen material and even brown trousers were issued. A surprising number of Pennsylvania volunteer soldiers were still wearing gray uniforms even after 1862. The Philadelphia Home Guard wore gray uniforms for much of the war which must have looked very unusual when the gray uniforms were worn with full dress Hardee hats.

Many men of the Pennsylvania Reserve Corps formed from surplus regiments in the rush of men volunteering for Union service, were meant to wear regulation Union Army uniforms but many wore gray jackets and trousers. Buttons on Pennsylvania uniforms bore the state coat of arms and brass oval belt plates were also issued, often marked with individual unit designations. More often than not regulation army belt plates marked US were worn. It doesn't seem that Pennsylvania had any trouble arming its men. Most of their weapons came directly from the government.

Illinois had very sparse dress regulations for its troops, merely requiring that volunteer officers should wear close approximations of the uniforms worn by regular officers in the Union Army. Illinois was hoping that the Federal government would arm and equip its men right from the start of the war, but the government was not forthcoming. Illinois troops at first received a sparse state issue of gray shirts, blue forage caps, and red blankets. The state authorities appear to have been so desperate for uniforms that a consignment of clothing was even ordered from suppliers in New York, but these uniforms which featured gray jackets and trousers and even Zouave caps, wore out very quickly.

When more regiments were raised in Illinois uniforms were locally made usually by seamstresses in the men's hometowns. Illinois soldiers could expect to receive gray or blue jackets and trousers but when the state made greater provisions for uniforms, volunteers were supposed to receive blue or gray jackets and trousers cut in the same style as U.S. regulation jackets, two flannel shirts, two pairs of socks and a stout pair of shoes. In practice it seems that most Illinois volunteers wore gray uniforms with gray broad-brimmed hats turned up at the side like regulation Hardee hats. Hats issued to a number of Illinois regiments featured the unusual ornamentation of a brass button attached to a red, white and blue cockade.

The 8th, 9th, 11th, and 12th infantry regiments in the first brigade of Illinois volunteers received gray coats edged in blue while artillery units received gray coats edged in red. Fatigue uniforms featuring Zouave caps were also issued. Cavalry regiments were issued with red shirts and dark blue trousers, but they were later issued with Union Army regulation dress. In 1862, doubtless much to the relief of state officials, the U.S. Quartermaster took over supplying Illinois troops with uniforms and a huge amount of uniform items were issued including more than 17,000 coats. Unlike the troops in many other states, Illinois soldiers are not thought to have worn any distinctive buttons with their uniforms. Illinois soldiers were mainly armed with Springfield rifle muskets.

Broad-brimmed black hats originally issued to troops from Minnesota and Illinois were also a feature of the original state uniforms issued to volunteer soldiers from Indiana. Uniforms from Western states tended to be much more functional and far less decorative than the uniforms issued by their Eastern counterparts, largely because Western states didn't have such an old militia system as their Eastern comrades-in-arms. Regiments in Indiana were issued uniforms made out of satinet or jean cloth, the latter material is a form of cloth usually associated with uniforms manufactured in the Confederacy. Hats were meant to be looped up at each side.

It seems that two of Indiana's regiments began the war wearing gray jackets and trousers and blue shirts, while the others wore light blue jackets. In September 1861 gray uniforms trimmed with black were issued but it seems that when new regiments were raised they were outfitted in standard army dress although many gray and blue jackets would have survived. Indiana's regiments received 1842 pattern smoothbore muskets and Enfield rifle muskets.

The State of Iowa took little pride in militia units before the Civil War and at the outbreak of hostilities Iowa State authorities were forced to buy cloth from Chicago to make enough uniforms for Iowa troops. some troops wore loose fitting baggy shirts with green grim and dark gray trousers, while others wore similar uniforms trimmed red, but these uniforms wore out in a matter of weeks. After the Battle of Wilson's Creek, Iowa

troops were so destitute, that many were reduced to patching their trousers with material from flour sacks. Some even wore aprons made out of these sacks, because their trousers were beyond repair.

Replacement uniforms were ordered from Boston and these proved to be far sturdier. Troops from Iowa's first three infantry regiments were issued with gray frock coats and trousers, flannel shirts and felt hats. Later issues of clothing were made by the Federal government. Iowa troops were issued with a variety of weapons including French and Belgian rifles.

Wisconsin wanted its troops dressed in blue, but again there wasn't enough blue material to go around, so the majority of Wisconsin's volunteers wore gray uniforms. It was a particularly smart dress with single-breasted frock coats, gray trousers ornamented with a black cord down each seam, gray kepis trimmed black and a gray overcoat with black piping.

The 3rd Wisconsin's uniform featured gray hunting shirts and light gray trousers. Other regiments wore single-breasted jackets, with black shoulder straps and black decoration on the cuffs and collars. The jackets also had loops at the bottom so that a belt could be passed through and the rest of the uniform included gray forage caps, gray trousers with the popular black stripe down the seams and gray overcoats. Wisconsin volunteers were later largely dressed in blue uniforms issued by the state, including dark blue coats with stand up collars. Black hats, sky-blue trousers and forage caps were also issued. Later in the war, Wisconsin regiments received their clothing from Federal supplies and were armed and dressed with regular uniforms, weapons and equipment.

Massachusetts had authorized a state uniform for its troops as far back as 1852, but many of its militia units were inadequately clothed at the beginning of the war. Many soldiers were just issued basic uniform parts such as shirts, but little else. Gray flannel uniforms were quickly made, which came with red Zouave fezzes. This distinctive headgear was later replaced by felt hats, but doubtless many volunteers wore their fezzes for at least the first two years of the war. Massachusetts procured over 9000 gray infantry jackets and over 1000 cavalry and artillery jackets.

Right: This private of the 65th New York Volunteers who were known as the 1st U.S. Chasseurs, is wearing a New York Chasseur jacket trimmed light blue. The 65th's forage caps were very unusual. They were standard issue forage caps with the peaks and chinstraps removed. (David Scheinmann)

Two Massachusetts regiments never wore gray uniforms and were outfitted in blue right from the start of the war, and eventually all units from the state wore regulation blue. An interesting aspect of the accoutrements carried by Massachusetts volunteers is that many of them were British made. Ten thousand British accoutrement sets were distributed to Massachusetts soldiers.

The dated long-tailed coats that many New Hampshire Volunteers began the war in were considered to be out of step with uniform trends and they were replaced with state issued gray frock coats of a light or mid gray shade. Collar and cuffs were trimmed in red like the old coats, but the cuff trim like the regulation army frock coats was pointed. The coats had nine buttons down the front and the rear skirts of the coat were similar, if not identical to regulation frock coats.

The most distinctive part of New Hampshire's state issued uniforms was an unusual cap called a New Hampshire Cap that was similar to the unusual caps first issued but later rejected by Berdan's Sharpshooters. One New Hampshire soldier described his cap as: 'A helmet like structure of waterproof cloth with a visor before and behind, the top resembling a squash and the whole lined and padded. This was the New Hampshire cap and although it would do in a row to keep blows from the head and was good to protect the neck from rain, yet in summer it was a sweltering concern.'

The hat visors were made out of leather, while the flaps at the back were made out of the same material as the main body of the caps. The caps had leather chin straps were fastened with a buckle. New Hampshire troops were later provided with regulation dress that had a few subtle differences from standard Union Army uniforms. Frock coats did not have piping on the cuffs or collar and the shoulders had shoulder straps with

pointed ends, held in place by a small button which didn't reach quite to the collar.

The famous blouses supervised by Ambrose E. Burnside for the 1st Regiment Rhode Island Detached Militia became the State's issued dress. Rhode Island had an array of individually clad militia units who wore different uniforms, many of them very dated. The Providence First Light Artillery who formed Companies C and D of the 1st Regiment wore scarlet tail coats trimmed light blue and buff with red and white epaulettes, light blue trousers with white stripes. The Pawtucket Light Guard, Company E of the same regiment wore a gray uniform trimmed yellow with red cuff flaps and a dress cap with a red pompon.

Surprisingly, it seems that Rhode Island's volunteers didn't mind swapping their elaborate uniforms for the more simple state outfits. Perhaps it was because their distinctive clothing picked up a lot of attention. The *Washington Star* wrote: 'Their dress is characteristic. At the bottom they were stout, thick soled cowhide boots; their pants are homemade gray and over this they wear a dark blue jean frock or hunting shirt, added to which they mount the new army hat turned up at the side.' Officers wore variations of the standard blouse, some had five small buttons reaching down from the neck, some blouses had a large inside pocket, and some were double breasted.

The 1st Rhode Island Artillery Battery wore dress uniforms based on U.S. Army regulations, which had dark blue frock coats and sky-blue trousers. For fatigue dress enlisted men wore dark blue shell jackets piped in scarlet at the collar and cuffs and which had nine buttons down the front. Trousers were the standard reinforced issue. On campaign, officers wore dark blue Rhode Island blouses, dark blue trousers and forage caps. The second battery originally wore Rhode Island blouses and dress hats, but they were later issued with regulation light artillery dress.

Insignia and Medals

Ten years before the outbreak of the American Civil War, several changes were made to United States military insignia. Metal insignia for all branches of the service was cast in brass. Distinctive colors were also adopted for branches of service; blue for infantry, red for artillery and yellow or orange for the cavalry.

The regulation embroidered bugle horn insignia is shown in this photograph of an officer holding his Hardee hat. (David Scheinmann)

The yellow cavalry trim dated back to the dragoons' yellow trim authorized in 1833. At first, this trim clashed with the artillery who were already wearing yellow facings as their branch of service color, and as some dragoon officers favoured wearing orange sashes, orange became the dragoons' branch of service color. The cavalry in general adopted yellow when the facing color of the artillery was changed to scarlet. Traditionally, the artillery had yellow as its facing color, to match the yellow metal of its guns. But scarlet which had first been adopted by the American army in the Revolution was much more appropriate.

White facings had originally been adopted as the infantry's branch of service color in 1832, but the infantry's facings were eventually changed to light blue or dark blue because the white cloth soiled too easily.

The War Department issued insignia which went on a soldier's accoutrements, while the Ordnance Department was largely responsible for issuing insignia which soldiers wore on their clothing. Some insignia has already been mentioned in this book, but the subject of Union insignia during the Civil War is so complex that it deserves a detailed study. One of the most distinctive forms of Union insignia was the eagle cap badge. Introduced in 1851, it was made out of gold embroidery for officers and yellow metal for enlisted men. The brass version featured a stamped design showing the United States national bird, the eagle. Eagle badges were slightly under 2½ inches high and measured 1¾ inches between the wing tips.

Officers' eagles were richly embroidered in gold on an oval of black velvet fixed to a small tin plate which had two wire loops attached, so that the eagle could be fixed to the officer's headgear. There was no regulation for which way the eagle should look, eagles 'looking' both to the left and right were common.

Eagle symbols were also an important feature on officers' and NCOs' sword belt plates. In 1851 a new pattern for these plates was adopted that remained virtually unchanged until World War II. Regulations stated that the belt plates should be: 'Gilt, rectangular, two inches wide with a raised rim, a silver wreath of laurel encircling the Arms of the United States, eagle, shield

scroll, edge of cloud and rays bright. The motto "E Pluribus Unum" in silver letters, upon the scroll, stars also of silver; according to pattern.'

Sword belts were attached to the plates usually by passing the right end of the belt through a slot in the right side of the plate. Despite regulations belt plates varied in design. Most were cast but others were stamped out of metal. Some had the silver wreath cast as an integral part of the plate but on many plates the wreaths were separate items added to the plates as a finishing touch.

Not only did officers of the 8th Wisconsin Infantry have eagle sword belt plates, the regiment actually carried a live eagle as part of its insignia. Bought from a Chippewa Indian, Old Abe the Battle Eagle was carried into battle tethered on top of a special perch and saw action several times, including the siege of Vicksburg in May 1863. Old Abe survived the war only to die of smoke inhalation when fire swept through the Wisconsin Capitol building where he spent his retirement.

Eagle plates used decoratively on shoulder belts supporting the infantryman's cartridge box, had a raised rim with an eagle holding three arrows and an olive branch. The plate itself was made out of stamped thin brass with a lead filled back with imbedded hooks for fastening it to the belt. The plates were also used to fasten the two halves of sergeants' shoulder belts together. Shoulder belt plates had a regulation diameter of 2½ inches and while there were variations in design most shoulder belt plates followed a similar pattern.

Regulations stated that each infantryman should have an oval plate holding his waist belt together and another on the flap of his cartridge box. Classic U.S. plates dated as far back as the 1840s and came in two sizes; 3.5 by 2.2 inches and 2.8 by 1.6 inches. Usually the plates were made out of stamped brass filled with lead solder on the back. Most commonly they bore the letters US but many carried state initials.

Some of the most unusual cartridge box plates were the ones carried by the company of Zouaves raised by Captain H. T. Collis as a bodyguard for General Banks. These carried the initials Z.D.A. standing for Zouaves d'Afrique. When the company was expanded to become the 114th Pennsylvania

Left: Rectangular belt plates like the one worn by the officer here, found much favour with cavalrymen. A brass eagle motif was surmounted by a silver wreath on these plates. (David Scheinmann)

Volunteer Infantry, the men were issued with standard cartridge box plates, but some of the distinctive Z.D.A. plates probably saw service throughout the war.

Standard issue plates were made in Federal armouries, but more than 250,000 were also manufactured by private contractors. Circular brass two piece belt plates also saw service on white buff leather sword belts for carrying artillery swords or sabres.

In 1851, after years of unofficial use, insignia identifying infantry, cavalry and artillery were officially authorized. General officers and staff officers had an embroidered cap badge insignia with a silver 'U.S.' in old English characters in a golden laurel wreath. Cavalry insignia developed from the insignia worn by the old regiments of dragoons. The cap insignia authorized for the dragoons in 1851 was an orange pompom for enlisted men and crossed sabres for officers. The crossed sabres were in gold and had their edges upward. In the upper angle the regimental number was placed. This insignia was usually embroidered directly on to the cap, but crossed brass sabres began to become popular as well.

Enlisted men were later authorized to wear a brass company letter 1 inch high on their hats. When the dragoon regiments were authorized to wear felt hats in 1858, officers' insignia was worn on a black velvet background; an oval of velvet with a narrow embroidered border and tin backing. Enlisted men were now authorized to wear cross sabres, which came to be forever associated with the United States cavalry. Officers also continued to wear crossed sabres, either embroidered on black or blue cloth or in metal like their men.

The most distinctive Union infantry insignia was the bugle horn which was heavily influenced by the bugle horn insignia of the French voltigeurs. Bugle horn insignia had been adopted by the United States Army as early as 1831 but in 1851 the metal was changed from silver to gold and officers were authorized to wear a gold embroidered bugle on their caps within the number of their regiment in silver in the centre of the horn. Interesting variations on this are some Zouave officers who wore the letter Z in the centre of the bugle horns on their kepis.

Left: This officer's crossed sabres are embroidered on a black piece of oval cloth. The number of his regiment and company letters also appear to have been added. (David Scheinmann)

Enlisted men often displayed insignia on the tops of their forage caps, as shown here by these pipe smoking comrades. (David Scheinmann)

This infantryman wearing an overcoat clearly displays the eagle buckle on his shoulder belt. (David Scheinmann)

Some unique items of infantry insignia were the special cap plates worn by the 10th New York Volunteer Infantry, National Zouaves usually on the turbans wrapped around their fezzes. Not much is known about them, but they were over an inch long and were inscribed 10 NZ. Infantrymen were specialists in arranging brass letters and numbers of their clothing and kepis. Many of the 14th Brooklyn Regiment proudly bore the brass numerals 14 on the fronts of their kepis while the 11th new York often sported FZ letters standing for Fire Zouaves.

The distinctive castle insignia worn by the engineers and topographical engineers dated back to 1840 and it was used on the dress cap of U.S. Military Academy cadets in 1842. Engineer officers in the Civil War also wore an embroidered star within a laurel wreath on the collars of their coats. Apart from their distinctive buttons, officers of the topographical engineers also wore a gold embroidered shield surrounded by a wreath of oak leaves.

The Ordnance Department wore an embroidered shell and flame motif. Very much influenced by the French style, the Ordnance Department had worn its distinctive badges since 1833 and the unique design became exclusively theirs in 1851.

Officers wore it in gold embroidery on their forage and dress caps, and embroidered in silver it was also worn on the crescents of their epaulettes. Enlisted men wore a similar design made out of brass on their caps and the collars of their uniforms, but eventually gave up wearing the device on their collars.

The famous crossed cannon of the artillery had been worn since 1833 and was officially adopted in 1851, when regulations stated that officers should wear gold embroidered badges with crossed cannon on their caps. They were also to have the regimental number in silver above the intersection of the cannon. These badges were also made in metal. Embroidered cannon badges came in different shapes and many featured different motifs but a common feature was the fact that the muzzle ends of the cannon designs were longer than the breech ends. Enlisted men had originally only been authorized to wear brass crossed cannon insignia with a brass regimental number and a company letter. The brass crossed cannon was reminiscent of the insignia worn on artillery dress caps before 1851, but the 1858 crossed cannon badges were flatter and had slimmer and longer cannon barrels. Like infantrymen, artillerymen put their badges and company letters either on the fronts of their forage caps, or on top.

In 1858 artillery officers' cap devices were changed to black velvet ovals of material bearing the gold embroidered cross cannon which also had the regimental number embroidered on a black base in a small circle of gold embroidery. Artillery officers' black velvet ovals were a little smaller than those worn by the cavalry. Miniature size cannon badges were also widely available and embroidered crossed cannon badges without the ovals were also widely worn.

Late in the Civil War, it seems that some horse artillery officers adopted a unique badge with a laurel wreath, a horse, crossed cannon and the words 'Horse Artillery'. Whether it was officially authorized or not isn't known and it represents just one of the many badge variations found in the Union Army.

Corps Badges

One of the most distinctive features of Union Civil War uniforms were the corps badges worn by soldiers on their forage caps or on their uniforms. Such badges gave soldiers a sense of identity and increased the esprit de corps of the Union Army. Unlike insignia or uniform regulations, the corps badge system

This private of the 146th New York Volunteer Infantry, Garrard's Tigers, wears his corps badge on his chest. It was not unusual for men to make their corps badges out of wood or bone and also inscribe them with their name and the letter of their regimental company. (Michael J. McAfee)

was developed during the American Civil War and was unique to the conflict.

Corps badges were originated by Major General Philip Kearny as a means of identifying soldiers from a particular command after he mistakenly reprimanded some officers who were not under his direct orders. In May 1862, Kearny ordered that the officers of his Third Division, Third Corps, Army of the Potomac, should sew a piece of red flannel 2 inches square on

Ogden painting of Union uniforms and corps badges. (Peter Newark's Military Pictures)

Right: This colonel wears a particularly large set of epaulettes. These uniform ornaments were favoured by the commanders of volunteer infantry regiments. (David Scheinmann)

Infantry sergeant with chevrons. (David Scheinmann)

the fronts of their caps for identification purposes.

Legend has it that these badges, nicknamed 'Kearny patches' were cut from scarlet blankets bought by Kearny from France. Before the war Kearny had seen a lot of service with the French Army in North Africa and even charged with the French cavalry during one battle. Kearny was highly esteemed in the Union Army and when he was killed at the Battle of Chantilly in 1862, the distinctive red badges continued to be used as a tribute to him.

General Orders No. 49, Headquarters of the 1st Division, Third Army Corps, issued to announce General Kearny's death, stated: 'To still further show our regard for him and to distinguish his officers as he wished, each officer will continue to wear on his cap a piece of scarlet cloth.' General Hooker widened the use of corps badges in a circular issued on 21 March 1863, recommending the adoption of original corps badges 'for the purpose of ready recognition of corps and divisions of this army and to prevent injustice by reports of straggling and misconduct through mistake as to their organizations.'

Soon the entire Army was wearing corps badges. Union Corps were usually divided into three divisions and the color of the badge corresponded to the number of the division. The 1st division wore red badges, the 2nd white, and the 3rd blue. When more than three divisions existed in a corps, green was used for the 4th and orange for the 5th.

Corps badges were also used on flags and drawn on ambulances and wagons belonging to the particular corps. Regulations authorized that the 1st Army Corps should have a sphere symbol, the 2nd a trefoil, the 3rd a lozenge, the 4th an equilateral triangle, the 5th a Maltese Cross and the 6th a Greek cross. The 7th Corps was discontinued before any orders for a badge were given and the 8th Corps unofficially used a star with six rays.

The 9th Corps saw duty in the South, East and West, and adopted a shield with a figure 9 as its badge. The centres of these badges also featured an anchor and a cannon. The 10th Corps spent a lot of its time building fortifications and a badge showing a four bastioned fort was selected for it.

On 21 March 1863, a crescent was prescribed for the 11th Corps and the 12th Corps was to wear a 12-pointed star. When the Army of the Potomac was reorganized in March 1864 it was stipulated that transferred troops should preserve their badges. The combined 1st and 5th Corps used a circle surrounding a Maltese Cross as their badge when the new 5th Corps was formed, while the 6th Corps retained a Greek cross.

The 13th Corps never had an official authorized badge during the war, but seems to have adopted an elipse shape surrounding a canteen. Corps serving in the Department of the Cumberland also had distinctive badges. General orders stated that they were 'For the purpose of ready recognition of the corps and divisions of this army and to prevent injustice by reports of straggling and misconduct through mistakes as to organizations.'

On his unusual three-button coat with pockets, this infantry first sergeant wears chevrons with a diamond shape above. (David Scheinmann)

Left: The epaulettes worn by this cavalry or artillery sergeant do not have shoulder scales but appear to be cloth boards with metal crescents and worsted fringes. They are certainly non-regulation. (David Scheinmann)

It was claimed the 14th Corps was given the distinctive acorn badge in memory of the bad times they went through in the autumn of 1863. The weather was so bad that supplies couldn't get through and the men were reduced to eating the acorns from a grove of oaks growing near their camp. Ingeniously, the men roasted and boiled the acorns and even ground them between stones to make bread. Not surprisingly, they were known ever after as the 'Acorn Boys'.

The 20th Corps, which was formed by consolidating the 11th and 12th Corps, adopted a five-pointed star, the old badge of the 12th as its badge, but men of the 11th Corps jealously stuck to their crescent badges for a long time, using it in combination with the star.

The badge of the 15th Army Corps was described in general orders issued on 15 February 1865: 'The following is announced as the badge of this corps: A miniature cartridge box, black, set transversely on a field of cloth or metal: above the cartridge box plate will be stamped or marked in a curve, the motto "Forty Rounds".'

This distinctive badge came about as a result of the rivalry between the Eastern soldiers of the 12th Corps and the Western soldiers of the 15th Corps. A soldier of the 15th Corps joked that the star badges then carried by the 12th Corps made them all look like brigadiers, and when the 12th Corps men asked what the 15th Corps badge was he patted his cartridge box and said: 'this is the badge of the 15th Corps, 40 rounds.' The 15th Corps' commander, General Logan, later heard the story and this decided him on the 15th's corps badges.

No official order was ever given for a badge for the 16th Corps. Instead several designs were put into a hat and the first drawn out was accepted as the design for the corps badge. The rough drawing plucked out of the hat was a circle crossed by two bars at acute angles and this was modified into a figure resembling a Maltese Cross with curved lines for the 16th Corps' badge. The badge was called the A. J. Smith Cross, in honour of the first commander of the corps.

The 17th Corps badge was an arrow design and though simple it was very memorable. In general orders issued on 25 March 1865, General F. P. Blake wrote: 'In its swiftness, in its surety of striking where wanted and in its destructive powers when so intended, the arrow is probably as emblematical of this corps as any design that could be adopted.'

The 18th Corps had a cross with foliated leaves as its badge, while the 19th Corps badge was changed from a four-pointed

star to a fan-leaved cross with an octagonal centre on 17 November 1864. Ironically the 19th hardly fired a hostile shot while they had this badge late in the war.

No official orders were ever made concerning badges for the 21st and 22nd Corps, but as the 22nd Corps served in the defences of Washington, a pentagon was chosen with the edge cut into five equal sections and a circle in the centre. The 23rd Corps used a shield as its badge, while the 24th Corps, largely composed of veterans from the 10th and 11th Corps, adopted a heart as its badge in the closing stages of the war.

Orders dated 18 March 1865, explained the poignant feelings behind the choice of symbol: 'The symbol selected is one which testifies our affectionate regard for all our brave comrades – alike the living and the dead – who have braved the perils of this mighty conflict and our devotion to the sacred cause – a cause which entitled us to the sympathy of every brave and true heart and the support of every strong and determined hand.'

The 25th Corps composed of colored soldiers from the 10th and 18th Corps had square corps badges, featuring a smaller square superimposed into the main design. These badges were very distinctive and when they were issued on 20 February 1865, General Weitzel had these words to say: 'Soldiers, to you is given a chance in this spring campaign, of making this badge immortal. Let history record that on the banks of the James thirty thousand freemen not only gained their own liberty, but shattered the prejudice of the world, and gave to the land of their birth peace, union and glory.'

The men of Hancock's First Corps, Veteran Volunteers, were never officially authorized a badge, but adopted badges with particularly elaborate motifs, which one account describes as: 'A circle is surrounded by a double wreath of laurel. A wide red band passes vertically through the centre of the circle. Outside the laurel wreath, rays form a figure with seven sides of concave curves. Seven hands, springing from the circumference of the laurel wreath, grasp spears, the heads of which form the seven points of the external radiated figure.'

Cavalry corps also adopted badges, even though no official orders were ever given authorizing them. General J. E. Wilson's

Left: Thomas Francis Meagher, wears an ornamental baldric in this picture. His green frock coat was one of the several dazzling outfits he appeared in throughout the war. (David Scheinmann)

Cavalry Corps had a red swallow tailed cavalry guidon with crossed sabres suspended from a rifle, or alternatively, a carbine. The badge issued to Kilpatrick's Cavalry Corps had a swallow tail flag. It also had three gilt stars and an eagle motif. The Signal Corps badge had two flags crossed over the handle of a blazing torch, signifying that by day the signal corps used flags to signal, and by night they used torches.

Corps badges proved so popular that Union soldiers were given the legal right to wear them, even when they left the Army. Orders stated: 'All persons who have served as officers, non-commissioned officers, privates or other enlisted men in the Regular Army, volunteer or militia forces of the United States, during the war of the rebellion and have been honourably discharged from the service, or still remain in the same, shall be entitled to wear, on occasion of ceremony, the distinctive army badge ordered for or adopted by the army corps and division respectively in which they served.'

Epaulettes

American officers had traditionally worn epaulettes as a badge of rank and although their use was beginning to die out in the early years of the Civil War, it was not unusual to find them particularly on the shoulders of some militia officers. The 69th New York State Militia had worsted epaulettes on its new jackets adopted shortly before the war. These epaulettes had a broad bullion fringe for NCOs, a medium fringe for sergeants, and a narrow fringe for corporals and privates.

Epaulettes were expensive uniform accessories and were individually tailored to fit the left and the right shoulder. Epaulettes were fixed on the shoulder by an open brass strap on the underside which passed through cloth loops on the wearer's shoulder and were secured by a spring clip. Epaulettes came with three sizes of bullion fringe. For general and field officers the fringe was 3.5 inches long and 0.5 inches in diameter, for captains it was 2.5 inches long and 0.25 inches in diameter and for lieutenants it was the same length. Colonels had a silver embroidered eagle on their epaulettes, lieutenant colonels had a silver embroidered oak leaf, captains had two silver embroidered bars and first lieutenants had one silver embroidered bars.

The cost of epaulettes helps to explain their declining use and why they were usually reserved for full dress occasions. Replacing epaulettes for widespread use were shoulder straps

Andrew Scott, a freed slave who served in the Union Army. (Peter Newark's Military Pictures)

were sewn on cloth designating the branch of service the officer belonged to. The rank indications on shoulder straps were the same as for epaulettes.

Prior to the Civil War, worsted epaulettes were worn by enlisted men in all branches of the Army. Artillerymen wore scarlet epaulettes, and infantry light or Saxony blue. Enlisted men's epaulettes had crescents made out of worsted cord and straps made out of coarse material attached to a piece of tin plate. The epaulettes had three rows of fringes which were 3 inches long often held in place at the bottom by a cord running through the ends. Epaulettes were fastened to the men's coats by a hook at the pointed end of the strap and a loop of cloth on each shoulder which the strap could be passed through.

Worsted epaulettes were eventually withdrawn and replaced by brass scales which had previously only been worn by cavalrymen as shoulder protectors and can be regarded as the last vestiges of medieval armour. Scales were called different names. 1851 regulations called them shoulder knots, which was a little peculiar because they didn't resemble shoulder knots at all, but they were usually officially called 'shoulder straps (brass)' or 'metallic scales'. The scales were originally issued in two patterns, one for non-commissioned staff and the other for dragoons and light artillery.

Brass scales issued to privates had seven scalloped pieces of metal, mounted on a strap which was slightly over 2 inches wide with a rounded end and 4-inch wide crescent. Sergeants' scales were similar in design, but their crescents were slightly larger and the scales and six of the scallops each had three small round head rivets. The scales were attached to soldiers' coats by open brass straps that were fixed to cloth or brass straps on the shoulders and over brass staples near the collar.

Chevrons

The French Army had originally introduced chevrons in the mid-18th century as a mark of long service for soldiers. The British adopted chevrons as badges of rank in 1802 and the American Army began using them shortly after the end of its second war with Britain in 1817. Chevrons were first worn by cadet military officers at the West Point Military Academy and in 1821 the United States Army authorized them to be worn by commissioned and non-commissioned officers. Around 1830, chevrons were banned for officers and from then on were worn by non-commissioned officers only.

and these came in a regulation size of 1.375 by 4 inches. Shoulder straps all had gold embroidery trim on the borders and regulations stipulated that the borders should be 0.25 inches in width; but many officers bought shoulder straps which had wider borders. Originally, shoulder strap borders

A proper chevron system in the United States Army began in 1851. With some exceptions like the chevrons worn by United States Marines, chevrons pointed down and were in the cloth of the sergeant's branch of service. They were worn on the upper arms and had a small space between the seams. Diagonal pattern half chevrons were also authorized to be worn on the lower sleeves marking each period of five year service a soldier may have attained.

In the Civil War, these chevrons were issued to soldiers whose terms of service had expired but who had re-enlisted voluntarily in the army for another tour of duty. Sometimes the veterans wore their chevrons in the shape of an inverted V on their left coat sleeves.

Sergeant majors' chevrons were three stripes with an arc of three stripes above. Regimental quartermaster sergeants had three stripes and a tie of three stripes, ordnance sergeants had three stripes and a star, first sergeants had three stripes and a lozenge, sergeants had three stripes and corporals had two stripes. Sergeants and corporals of the 5th new York, Duryée's Zouaves, had particularly gaudy chevrons, with gilt on the stripes.

Aiguilettes

Aiguilettes, twisted strands or metallic cord or braid, were popular with some officers. Usually they were made out of twisted gold or silver and were suspended from the right shoulder under the epaulette. Aiguilettes had a practical as well as a decorative use, the ends sometimes contained pencils which meant officers could conveniently take notes or write out orders in the field. Regulations never prescribed the wearing of aiguilettes and they usually had to be privately purchased.

Baldrics

Baldrics were leather shoulder belts carried by some officers. They were often festooned with gold lace and a lion's head usually of gilded brass was fixed to the front. Three brass chains were suspended from the lion's mouth with pins on the end that fitted behind a shield made out of the same metal. Suspended by rings from the belt was a small brass mounted leather box. The length of the belt was adjusted by a brass buckle with a brass tip and loop and the purpose of the baldric was purely ornamental. Baldrics had originated in the 16th century when the boxes were used to hold cartridges and the pins were used to clear out the touch holes of muzzle-loading pistols.

Medals

On the eve of the Civil War, the Union didn't have a medal for gallantry. The first such medal issued was the Medal of Honor authorized by President Lincoln on 21 December 1862. The first recipient of this medal was Corporal Francis Edward Brownell of the 11th New York Fire Zouaves, for his action in gunning down a Virginia tavern keeper James T. Jackson who shortly before had shot the Fire Zouaves' leader Elmer E. Ellsworth dead, after Ellsworth had removed a Confederate flag flying from the roof of the Marshall House tavern in Alexandria.

Brownell's action wasn't exactly a great act of bravery, but in the wave of grief that swept across the North after Ellsworth's demise, it was certainly a smart, politically correct move, to award him with a medal.

The Army Medal of Honor was similar to the Medal of Honor struck for the Navy, except that Union Army's medal was attached to its ribbon by an American eagle and a crossed cannon. The Navy's had an anchor and a star.

The Medal of Honor hung from a ribbon which had 13 alternating stripes of red and white with a solid blue stripe running across the top and it was attached to a small shield. The medal featured a five-pointed bronze star and on the obverse was a female warrior representing the Union, holding back an attacker carrying writhing snakes with her shield.

During the Civil War many other medals were officially proposed. The Sumter Medal, issued by the New York State Chamber of Commerce was given to the men who had defended Union Fort Sumter at the beginning of the war and more than 100 were awarded. The Butler medal for colored Troops was awarded to black soldiers in the 25th Corps for gallantry displayed in the storming of New Market Heights and at the Battle of Chaffins' Farm in 1864. Two hundred of these medals were issued and today they are very collectable.

Kearny Medals, named after General Philip Kearny were awarded to officers and men who had served with distinction in the late General's command. The medals had a gold medal cross and an inscription in Latin and more than 300 men received them. The Kearny Cross, another medal named after the popular general, was awarded as a cross of valour by Kearny's successor Brigadier General D. B. Birney. Kearny Crosses supplemented Kearny Medals and it was ruled that soldiers could not receive bronze medals. The medals, which were cast in bronze, were inscribed Kearny Cross on one side and Birney's Division on the other.

General Philip Henry Sheridan (standing extreme left) holding war conference with his officers. General George Armstrong Custer sits extreme right. (Peter Newark's Military Pictures/M. Brady)

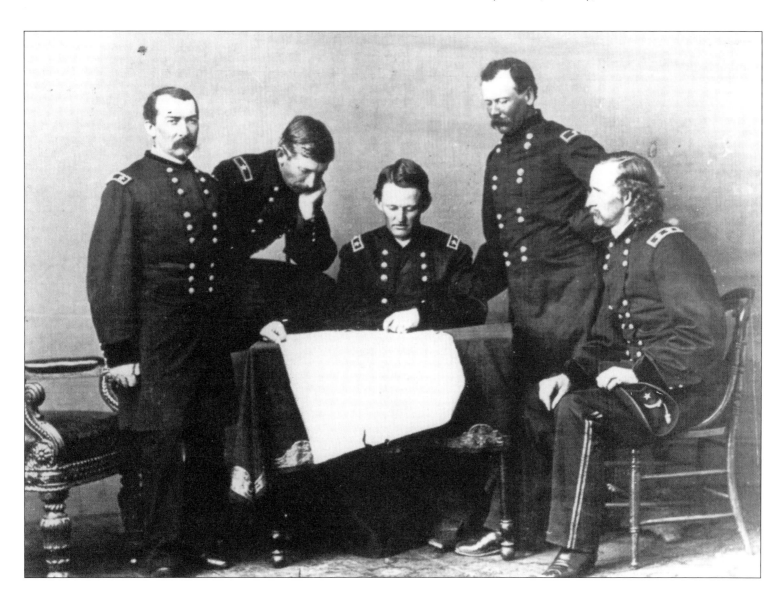

Uniforms of the Confederate Army

by Ron Field

South Carolina	142
Mississippi	165
Florida	174
Alabama	178
Georgia	186
Louisiana	195
Texas	210
Virginia	219
Arkansas	231
Tennessee	238
North Carolina	243
Missouri	250
Kentucky	254
Maryland	257
Confederate Quartermaster Issue	261

South Carolina

Following the act of secession on 20 December 1860, the small Republic of South Carolina began to organize an army of defence in preparation for an inevitable Northern invasion. The militia of the 'Palmetto State' by that time consisted of five divisions, each composed of two brigades of either five or six regiments of generally non-uniformed beat militia, or heavy infantry. Attached to most of these regiments were several companies of uniformed volunteer militia consisting of either light infantry of riflemen. A regiment of uniformed volunteer militia cavalry was also attached to each brigade. The 17th Regiment of Infantry, the 1st Regiment of Rifles, and 1st Regiment of Artillery, of the 4th Brigade, 2nd Division, at Charleston were exceptions to this rule being composed entirely of uniformed companies. Small volunteer battalions at Columbia and Beaufort were also uniformed.

As early as October 1860, many of the Charleston companies were beginning to think about the adoption of fatigue clothing or 'service uniforms'. Towards this end they were prompted by several of the military outfitters and hatters of the city. Steele & Co., 'Military Hatters' on King Street, advertised a large stock of 'Fatigue Caps' priced between '50 cents, $1 or $1.25', adding 'There is no use of being killed in a Ten Dollar Hat!' During January 1861, Walter Steele advertised 'Blue and Gray Cloth Fatigue Caps', 'Glazed Fatigue Caps', and 'Black and Brown Felt Hats, suitable for Military Companies'. Merchant tailor and draper H. Koppel, also on King Street, had supplied 'cheap, excellent and serviceable' fatigue uniforms to units including the Charleston Riflemen, the Palmetto Guard, the Meagher Guard and the Washington Light Infantry. C. F. Jackson & Company made up uniforms for companies such as the Moultrie Guards, the Vigilant Rifles,

Henry Middleton Rutledge was photographed at the studio of Quinby & Company in Charleston wearing the uniform of the Rutledge Mounted Riflemen, a volunteer militia unit organized on 9 November 1860. His gray coatee was bordered with 1-inch wide orange braid, and his gray pants were made 'small at the ankle and fastened by a strap of tape', and had orange worsted seam stripes. A 'French fatigue cap, of blue cloth, with the letters R. M. R. upon the front', as prescribed for this unit, is held in his left hand. (North Carolina Division of Archives and History)

The Charleston Zouave Cadets were formed on 17 August 1860 and modelled themselves on Elmer E. Ellsworth's United States Zouave Cadets. This group study was taken during the winter of 1860/61, when secession fever was at its height in South Carolina. First Lieutenant Charles Edward Gilchrist, who commanded the unit at this time, is seated second from the right. Third Lieutenant Benjamin M. Walpole is sat next to him, third from the right. The enlisted men wear their 'winter uniform' consisting of chasseur tunic and trousers, and are holding Model 1841 'Mississippi' rifles with brass furniture and patch boxes. Note the 'Tiger head' on the two-piece brass belt plates worn by the two men on the left. (Valentine Museum)

the Cadet Riflemen, and the Ætna Guards.

Most of these uniforms were made of some shade of gray cloth, but there the similarity ended. On 21 April 1861, William H. Russell, correspondent for *The Times* of London, wrote:

'At the present moment, Charleston is like a place in the neighbourhood of a military camp where military and volunteer tailors are at work trying experiments in uniforms, and sending their animated models for inspection. There is an endless variety – often of ugliness – in dress and equipment and nomenclature among these companies. The headdress is generally, however, a smart cap like the French kepi; the tunic is of different cuts, colors, facings, and materials – green with gray and yellow, gray with orange and black and white, blue with white and yellow facings, roan, brown, burnt sienna and olive – jackets, frocks, tunics, blouses, cloth, linen, tweed, flannel.'

The uniformed companies of the Charleston regiments were the first South Carolinians to see active service. The 1st Regiment of Rifles, elements of which occupied Castle Pinckney in Charleston Harbor on 27 December 1860, wore a variety of service dress. The Washington Light Infantry had adopted a cadet gray cassimere frock coat, overcoat and pants, the latter being trimmed with ¾-inch black seam stripes; a 'plain felt, brownish color' hat looped up on one side; and 'Leggins of calf-skin,' which laced up as high as the calf of the leg, and fitted 'snugly over the feet'. The Moultrie Guards wore a 'blue cloth cap, a gray jacket . . . made of North Carolina (cassimere) goods, with standing collar, and one row of palmetto buttons in front, and black pants'. The Carolina Light Infantry adopted 'Black Pants and Fatigue Jacket'.

The Charleston Zouave Cadets first saw service in 'a neat undress gray suit, with white cross belts.' They also adopted a 'full dress Zouave uniform,' subsequently referred to as a 'winter uniform', which consisted of a gray, nine-button chasseur jacket with 4- to 5-inch skirt, slit in the sides. Modelled on the *habit-tunique* adopted by the French Army in 1860, the jacket worn

(Continued on page 154)

An officer in the dark blue 'Volunteer Forces' uniform prescribed for those who received commissions in the regiments raised by the 'Palmetto State' at the beginning of 1861. Buttons where white metal and trousers stripes were white. (From a photograph by Ron Field)

Previous page: At Seven Pines, or Fair Oaks Station, on 31 May 1862, Hampton's Legion made at least three charges through dense woodland raked by murderous grape, canister and musketry fire. An anonymous staff officer present recalled: '…on getting to the woods our little brigade found itself unsupported within fifty yards of a heavy battery, flanked by fifteen thousand infantry, strongly entrenched.' The 363 strong Legion lost 21 killed, 118 wounded and 13 missing. This was a greater loss by far in proportion to its numbers than any other regiment in Brigadier-General W.H.C. Whiting's division.

The plate depicts a private of the Washington light Infantry Volunteers, Co. A, (left) wearing tattered remains of the frock coat and trousers issued to Hampton's Legion in October 1861. Made at the 'Industrial School for Girls' on Ashley Street, Charleston, it consisted of various gray jeans material of mixed cotton and wool, yellow or buff braid. The choice of trim color, which

was coincidently worn by the U.S. Army Regiment of Voltigeurs and Foot Riflemen during the Mexican War, may echo Wade Hampton's original intention that the Legion infantry should fulfil that branch of service.

A second member of the same company (right) wears a well worn collarless green flannel shirt, with two breast pockets, under which is a dirty white cotton shirt. His gray pants are the same as those worn by the first figure. Both men wear short off-white gaiters and are equipped with waist belts, shoulder belts supporting cartridge boxes, cap pouches and bayonet scabbards, and are armed with Enfield Short Pattern Rifles, cal. .577, with sabre bayonets.

The field officer (top) is based on descriptions of Major James Conner. He wears his blue militia frock coat over a red French shirt, and gray checked pants. Rank is indicated by an embroidered star on each side of the collar and red waist sash. His cap is a plain gray Model 1858 pattern, which was basically a Model 1851 dress cap with stiffening removed from all but the crown. A

gold-embroidered palmetto tree graces its front. A black leather sword belt is fastened around his waist by a brass clasp bearing the palmetto device. He holds a Colt Navy Revolver, Model 1851, which he has drawn from a black leather flapped holster. (Painting by Richard Hook)

Above: When the Confederate soldier marched off to war, he carried aloft a multitude of different flags. The largest flag seen above is a bunting camp flag of the 'Maryland Guards', a unit which enlisted as Company B, 21st Virginia Infantry. This company of Marylanders 'escaped' South in 1861 and joined the Virginia regiment. The 12-star First National flag of the 'Dixie Rangers' seen at top right was captured near Barnesville, Georgia, on 19 April 1865 by Wilson's Cavalry Corps. It may originally have been carried by Company C, 65th Georgia Infantry, the only Georgia unit designated the 'Dixie Rangers'. At bottom right is an unidentified cavalry-size flag of the Charleston Clothing

Depot pattern, apparently issued during the Civil War to a few units in the Military Department of South Carolina, Georgia, and Florida. This flag was loaned to the Boers during the Boer War in South Africa in 1899, and was later returned to a Confederate veteran in Florida. Hence, the bullet holes in its folds may be circa 1900 machine gun bullet holes! The flag fragment at bottom left bears the battle honor 'Second Battle of Manassas', and is tentatively identified as having been used at the battle of Second Manassas by Company E, 4th Virginia Infantry. However, according to the 'history' associated with this flag, it was sent home by company member William H. Haynes when he was discharged in February of 1862. Hence it could not have been used at Second Manassas. Also, as a company flag, it is unlikely that it saw service in combat after 1861. (Artifacts courtesy of The Museum of the Confederacy)

The Confederate battle flag was conceived after confusion identifying friend from foe during the Battle of First Manassas (Bull Run), 21 July 1861, and was approved in September 1861. The design as originally adopted was roughly square, but later patterns took many different shapes and forms. The battle flag seen at top was made at the Augusta Clothing Depot and issued at Dalton, Georgia, to the 7th Mississippi Infantry. Seen right is a 2nd pattern Richmond Depot bunting battle flag tentatively identified as belonging to the 4th North Carolina Infantry. It was captured by the 7th Ohio Infantry on 3 May 1863 at Chancellorsville. (Courtesy of The Museum of the Confederacy)

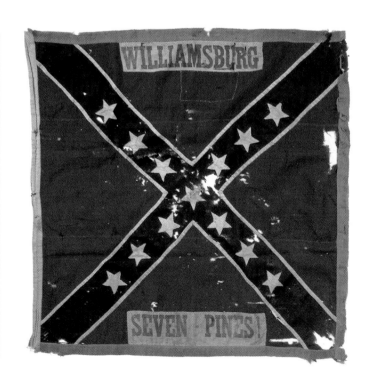

The unusual battle flag seen at top was presented to the 1st and 3rd (combined) Regiments, Florida Volunteer Infantry in 1864. As it bears the battle honour for Jonesboro, which was fought on 31 August–1 September 1864, and since the honours are uniformly applied, it must have been decorated after that date. The crossed cannon in the bottom quarter indicate that this regiment captured an enemy battery.

The first flag used by the Confederate States became known as the First National flag, and was adopted on 4 March 1861 at Montgomery, Alabama. According to a remnant of writing on the heading of the flag at bottom, this unidentified example was captured at Logan's Cross Roads (Mill Springs), Kentucky, on 19 January 1862. (Courtesy of The Museum of the Confederacy)

Confederate army manuals and record books were an essential tool of command. The uniform plate is part of 'Uniform and Dress of the Army of the Confederate States', published in Richmond, Virginia in 1861. The record book at right belonged to Captain B.F. Howard, Co. I, 1st Virginia Infantry, Kemper's Brigade, Pickett's Division, 1st Corps, A.N.V. It is open at pages dated for the years 1863 to 1864, with references to prisoner exchanges. Other volumes include letter and payroll books, and various editions of the 'Regulations for the Confederate Army'. The spectacles and case at bottom were possibly used by President Jefferson Davis. (Courtesy of The Museum of the Confederacy)

Left: The infantryman of the Army of Northern Virginia is wearing an 'English blue', eight-button shell jacket with shoulder straps of the type made by Peter Tate, an Irish clothing manufacturer. His trousers are wool-and-cotton homespun. His high-crowned, mid-gray, enlisted man's infantry kepi is made from inexpensive cotton jean cloth and finished with a polished mid blue band of the type manufactured by a clothing depot in the Deep South. He is armed with a Short Enfield Rifle with sabre bayonet, and accoutred with cartridge box on belt, cap pouch, haversack and strap, canteen and strap. Note that his straps are shortened and knotted in order to prevent haversack and canteen banging against his thigh, as this was an impediment to the Civil War infantryman. Note infantry 'block I' buttons (top centre); tin drum canteens (top right); sabre bayonet and waist belt plates (centre right); haversacks (bottom right); cap pouches (bottom); cartridge boxes (left). (Painting by Richard Hook)

Right: An unidentified member of the 11th Virginia Infantry. Wearing a hunting shirt possibly made by tailor Charles J. Maine, of 130 Main Street, Lynchburg, he is armed with a M1842 'Mississippi' Rifle, revolver, Sheffield-type Bowie knife, drum canteen, and rigid box knapsack, complete with waterproof blanket roll.

New Orleans resident George Auguste Gaston Coppens proposed raising a battalion of Zouaves based on those of the French Army in March 1861. The organization, drill, orders and dress were modelled on that of the French zouaves, which made it a most distinctive Confederate command. The unit saw service at Pensacola in Florida, and in the campaigns of Northern Virginia, Maryland and North Carolina. Enlisted men wore a red flannel skull cap with deep blue tassel; a dark blue vest trimmed with red; a flannel jacket similar in cut to the original 1830 French zouave uniform, without the characteristic 'tombeau', or false pocket, but trimmed with red around the cuff and jacket edges; sky-blue waist sash; bright red baggy trousers, or serouels; and white gaiters, over which were worn black 'gutta percha' leggings, or jambieres. NCO's rank was indicated in French style with gold lace chevrons on the fore

arm. Gray blanket rolls that doubled as knapsacks were worn across the body from left to right. They were armed with the U.S. Musket, Model 1842, a smoothbore, percussion cap muzzleloader of caliber .69, firing a round lead ball. Vivandieres, or ladies armed with barrels of brandy, were quite common in the earliest volunteer units, both Norh and South. Those in Coppens' command wore a version of the battalion uniform, over which was a blue skirt with red border. Officers wore a dark blue single-breasted frock coat with rank indicated by gold lace Hungarian knots on each sleeve that reached almost to the shoulder. The color of their full cut trousers is conjectural. Their kepi appears to have had a red crown, sky-blue band and gold lace quartering and quatrefoil. Belts and swords appear to have been left up to personal choice. (Painting by Richard Hook)

by the Zouave Cadets had a solid red collar, narrow red braid on the front and bottom edges, red shoulder straps secured by single small buttons, and slash (a tailoring term for an opening on the outside of a cuff closed by two or more buttons) pointed red cuffs fastened with two small buttons. It was apparently without the belt loops often found on chasseur jackets. Most of the jackets worn by the Charleston unit had external pockets on the breast. Non-commissioned officers' chevrons were worn above the elbow with points up.

Trousers were also gray with red seam stripes, and cut in the chasseur style, probably being gathered at the waist with pleats, and below the knee into wide cuffs fastened by buckles or buttons. These were worn with white buttoned gaiters, over which were russet leather *jambiere*, or greaves, buckled at the top and laced down the side opening. Red cadet-pattern caps with lighter-colored bands, of the small-crowned chasseur pattern were worn with this uniform. Black oilskin covers were required for winter wear.

The uniform worn by officers of the Charleston Zouave Cadets at the time the 'winter uniform' was adopted consisted of a dark blue, nine-button frock coat with red collar and cuffs edged with gold braid, the cuffs being slash and pointed, the back seam being fastened by three small buttons. Rank was indicated by Federal-style shoulder straps with red ground, and a crimson net waist sash. Straight-legged dark blue trousers were trimmed with broad gold-colored seam stripes. Their red caps resembled those of other ranks but were embellished with one or more horizontal stripes of ¼-inch gold braid encircling the band; above them similar stripes rose vertically to a circle of braid around the top of the crown. The Austrian knot usually associated with this pattern appears not to have been adopted by the Zouave Cadet officers.

Companies of the 17th Regiment, of Charleston, wore an equally diverse range of service uniforms. The Union Light Infantry, a unit with many Scottish members, wore a 'Scotch bonnet, [and] blue hunting shirt and pants'. The 'camp suit' chosen by the Palmetto Guard consisted of a 'gray woollen jacket and pants,' described as being made 'of light gray Kersey trimed [sic] with yellow braid'. The headgear consisted of 'a blue French Cap'.

Richland Volunteer Rifle Company, Co. A, 1st South Carolina Volunteers (Gregg's). (From a photograph by Ron Field)

John Edward Harrell (or Horrell) of an unidentified South Carolina regiment, wears distinctive South Carolina trim around the skirts of his gray frock coat. The small brass 'Palmetto Tree' which graces the front of his cap dates back to 1840, and was often worn on leather cockades and dragoon helmets. (David Wynn Vaughan collection)

Volunteer companies raised by the Charleston Fire Department also adopted a variety of uniforms. The Ætna Guards wore 'a gray pea jacket, trimmed with red, gray pants, and the "kepi" with the initials Æ. G. in gilt letters'. The Phoenix Rifles paraded in frock coat and pants of 'bluish-gray plains' trimmed with black braid, and a cap of 'Blue Cloth of recent French military style, with the letters P R [white] in front'. The Vigilant Rifles uniform was made of 'the excellent product of the Rock Island Mills, near Charlotte, North Carolina,' and consisted of a shell jacket and pants of dark gray cassimere trimmed with scarlet braid, and 'a light French fatigue cap of blue, with the initials V. R. in gold embossed'.

Regarding artillery companies of the volunteer militia, the Lafayette Artillery of Charleston acquired an undress uniform by April 1861 which, according to a photograph taken of the unit on Cole's Island by Osborn & Durbec, consisted of a five-button sack coat or smock, probably light gray in color, worn loose without waist belt, with two large, waist level patch pockets at the front. The falling collar was trimmed in solid dark-colored cloth, probably red in line with the unit's dress uniform of blue and red. Cuffs were similarly trimmed with upper edge forming an inverted 'V' shape, whilst the front buttoning edge and top of the pockets were also embellished with a wide band of trim. Trousers were the same color as the coat, with a narrow dark-colored stripe on outer seams. Headgear consisted of the Model 1858 forage cap, which was essentially a non-rigid version of the M1851 dress cap with only the top of the crown stiffened. Solid gray in color, and apparently trimmed with a thin band of dark-colored cord round the top edge, some of these caps were decorated with a small brass crossed cannon insignia, either side of which were the brass letters L and A.

During November 1860, the 'Zouave Drill Club' of the German Artillery of Charleston had adopted a fatigue suit consisting of 'a gray satinet jacket, bound with yellow braid; French undress cap, with glazed cover; and dark pants'. The

Far left: William R. Atkinson joined the Richland Volunteer Rifle Company on 1 January 1861, the day it left Columbia for Charleston. He wears the gray pleated hunting shirt of this unit over his civilian clothing. Note the six-pointed star pinned to his neck tie and silver M1834 horn on his fatigue cap. (South Caroliniana Library)

Left: Captain W. T. Livingston raised the Keowee Riflemen, later to become Co. A, 1st Regiment of South Carolina Rifles (Orr's Regiments of Rifles), during January 1861. He wears the blue uniform prescribed for this regiment in May 1861. Note the captain's bars on the collar, and two straight strips of braid on his sleeves, representing an oversimplified interpretation of official C.S. regulations. His coat is trimmed, in distinctive South Carolinian style, with a broad band of dark green velvet. His broad, light-colored trouser stripes do not conform to Orr's Rifles regulations. (South Caroliniana Library)

Above: Frock coat and trousers supplied to Robert Hayne Bomar, Washington Light Infantry Volunteers, Hampton's Legion, by the South Carolina Quartermaster Department during October 1861. Made of gray jeans cloth, they were trimmed with yellow, or buff, tape. (From photographs by Ron Field)

Beaufort Volunteer Artillery appeared in 'a French fatigue cap, a blue frock coat with standing collar, and a single row of Palmetto buttons on the breast; pants blue with red stripes' during the same month.

The Charleston Light Dragoons, renowned for their 'Bottle Green' coatee with 'trimmings of red Casimere'; 'Helmet of black Patent leather trimmed with brass' and 'white horse hair' plume, had their 'Measures taken for the Service Uniform' on 28 November, and paraded in 'full Fatigue Dress' on 11 December 1860. A visitor to Charleston during January 1861 described this as consisting of a 'small French military cap' and fatigue jacket: '. . . charily trimmed with red worsted, and stained with the rains and earth of the islands. One young dragoon in this sober dress walked into our hotel, trailing the clinking steel scabbard of his sabre across the marble floor of the vestibule with a warlike rattle'.

The only state uniform regulations in use at this time were for officers and were modelled on the antiquated U.S. pattern of 1839. Clearly something more modern was needed for the officers of the State Volunteer Forces being grafted on to the existing South Carolina militia system by an act of 17 December 1860. The new regulations subsequently published by the State Adjutant General and entitled *Uniform and Dress of the Officers of the Volunteer Forces*, consisted of a plain dark blue frock coat of M1851 U.S. army pattern, with dark blue trousers and forage caps. General officers wore gilt buttons bearing 'the palmetto device' and gold lace seam stripe on trousers. Silver metal and white leather and facings, abandoned as a distinction for U.S. infantry officers in 1851, were retained as the infantry branch service color by South Carolina. Hence, field and company grade officers wore silver metal buttons, with white leather sword belts. Field officers' trousers bore 1-inch-wide silver seam stripes, while those of company grade officers were white. Insignia for the 'dark blue cloth military caps' of company-grade officers consisted of a 'silver palmetto tree on the front, with the figure indicating the number of the Regiment on one side, and the letter R on the other.' Full dress headgear for field officers was the plumed cocked hat prescribed for the state militia in 1839. For undress, they wore forage caps with a silver wreath encircling the figure indicating the number of their respective regiment.

The eight regiments commanded by these officers initially wore a wide variety of uniforms. Whether formed by existing uniformed volunteer militia companies, or raised amongst the

This tinted image of a South Carolinian officer is tentatively identified as Captain James M. White, Company I, 1st South Carolina Volunteers (Hagood's). Note his ornate militia staff officer's sword attached to a white leather waist belt. (David Edelen)

ranks of the beat militia, each company was originally provided with a 'service uniform' generally paid for by public subscription, and made up by local tailors and seamstresses. A style of 'hunting shirt' with pleats on the chest and broad band of trim around the skirts was uniquely associated with South Carolina. The Richland Volunteer Rifle Company left Columbia in January 1861 to become Company A of Colonel Maxcy Gregg's 1st South Carolina Volunteers (six months volunteers), wearing a dark gray hunting shirt made from cloth produced at the Rock Island Mills, at Charlotte, North Carolina. Pleats embellished the chest, whilst the trim below the waist was probably green if based on their volunteer militia uniform, which was a 'dark blue green frock coat, trimmed with three rows of gilt buttons . . . faced with green velvet'. A forage cap and dark gray trousers completed the service uniform of this company, although they also appear to have worn the U.S. Model 1858 dress hat, or Hardee hat, associated with their militia full dress uniform.

The Rhett Guard of Newbury enlisted as Company L of Colonel Maxcy Gregg's 1st South Carolina in January 1861 wearing 'a fatigue dress, composed of a hunting frock of green, with scarlet sash and oil-silk cap'. During July of the same year this company received new 'outfits for the service' consisting of a gray pleated hunting shirt and pants trimmed with green velvet, and dark-colored slouch hats pinned by star-shaped insignia, with black ostrich feather plumes. The Pee Dee Rifles of Darlington became Company D of Gregg's re-organized 1st South Carolina Volunteers, and during the summer of 1861 received a uniform '. . . of dark gray goods manufactured at Salem, North Carolina. The bodies of the coats were pleated, making a neat appearance and proving, in the absence of overcoats, warm and serviceable.' The Gist Riflemen of Williamston, in Anderson District, were wearing a 'green, hunter-like, loose-fitting coat' when they paraded in front of President Davis within the ranks of the infantry battalion of the Hampton Legion at Camp Chimborazo, near Richmond, on 8 July 1861.

Other South Carolinian companies volunteering for Confederate service wore single-breasted frock coats with the distinctive broad bands of trim around the skirts. The Edisto Rifles of Orangeburg enlisted as Company A of Colonel Johnson Hagood's 1st South Carolina Volunteers (twelve months volunteers) wearing their volunteer militia uniform consisting of a gray frock coat fastened by eight buttons, with

a standing collar faced with green, and wide band of green velvet edging on coat skirts. Their gray pants had green seam stripes, and their dark-colored fatigue caps bore the brass letters ER on the front. On 27 October 1861 the Brooks Grays, Company G of the 7th South Carolina Volunteers (Bacon's), received a new uniform, courtesy of the Ninety-Six Aid Association of Edgefield District. Made of 'gray cloth', their frock coats were fastened by nine 'silver Palmetto buttons,' and had solid black velvet collars and a narrow band of black velvet trim around the skirts. Their gray trousers had black seam stripes, whilst their gray forage caps had black bands and brass 'Palmetto Tree' insignia in front. The Southern Guards, another company in the 7th South Carolina, were supplied with a uniform of 'dark gray with brilliant orange stripes' on 27 October 1861.

The companies of the infantry battalion of the Hampton Legion originally wore a variety of uniforms off to war in Virginia. That of the Washington Light Infantry Volunteers was described as 'cadet gray, frock coat and pants, with black trimmings; black felt hat, looped up on left side with a Palmetto cockade'. The green hunting shirt of the Gist Riflemen has already been described. The Davis Guards wore a dark gray or black frock coat and pants with either brown or black felt hats. The South Carolina Zouave Volunteers, raised initially from the ranks of the Charleston Zouave Cadets, left Charleston to join the Legion wearing 'a gray jacket, well lined, and trimmed with blue. The pants of yellow woollen, very loose about the body, tight around the ankles, so as to go under a gaiter'. Their cap probably consisted of 'a red turban, lined inside with gray, so as to be used either way'. Overcoats were gray, and 'Undershirts' were made of gray flannel.

The Regular Army of South Carolina was established in late December 1860, and consisted of one regiment of infantry, which was eventually designated the 3rd Regiment, South Carolina Artillery; a battalion of artillery, which was expanded and re-organized into the 1st Regiment, South Carolina Artillery; a squadron of cavalry, which later evolved into the Dismounted Dragoon Battalion; and a 'Corps of Military Engineers'. Volunteers enlisted as 'regulars' were informed that their uniform would be 'the same as that of the U.S. Army'. Certainly, officers' dress was based on M1857 U.S. Army regulations, which in general terms consisted of a dark blue frock coat, sky-blue trousers, with the kepi, or 'new U.S. Army fatigue cap', replacing the Hardee hat and dress cap.

Regarding the uniform worn by enlisted men of the Regular Army, the 'Clothing Emporium' of C. F. Jackson, 199 King Street, Charleston, was reported in the press to have 'filled numerous orders for . . . uniforms for the regular service' by 14 February 1861. A report entitled 'Carolina Caps – Williams & Brown' indicates that this firm was busily engaged 'filling a large order for the South Carolina Army of the regular line'. Artists' impressions of the bombardment of Fort Sumter depict the artillery battalion wearing forage caps and plain uniform trousers. Several wear shell jackets. Company A of this unit was photographed in battle order standing by the guns of Fort Moultrie in caps, plain gray coats and gray pants with dark-colored seam stripes. During August 1861, several published descriptions of deserters from the Regulars are of value. Private William Bond of Company C, Battalion of Artillery, was described as wearing his 'Uniform Coat, Cap and White Pants' when he went missing from duty at Fort Sumter on 8 August 1861. Private Albert Leildke, of the Third Company (C), 1st Regiment of Infantry, was similarly clad in a 'Uniform Coat, and Cap marked 1, C.S.A., and white pants' when he disappeared from Sullivan's Island the next day!

Several regimental uniforms were also supplied by the State to its volunteer forces. That received by Gregg's original regiment of 1st South Carolina Volunteers (six months state service), consisted of frock coats and pants of 'dark gray cloth', and was made up under the direction of the Rev. A. Toomer Porter, an Episcopal priest and proprietor of the 'Industrial School for Girls' in Ashley Street, Charleston. In his memoir, *Four Years in Rebel Capitals*, Thomas Cooper DeLeon recalled the 'dirty gray and tarnished silver' of Gregg's regiment arriving in Richmond, which would indicate that they wore white metal state buttons, in line with those prescribed for officers in the Volunteer Forces regulations.

Based on a photograph of Private Joseph Brunson of the Edgefield Riflemen, Company C of Gregg's unit, the frock coat supplied with this uniform was single breasted and fastened by nine buttons, and had ½-inch wide dark tape trim around the collar, with plain cuffs. His headgear consisted of a gray chasseur pattern forage cap bearing in front the numeral 1 above the letters SCV over ER. Presumably this was one of the caps 'supplied throughout the First South Carolina' by 'Williams and Brown' of King Street in Charleston.

Established in 1858 to teach 'plain sewing' to the 'poor girls'

Private John Bagnal Brogdon enlisted in the cavalry battalion of the Holcombe Legion on 13 November 1861. He had a horse valued at $225 and equipment worth $25. For reasons unknown he was discharged five weeks later. Hence his eight-button plain gray frock coat may be identified to a specific period of issue. Note his oval SC belt plate. He grips a derringer-type pistol in right hand, and a U.S. Model 1840 sabre, or Palmetto Armory copy, in his left. (S.C. Confederate Relic Room & Museum)

of the city, by April 1861 the Rev. Porter had contracted with the Colonel Lewis M. Hatch, of the Quartermaster Department of South Carolina, to supply uniforms for troops in State service. City tailors undertook the 'pressing and cutting' of the cloth, whilst 59 women at his 'Industrial School' worked 32 sewing machines. These labours were variously supplemented by upwards of 350 'out-workers' who presumably sewed by hand. At the end of July 1861, the 'Industrial School' was taken over by the Quartermaster Department. Assisted by Colonel S. L. Glover, Hatch had 'constantly employed . . . under the foremanship of Messrs. H. Koppel ["Merchant Tailor" on King Street] and D. H. Kemme ["Draper and Tailor" on Broad Street], forty experienced cutters, who supply about 1500 needlewomen, who make a fair weekly salary'. These two tailors received payment between 14 December 1861 and 31 January 1862 for cutting '3019 frock coats, 1157 overcoats, [and] 113 pairs of pants . . .'

As chaplain of the Washington Light Infantry Volunteers of Charleston, the Rev. Porter next turned his attention to supplying the Hampton Legion with uniforms to replace those worn off to war which, by August 1861, were 'in rags'. After contacting every factory in Virginia and North Carolina 'in vain for a sufficient quantity of cloth of the same color to uniform one thousand men . . .', Porter returned to Charleston where he purchased from 'Messrs Wm. Ravenel and Co. . . . ten different kinds of cloth for the ten companies' of the Legion. This was duly taken to the State Quartermaster's Department situated at his old 'Industrial School' and turned into frock coats and pants which, by the Fall of 1861, had been delivered to the Hampton Legion.

Evidence for the style of uniform supplied to the Hampton Legion by the Industrial School survives in the frock coat and trousers of Corporal Robert Hayne Bomar, held today by the South Carolina Confederate Relic Room and Museum at Columbia, South Carolina. Bomar enrolled as a private in the Washington Light Infantry Volunteers, Company A of the infantry battalion of the Hampton Legion, on 12 June 1861, and was wounded at First Manassas. Private C. W. Hutson of Bomar's company noted on 27 September 1861 that Bomar, since his promotion to sergeant, 'has never exercised his office, not having yet recovered from his severe wound'. It is probable that the surviving coat and pants were issued to him in hospital shortly before 1 October 1861, the date of his discharge because of these wounds, or were sent home to him later

because they were not needed by other members of his company. Although the exact date when Porter brought the uniforms to Manassas is unknown, he was with the Legion by 6 October. Curiously, the bulk of the uniforms do not seem to have been distributed until 20–21 October.

The Bomar coat and trousers are of a grayish-brown jeans material of mixed cotton and wool, which was originally gray, as may be seen in an area once covered by the trousers stripe. The coat was based in certain respects on M1851 U.S. dress regulations, and has H-inch light yellow or buff tape edging round the collar, and eight buttons on the front, which are brass eagle buttons with a V on the shield, of the type made by Scovills & Co., Waterbury, Connecticut, for enlisted men of the Regular United States Army's Regiment of Voltigeurs and Foot Riflemen (1847–1848) in the Mexican War. These were attached by pushing the looped shank of each button through the coat cloth, and threading a long piece of braid through each shank. Not coincidentally, the Regiment of Voltigeurs was originally designed to be a 'legion' comprising infantry, artillery and dragoons, and to have a uniform of 'dark gray' with yellow trimming. It is possible that, following the lead of the U.S. Voltigeur Regiment, it was intended to dress the infantry, cavalry and artillery of the Hampton Legion all in the same uniform with yellow trim. In addition, yellow trim was appropriate for the infantry of the Legion, originally designated 'voltigeurs', because yellow had been a distinctive branch trim of the French voltigeurs and their successors, the Chasseurs a pied, since the Napoleonic Wars.

Except in having 8 buttons rather than 9 or 10 (not a very consequential difference in Confederate uniforms), the Bomar coat matches those made earlier in 1861 at Porter's Industrial School for the 1st South Carolina Volunteers (Gregg's). The sleeves were plain without buttons or slashes. The rear skirts were divided from the waist seam down, and one pocket was set inside each skirt. Bomar's trousers were also originally gray with a light yellow or buff strip of 1-inch wide braid on the outer seam. In the rear was a slit some 4 inches long, originally held together to adjust the waist size by two 4½-inch long straps probably once fastened by a buckle. In a style frequently found in U.S. Army officers' trousers, two 'frog pockets' in the front were fastened by small buttons.

When Private Hutson of the Washington Light Infantry received his regimental uniform on 20 October, he was not impressed: 'This morning we were furnished with the new

Turner T. Wright, Co. K, Orr's Rifles, possibly wears the brown uniform supplied to his regiment during the Fall of 1861. Alternatively it may be that worn after his transfer to Co. E, 20th South Carolina Volunteers, in which case it is representative of the six-button frock coat issued by the state Quartermaster Department between 1862–63. (Courtesy of his great-great-grandson, Dan Snipes)

uniform coats & pants, two pairs of socks & two warm flannel shirts apiece. The stuff of which the coats & pants are made is wretched. They are not as warm as those we have worn through the summer.'

The 1st Regiment of Rifles, South Carolina Volunteers (not to be confused with the similarly titled militia regiment mentioned earlier), commanded by James Lawrence Orr and organized during the summer of 1861, received a uniform based on a very specific set of regulations published in contemporary South Carolina newspapers in two slightly different versions. According to the *Keowee Courier*, of Pickens Court House, field officers were to wear dark blue double-breasted frock coats with two rows of nine buttons. The standing collar was of green velvet, edged with gilt lace. Cuffs were 2½ inches deep of solid green velvet, with two small buttons on the under seam. Coat skirts were trimmed with a 1-inch wide green velvet stripe. The Abbeville Press stipulated two rows of eight buttons. Field officers' pantaloons were also of dark blue cloth, 'made full in the legs' and trimmed with 1-inch wide gold lace on the outer seams. Their hats followed 1861 U.S. regulations, and were broad-brimmed black felt, 6 inches in the crown, with a black ostrich feather, and right side looped up by a gold cord to a small button. A gilt Palmetto Tree was specified for the side of the turn-up brim, whilst a gilt bugle horn, identifiable as the M1834 U.S. Infantry cap insignia, adorned the front of the crown.

Officer's rank insignia for Orr's Regiment of Rifles was influenced by a version of the Confederate States uniform regulations released unofficially in the Southern press during May 1861, but some chose to change them to comply with the official C.S. dress regulations issued the next month. Based on the 'leaked' version, sleeves remained plain, whilst a system of gilt stars decorated the collar. However, those officers in Orr's Regiment who did choose to follow C.S. regulations adopted the stars or bars collar insignia, but misinterpreted the wording of these regulations and placed straight gilt bars of braid running along the outside seam of the sleeve from the cuff to the elbow (two bars for captain and one for lieutenant), simply including the number of braids but not the specified Austrian knot shape.

Staff and company officers wore single-breasted, nine-button, dark blue frock coats trimmed on collar, breast, skirt, and cuffs with green velvet. Pants were also dark blue with green seam stripes. The Surgeon and Chaplain were the exception with black seam stripes. Hats were the same as field officers. The sergeant major and quartermaster sergeant wore the same uniform as company officers, minus green trim on the coat, with gold lace chevrons on each upper arm. Sergeants, corporals and privates wore a 'Dark blue jeans' frock coat and pants trimmed in the same style as company officers with narrow green worsted braid. Non-commissioned officers' chevrons were green worsted, point down above the elbow for sergeants, 'commencing with four for the First Sergeant, and diminishing one for each Sergeant.' Corporals were worn point upwards below the elbow, 'four for the First Corporal, and diminishing one for each Corporal'. Hats for NCOs and privates were the same as officers, minus feather, with a 2-inch high gilt Palmetto Tree insignia in front, with 1-inch high company letter underneath.

For fatigue dress, officers were prescribed frock coats and pants of dark blue jeans trimmed with green velvet, whilst NCOs and privates wore a 'roundabout coat', or shell jacket, of the same material trimmed with narrow green worsted braid. All ranks wore forage caps of 'Glazed silk or oil cloth'.

These uniforms were to be furnished by 'patriotic citizens' of the Districts in South Carolina from which the companies came. Furthermore, each soldier was requested to provide himself with 'a cape of oil or enamel cloth, to be fastened to the collar of the coat with three small buttons, and to extend three inches below the elbow . . .', plus 'one large Bowie knife, knapsacks, haversacks and canteens'.

By mid-August these uniforms were still being made up and, based on photographic evidence, many local seamstresses used gray rather than dark blue cloth, possibly influenced by C. S. regulations. Realizing that this clothing would be 'much worn before mid-winter', Colonel Orr issued an appeal on 23 August 1861 for a more suitable uniform for the regiment, to consist of 'a thick heavy woollen plains or jeans coat, overcoat and pants.' The 'Ladies of Pickens, Anderson and Abbeville Districts' were advised to 'Dye the cloth brown; this you can do from the trees and shrubs of our own forests . . .' The skirts of these 'Dress-coats' were to extend 'to within three inches of the knee,' with 'stand-up collar, one and three fourth inches high; single-breasted; . . . buttons, covered with the same material of the coat.' Overcoats were to be 'double-breasted, and to button all the way up; the capes to be fastened by buttons, so that it may be removed from the coat when not needed; the skirt of the coat to extend three inches below the knee.'

William Zachariah Leitner was commissioneed First Lieutenant of the Camden Volunteers, Co. E, 2nd South Carolina Volunteers (Kershaw's) on 9 April 1861. He rose to the rank of captain before losing his leg at Gettysburg, after which he served on the Bureau of Conscription as enrolling officer for Kershaw District. In this early war image, he wears a C.S. regulation officer's frock coat. (Camden Archives)

The State Quartermaster Department continued to supply locally-made uniforms and clothing to South Carolinian troops until at least the end of 1864. James A. Carter, of Charleston, made up '1745 frock coats, 131 overcoats and 74 pairs of pants' during January/February 1862. Earlier, during July 1861, the department had paid Porter's Industrial School 'for Making 50 Inft Uniforms' which indicates that some kind of branch service system was in effect – possibly using black or dark blue trim for infantry, yellow for cavalry, and red for artillery. The cloth used by the Quartermaster Department at Charleston for coats and pants included 'Cadet Jeans', 'Gray Woolens', 'Gray Satinet', 'Steel mix'd Tweeds' and 'Brown Plains'. Shirts appear to have been made from 'Striped Osnaburgs', 'Algonquin Twilled Stripes', 'Troy Cottonade', 'Checked Cottonade' and a variety of cotton plaids.

Returns exist for clothing received and issued at the Quartermaster Department at Columbia, the state capital, for the periods 1 June through 31 December 1862, and for the entire year of 1864. The most interesting is a monthly return for 1 June 1862, listing 8024 'Unif. Coats', 4107 'Pants', 2361 'O'Coats', 127 'Woolen Capes', 645 'Gray Caps', and 90 'Hats'. Very little clothing was issued from Columbia during the third quarter of 1862, but from October to December 1862 were issued 7957 coats, 3772 pairs of pants, 2518 overcoats, 1469 cotton drawers, 531 flannel shirts, 48 tweed shirts, 196 hickory shirts, 645 caps and 22 hats. These items were probably being transferred to Virginia for distribution to South Carolina soldiers in the Army of Northern Virginia. By 1864 the state was not issuing any clothing in Columbia except a few shoes.

The state issuance of 1862–63 appears to have consisted a slightly longer gray frock coat than that of 1861. It had only six (sometimes seven) buttons. Commonly the collar was trimmed with tape or cord forming the edging and a false buttonhole, and the pointed cuffs were trimmed in the same style, sometimes topped with an oval loop. some had a solid branch-color collar and cuffs, while others may have been completely plain. Trousers continued to be gray with 1-inch-wide branch-color seam stripes. Headgear appears to have been 'cadet-pattern' forage caps, either gray or (in early 1862) dark blue, to which brass company and regimental numbers and letters were sometimes attached. The six-button frock coat was superceded by a six-button shell jacket, with or without branch-service color trim, which was being issued by mid-1863. The collar 'buttonhole' was omitted from this jacket, and all other trimming was often omitted. The possible successor to this pattern was the plain five-button jacket issued by the Confederate Clothing Depot in Charleston by 1864.

Mississippi

Following the secession of Mississippi on 9 January 1861, the State Convention established a state military force called the Army of Mississippi, and a Military Board consisting of Governor John J. Pettus and five generals which, sometime during March 1861, published 'Orders' for the organization and maintenance of this force. Included within these orders were detailed uniform regulations, which were subsequently reprinted as part of the 'Southern Military Manual', published in both Jackson and New Orleans, which contained the collected 'military ordinances' of Mississippi and Louisiana.

The Army of Mississippi, according to the orders of the Military Board, was to consist of a division of 8 regiments of infantry or riflemen, 10 companies of cavalry and 10 of artillery. Unlike other seceded states who formed small 'regular' full-time state forces, the Army of Mississippi was not conceived as such. After mustering in, the men were furloughed and recalled for training when required. By mid-March, nearly 40 companies had been formed into the 1st–8th Infantry Regiments, within 4 brigades. Many of these were existing volunteer militia companies and since less than two years previously a militia act had attempted to organize the volunteer militia of the state into a division, it is difficult to understand why the 1861 Military Board should have wanted to duplicate this organization. As other volunteer militia companies were mustered into the Provisional Army of the Confederate States during 1861, the Army of Mississippi was by-passed. When some of the latter's commands did go into 'camp of instruction' late in the year, complaints of wasted resources were heard. The eight infantry regiments were disbanded in January 1862, whilst the cavalry and artillery seem not to have materialized.

The uniform for the Army of Mississippi was prescribed in detail. For full dress, gray frock coats were to be of U.S. regulation cut, although all double-breasted coats, for generals as well as field officers, bore two rows of seven buttons. Generals' cuffs were plain, but their collars were of black velvet, with an embroidered 1-inch gilt star each side for the Major-General, and silver stars for Brigadiers. Field officers wore black cloth collars minus the star, and black cuffs, all edged with ½-inch gold lace. Staff officers' coats were not braided. Company

Unidentified enlisted man in a uniform based on that prescribed for the Army of Mississippi. His coat is fastened by gilt Mississippi 'star'-pattern buttons. (Mississippi Department of Archives & History)

officers had collars and cuffs of branch service color, and horizontal silk braid of the same color running across from their nine buttons, the top braids being 5 inches in length, and the bottom 2. Enlisted mens' coats were similar, but with worsted braid. Branch service color was to be crimson for infantry and riflemen, yellow for cavalry, and orange for artillery.

Trousers were also gray, with black cord stripes for generals, and 1-inch cloth stripes for the rest, black for field officers, and of branch service color for the remainder. Hats were of black felt, broad brimmed and 'looped up on three sides', with cord, tassel and plume for parade. The plume was to be 'long flowing' for generals, field and staff officers, and 'short and standing' for all other ranks. Plume colors were – white for Major General, red tipped white for Brigadier-General, crimson for regimental field and staff, green for the Medical Corps, yellow for the Adjutant General's Corps, blue for the Quartermaster General's department, and blue tipped with red for the Ordnance Corps. Captains, lieutenants and enlisted men wore plumes of the color of the 'facings of their dress.' Yellow metal regimental numbers were to be worn below the plume socket for Regimental Field and Staff officers. These were probably substituted for company letters for Captain and all other ranks. Cords and tassels were to be gold for all officers, and worsted facing color for other ranks.

Officers' rank was to be indicated by a system of dark blue shoulder straps with gold borders. Like their full dress epaulettes, these bore a rank system consisting of a gold star for Major General, silver star for Brigadier General, gold crescent for Colonel, gold leaf for Lieutenant Colonel, silver leaf for major, two gold bars for Captain, one for First Lieutenant, and none for Second and Third lieutenants. Non-commissioned officers' chevrons were basically as per U.S. regulations, in facing colors, of silk for Sergeant-Major, Quartermaster Sergeant, and Ordnance Sergeant; of worsted for 1st Sergeant and below.

For fatigue, enlisted men were to wear flannel shirts with a white star on each side of the collar. Those for infantry and riflemen were to be red, gray for artillery, and blue for cavalry.

After these orders were issued, the Military Board apparently

Left: Unidentified officer in the uniform prescribed by the Military Board for the Army of Mississippi in March 1861. (Mississippi Department of Archives & History)

had second thoughts about the unusual, and possibly confusing, branch service colors prescribed. On 14 March 1861, the New Orleans *Daily Delta* reported: 'Mississippi regulation uniform (gray) changed by the Military Board to Infantry and Light Infantry . . . Green, Artillery . . . Red, Cavalry . . . Yellow or Orange.'

However, in a final version of these regulations, these colors were changed yet again. This was included as part of the collected 'military ordinances' of Mississippi in the the 'southern Military Manual', a handbook for officers published simultaneously in Mississippi and Louisiana, probably in May 1861. Here the facing colors were given as blue for infantry and riflemen, orange for cavalry, and red for artillery, while fatigue shirts were now gray for infantry, blue for cavalry, and red for artillery.

While there is considerable doubt that many Mississippi companies wore any of the three prescribed versions of these uniform regulations in their entirety, it is likely that they served as a partial guide for the war companies subsequently organized. A number of companies chose to wear three-cornered hats and/or coats with horizontal bars of trim on their chests. The Alcorn Rifles, Co. F, and the James Creek Volunteers, Co. H, 1st Mississippi Infantry, are both recorded as wearing horizontal bars on their coats. The Ben Bullard rifles, Co. B, 10th Mississippi Infantry, were photographed by J. D. Edwards manning heavy artillery at Pensacola in late April or early May 1861, wearing a uniform based almost in every detail on that prescribed by the State Military Board. Henry Augustus Moore of the Water Valley Rifle Guard, Co. F, 15th Mississippi Infantry, wore a gray coat with short 1-inch-wide bars across the chest. Sinclair B. Carter of the Choctaw Guards, Co. I, 15th Mississippi wore horizontal bars on his coat which appear to have been connected by two sets of short ties, thus securing the coat at the front. Both coats had solid branch service-colored collar and cuffs. The Lamar Rifles, Co. G, 11th Mississippi Infantry, wore gray frock coats with eight chest bars terminating with buttons at either end. Their hats were pinned up on one side only, and were adorned with infantry bugle horn insignia and, in some cases, a single black ostrich feather. The Natchez Fencibles, Co. G, 12th Mississippi Infantry, wore the same type of coat. The Jeff Davis Rifles, Co. D, 9th Mississippi Infantry, also wore thin bars of trim with buttons at either end of their gray tail coats. Regarding the last two units, discretion should be observed concerning their uniforms, as they were both organized prior to 1860, and formed part of the 2nd Regiment, 1st Brigade, of the Volunteer Militia established in

The Jeff David Rifles, of Holly Springs, enlisted into Confederate service as Co. D, 9th Mississippi Infantry. They paraded at Pensacola, Florida for photographer J. D. Edwards wearing their pre-war full dress uniform consisting of gray tail coats and M1851 dress caps. (Mississippi Department of Archives & History)

May 1860. As such, they may be wearing a company uniform adopted before the State regulations of 1861.

Three identified photographs survive of Mississippi soldiers wearing three-cornered hats. Thomas M. Barr of the Quitman Guards, Co. E, 16th Mississippi Infantry, and Thomas P. Gooch of the Carroll Guards, Co. C, 20th Mississippi Infantry, both had the popular large white metal star pinning up one side of their hats. William F. Parks of the Confederate Guard, Co. G, 17th Mississippi Infantry, was photographed holding a hat pinned up on at least two sides.

Regarding fatigue shirts, Frederick LeCand of the Natchez Fencibles was photographed wearing an example of that prescribed by the 'Manual'. Light gray in color, it had a small dark blue five-pointed star embroidered on either side of the turned down collar, thus combining elements of the original fatigue regulations prescribed by the Military Board. Other more elaborately-trimmed shirt types were worn minus the collar star. That chosen by the True Confederates, Co. C, 8th Mississippi Infantry, was typical, consisting of a light gray shirt buttoning all the way down the front, with dark blue trim on collar, along shoulders, around pocket and sleeves, and either side of the buttons.

The Bolivar Troop, Co. H, 1st Battalion of Mississippi Cavalry, adopted a gray pull-over woollen shirt with trim, possibly dark blue in color, on front, collar and around the sleeves. Their pants varied in color, with broad seam stripes. Hats were gray felt with low crown and 3-inch-wide brim pinned up on the right side with a star-shaped insignia. They were decorated with black ostrich feather plume, and had a wide silk band to which was fastened the brass letters BT. The Natchez Cavalry, Co. A, 2nd Battalion of Mississippi Cavalry, also wore a gray shirt with 1-inch-wide trim collar, cuffs, down the buttoned front, and along the top of slanting pockets. Two members of the Confederate Guards, an artillery company organized in Pontotoc County in 1861, were photographed wearing gray cotton over-shirts and pants with dark, probably red, facings and seam stripes, and light gray tricorne hats.

Numerous Mississippi companies volunteered for Confederate service in uniforms which owed nothing to the regulations of 1861. The Mississippi Rifles, Co. A, 10th Mississippi Infantry, wore a dress uniform described in 1860 as being 'of dark green cloth, Hungarian hats, ostrich plumes'. The collar, worsted epaulettes and cuff tabs on their single-breasted frock coats were red, as was their trouser stripes. Their 'Hardee'-style dress hat bore a red ostrich plume and was pinned up on the right by a regulation U.S. eagle; on the front was a Mounted Rifles-style bugle, placed horizontally, over large metal letters MR. During February 1861, this company acquired a fatigue uniform consisting of a seven-button gray coat with dark facings on collar, pointed cuffs and shoulder straps, plain gray pants and a gray cap with dark band. The Van Dorn Reserves, of Aberdeen, were mustered into service as Co. I, 11th Mississippi Infantry, in a uniform of 'red jeans'. The Prairie Guards, Co. E of the same regiment, originally wore a dress uniform consisting of gray frock

A member of the Natchez Fencibles, Co. B, 12th Mississippi Infantry (left), wearing a fatigue shirt patterned after that originally prescribed by the Military Board for the Army of Mississippi. Two further versions of fatigue shirts worn by Mississippi volunteers. The Shubuta Rifles, Co. A, 14th Mississippi Infantry (centre); and the Quitman Guards, Co. E, 16th Mississippi Infantry (right). (Based on photographs by Ron Field)

According to the 'Minute Book' of the Smith-Quitman Rifles of Jackson, who volunteered for 60 days' service in the 3rd Regiment State Troops during September 1861, they chose to wear a gray woollen shirt trimmed with ½-inch-wide green braid around the collar, cuffs and across the top of each chest pocket, with two stripes up the front from the waist to the neck. Their pants were of 'Blue cottonade' with ½-inch-wide green worsted braid down the outside seam. Hats were 'Black felt, crown 6 inches high, 3-inch brim – with left side hooked up – and fastened with [a] Large Military button.' This uniform was described as being based on that worn by the Burt Rifles, Co. K, 18th Mississippi Infantry, with 'some slight alterations.' (From descriptions by Ron Field)

First Lieutenant Israel Spencer, Issaquena Artillery, Captain Rice E. Grave's Company, Mississippi Artillery. His cap has an unusually-shaped cross cannon insignia patch, which may have been red, in keeping with branch service color. (Alice F. Sage Collection, USAMHI)

Right: John LeRoy Williams of the Sardis Blues, Co. F, 12th Mississippi Infantry, wears a plain gray fatigue shirt, and is armed with a M1842 Musket and hunting knife. Note the large frame buckle on his waist belt. Massachusetts Commandery Military Order of the Loyal Legion & the U.S. (U.S. Army Military History Institute/Jim Enos)

Unidentified member of the Moody True Blues, Co. D, 8th Mississippi Infantry. Raised in Clarke County, Mississippi, most of this unit was wiped out at the battle of Murfreesboro on 31 December 1862. (David Wynn Vaughan collection)

coat with dark-colored plastron front and epaulettes, gray pants with broad seam stripes, and black Hardee hat with ostrich plume and brim looped up on the left. A member of this company later informed his parents that he had sold his 'red jeans pants for four dollars', possibly indicating that more than one company of this regiment was thus clad for war service.

Predominantly an agricultural state with very few facilities to process cloth, Mississippi was virtually destitute of all supplies by February 1861. The government slowly realized that in order to provide clothing for their troops they would have to take stringent action. By the summer of 1861, it virtually monopolized the state's textile industry, and had directed that all penitentiary labour be, as far as possible, employed in producing supplies for the soldiers of Mississippi. The prison workshops had been established in the Mississippi State Penitentiary at Jackson in 1849. By 1860, this facility consisted of 2304 spindles, 24 cotton-carding machines, 76 looms for weaving osnaburgs, 4 mills for producing cotton twills, and a full complement of machinery for making woollen linseys and cotton batting. When Mississippi belatedly began to arm after secession, the entire penitentiary facilities were diverted to the manufacture of military goods. The extent of its services to the state's war effort can be gauged from the fact that its output during the last 12 months of its existence (July 1862 to July 1863) was reckoned at $172,608.

The 'Mississippi Manufacturing Company', established in 1848 by James Wesson near Drane's Mill, in Choctaw County, was the state's second largest textile factory, with 1000 cotton spindles, 500 woollen spindles, 20 looms, and a large wool-carding machine. The factory's labour force consisted of 85 well-trained white mill workers, who were comfortably housed in homes provided for them in the company-owned village of Bankston. The isolation of the Bankston factory, chosen originally to keep the labour force away from the temptations of the city 'grog shops', later paid unexpected dividends. Hostile Federal cavalry did not chance upon it until almost a year after the state's more accessible factories had been burned to the ground during the Vicksburg campaign of 1863. According to a letter written to Governor John J. Pettus by Wesson, this Company had by the beginning of August 1861 provided samples and prices of cloth for uniforms, and was investigating the cost of dyeing on a large scale. Other textile mills turned over to wartime production included the 'Green factory' on the Pearl River in Jackson County, and 'Wilkinson Manufacturing Company' at Woodville in Wilkinson County.

It is difficult to ascertain exactly what type of uniforms these establishments produced for the men who volunteered for service in mid-1861. The Satartia Rifles who were mustered-in as Co. I, 12th Mississippi Infantry, during April wore very neat nine-button gray frock coats with dark trim around collar, shoulder straps and cuffs. Pants and hats were plain gray. The Long Creek Rifles, Co. A, 15th Mississippi Infantry, adopted plain gray frock coats, gray pants trimmed with side black seam stripes, and black felt hats.

Mississippi regiments in Virginia were very poorly supplied. According to the diary of Robert A. Moore, a member of the Confederate Guards, camped near Leesburg, Virginia, during August 1861, the 17th Mississippi Infantry purchased 'for the Reg.[iment] goods for a uniform' which was taken 'back to the homes of the different companies' to be made up. Received by the end of October, these uniforms consisted of gray 10-button shell jackets with a single small button on either side of a black-trimmed collar. Cuffs were decorated with black cord forming a distinctive single loop. The front and bottom jacket edges were also trimmed with black cord. Some jackets had a single pocket on the right breast. Pants were also gray with 2-inch-wide seam stripes.

As 1861 drew to a close, the lack of clothing began to affect the Mississippi troops closer to home. The 1st and 3rd Mississippi were described as 'the poorest clad, shod and armed body I ever saw,' by Brigadier-General Floyd Tilghman, commanding Camp Alcorn in Kentucky on 2 November of that year. Though widespread, this shortage was not general. One survivor of the 2nd Mississippi Infantry, often reported as one of the worst dressed regiments, recalled 1861 as a time of plenty. Much of this clothing was paid for and supplied by 'volunteer aid societies' of Mississippi.

Florida

Nicknamed the 'smallest tadpole' in the Confederacy, Florida seceded from the Union on 10 January 1861. However, her war preparations had begun months earlier. Independent companies of 'Minute Men' were formed during 1860, and late that year began to offer their services to

William G. Denham was still a West Florida Seminary Cadet when this ambrotype was taken in 1861. He enlisted in the Leon Rifles, Co. A, 1st Florida Infantry, soon after. The unusual multi-pointed star insignia on his belt plate may be specific to his military school. (Florida State Archives)

Private Walter Miles Parker of Co. H, 1st Florida Cavalry, was photographed on enlistment wearing this uniform, which his commanding officer acquired via a Virginia contractor in 1861. His light gray six-button sack coat, with patch sewn along the shoulders, may indicate a North Carolina provenance. This regiment served as infantry before leaving Florida in Spring 1862. (Florida State Archives, used with permission of Richard J. Ferry)

It is difficult to believe that William D. Rogers wore this uniform when he was transferred to the Simpson Mounted Rangers, Co. E, 15th Confederate Cavalry, in early 1864! Note the brass letters SMR on his hat, and the very elaborate system of buttons and trim on his two-tone coat. (John Segreat & Florida State Archives)

an act of legislature on 14 February 1861. This called for an immediate enrolment of all able bodied men and their organization into companies and regiments. Consequently, the Governor was immediately authorized to raise two regiments of infantry and one of cavalry or mounted riflemen for a six-month state service. This was later supplemented by two more cavalry regiments, two battalions of State Guards, and a number of independent companies of artillery, mounted riflemen and infantry.

In response to the call of the Confederate War Department on 9 March 1861 for 500 men to garrison Pensacola, the state raised the 1st Florida Infantry which was largely composed of existing companies. Subsequent calls on 8 and 16 April led to the formation of the 2nd Florida Infantry, sent to Virginia, and the 3rd and 4th Regiments, which were initially used to defend the Florida coast line. Eventually, Florida provided some 15,000 troops for the Confederacy, which were organized into 12 infantry regiments, 2 cavalry regiments, and 7 independent companies of light artillery.

There were no state dress regulations and no regimental uniforms in Florida until 1861. As with other states, volunteer militia companies wore a variety of individual dress uniforms, which would have been replaced by fatigue uniforms for active service. On 8 February, an act was passed empowering the Governor 'to adopt a State Uniform, which shall be distinctive in character, with such variations for the different grades and arms of service as may be appropriate'. Nothing is known regarding the design of this uniform. It appears that the supply of clothing to the new regiments came from various sources. The companies entering the 1st Florida Infantry (the Magnolia Regiment) appear to have worn militia clothing, or whatever civilian groups at home could supply in the way of service dress. Private William Denham of the Leon Rifles, Co. A of that regiment, wore a nine-button light gray shell jacket, light gray pants with narrow seam stripes, and a light-colored forage cap, when he enlisted at Warrington in June 1861. The 2nd Florida Infantry were uniformed in cloth purchased by a combination of state and county funding, and made into garments by several ladies' societies. The 1st Florida Cavalry hoped for the same support; when that failed its commanding officer, Lieutenant-Colonel William Davis, on his own responsibility, contracted with Baldwin & Williams, of Richmond, Virginia, to supply a coat, two pairs of pants, two shirts and an overcoat for each of his men – 1000 suits in all.

the state, thereby supplementing its small number of volunteer militia units. Raised and equipped almost entirely by private means, these new companies were speedily accepted into state services by Governor Madison S. Perry. A reorganization of the dormant beat militia system, consisting of 21 regiments arranged in two divisions, was also begun by

This unidentified man in a fatigue shirt enlisted in the Trapier Guard, Co. C, 5th Florida Infantry. Note the reversed letters TG on his belt.(U.S. Army Military History Institute/Jim Enos)

Left: This soldier has been tentatively identified as Theophilus S. Luckie, Co. B, 6th Florida Infantry. He wears a further example of the type of uniforms acquired out-of-state by Florida authorities. His shell jacket is remarkably similar to those worn by many Georgia units, and may have come from a Savannah or Columbus supplier. Under this kepi he wears a 'Sicilian'-style stocking cap popular with early war volunteers throughout the South. (U.S. Army Military History Institute/Jim Enos)

Private Mathew A. Beck of the Gulf Coast Rangers, an Independent Company of Volunteers commanded by Captain John Chambers, which later became Co. A, 9th Florida Infantry, wore a substantially-made nine-button plain gray frock coat.

The cloth for these various types of uniform could not be produced in the state, so agents followed the lead of 1st Florida Cavalry and scoured the South for supplies. Main centres visited were New Orleans, Louisiana; Savannah and Columbus, Georgia; Mobile, Alabama; and Charleston, South Carolina. The latter city was visited in June 1861 by agent James Banks, who bid against agents from other states and private concerns for cloth brought through the blockade, or made in the South itself. The Palatka Guard, a volunteer militia company commanded by Captain A. F. Braham, negotiated directly with Charleston tailor C. F. Jackson to have uniforms made up for 60 men. Regarding the styles of uniform, a member of the Marion Light Artillery wrote in May 1861: 'Captain Powell intends visiting Atlanta . . . for the purpose of purchasing uniforms . . . Our uniform consists of cadet gray or if not[,] the cloth is left to the discretion of Captain Powell . . . failing this he intends to purchase flannel shirts and cheap pants.'

It took until November 1861 for the legislature to authorize the state's Quartermaster General to arrange a supply of clothing for all her soldiers. According to photographs taken in early 1862, this clothing consisted of gray shell jackets and pants. A number of jackets had various combinations of exterior pockets on the chest. Trim, where used, varied according to regimental or company choice. Jackets without pockets were also supplied to units organized that year.

Alabama

After secession on 11 January 1861, the 'Republic of Alabama' existed for almost a month before she joined the Confederacy. Military preparations had been underway for fully a year prior to this step as, on 24 February 1860, an act of legislature was passed creating the 'Volunteer Corps of the State of Alabama', more usually called the 'Alabama Volunteer Corps'.

Organized under the authority of a State Military Commission, this Corps was limited in numbers to 8150 officers and men who were carefully divided among the several counties. The old uniformed volunteer militia companies of the state were encouraged to join it, and moves were made to purchase arms. A substantial number of new volunteer companies were raised during the second half of 1860, but it is not clear to what extent

The Independent Blues of Selma, Alabama. Photographed in January 1861 wearing the uniform of the Alabama Volunteer Corps. (Alabama Department of Archives & History)

J. F. Gaines of the Montgomery Mounted Rifles. This unit appears to have preferred the Hardee hat with their Alabama Volunteer Corps uniform. (Alabama Dept. of Archives & History)

Joseph Skinner wears the uniform adopted by the Mobile Rifle Guard, a company of the 1st Regiment, Alabama Militia, in April 1861. This included a gray frock coat with a 12-button front, and broad trim on collar, shoulders, and cuffs. Note the letters MRG on his kepi. (Eleanor S. Brockenbrough Library, The Museum of the Confederacy, Richmond, Virginia)

the Corps absorbed them. On 15 January 1861, four days after secession, a bill called 'An Act for the Organization of the Army of Alabama' formed a stepping stone towards the final issuance of General Order No. 1, on 28 March 1861, which described the regulation uniform devised by the State Military Commission for the Alabama Volunteer Corps. All companies were expected to adopt this garb, but were given until 1 January 1862 to comply, by which time Alabama gray clothing predominated. The

Alabama Volunteer Corps as a distinctive organization was abolished in November 1861, after which time its units were disbanded or mustered into active service.

The uniform adopted by the Alabama Volunteer Corps by the State Military Commission basically consisted of a dark blue frock coat and cadet gray pants. Officers' coats had a skirt extending two-thirds to three-quarters from the top of the hip to the bend of the knee, and were double breasted for those

2nd Volunteer Regiment, Alabama Militia, 1860–1. Officer, Auburn Guards (left): black shako with white feather plume tipped red, brass AG in wreath on front; dark blue coatee with three rows of brass buttons; gold epaulettes; gold or white trim on edge of collar and cuffs. Dark blue pants with gold or white stripe; white shoulder belt; and red sash. Officer, Tuskegee Light Infantry (second from left): dark blue kepi with gold and wreathed TLI insignia; dark blue frock coat, single row of brass buttons; gold epaulettes; gold or light blue trim on collar and cuffs; dark blue pants with gold or light blue seam stripe. Officer, Alabama Zouaves (centre): dark blue frock coat with gold lace trim on collar, cuffs, edge of coat, and chest bars; gold epaulettes; medium blue pants with gold seam stripe; blue kepi with gold braid; and red sash. Private, Montgomery True Blues (second from right): black shako with brass front plate; red feather plume; dark blue coatee with brass buttons and red facings on collar and cuffs; red epaulettes; dark blue pants with red stripe; white cross belts; and black waist belt. Musician, Montgomery True Blues (right): dark blue Mexican War-style forage cap with red band; dark blue jacket with brass buttons and red collar and cuffs; white pants. (From photographs and descriptions by Ron Field. Confederate Historical Society)

above the rank of captain with buttons arranged as per U.S. Army regulations. Solid collar and parallel cuffs were trimmed with dark blue velvet and trousers were plain gray without seam stripes. Company-grade officers wore a nine-button, single-breasted coat with collar and pointed cuffs supposedly trimmed as per branch of service, e.g. light blue for infantry, scarlet for artillery, emerald green for riflemen, and orange for dragoons. Trimmings consisted of a 0.375-inch band of lace around the standing collar, and pointed cuff edges. Some company-grade officers' coats were tailored without trim. Officers' ¼-inch-wide pants seam stripes were white for infantry, and branch colors for the others. Headgear was patterned on the M1853 United States Military Academy dress cap, which consisted of a black felt body reinforced with leather. Smaller in the crown than in the band, it sloped slightly forward, with black leather crown, head band, chin-strap, and visor. Judging from photographs it was given a round pompom above a national 'eagle' of brass; below these were attached the letters AVC in a slight curve. Buttons for cap and uniform bore the letters AVC over the U.S. national eagle. These buttons were made in some quantity by Lambert and Mast of Philadelphia; and Horstmann and Allen of New York. Distinctive AVC waist belt and cartridge box plates based on U.S. Army regulation size were also made. These were supplemented by the plain brass militia type simply engraved with the initials AVC.

The coat worn by enlisted men was similar to that of company grade officers, except that the length of the skirt was 'between the hip and the knee'. Trim was the same as that specified for company-grade officers. Pants' seam stripes were 1¼-inch wide white lace in corresponding branch color.

With minor differences regarding insignia and pattern, this garb was widely adopted by the volunteer militia of Alabama, plus the 1st Artillery Battalion, and the 1st and 2nd Volunteer Infantry Regiments, composed mainly of newly recruited companies. More often than not the dress cap gave way to a cloth forage cap or felt hat within these units. Indeed, the state purchased 10,000 black felt hats with brims 'looped & buttoned on the left side', from R. & A. Cain of North Port, Alabama. Many officers tended to wear the Hardee hat. The unpopularity of the frock coat in certain quarters may be gauged by remarks in a letter written by Captain S. F. Nunnelee, a veteran riflemen of the Mexican War, and now in command of the Eutaw Rifle Company, who wrote to Governor A. B. Moore on 6 September 1860: 'The prescribed

Sergeant William Henry Phillips is believed to have enlisted in the Pickens Stars, a unit designated Co. E, 40th Alabama Infantry. The brass letters CG on his gold-braided cap may indicate that he belonged to another company, such as the Creagh Guards or the Clifton Guards, of Alabama. (U.S. Army Military History Institute/Jim Enos)

uniform is the same for the whole corps – the Rifle movement is different from that of any other branch of the service. Its movements are very rapid, and carrying the gun in the right hand, the frock coat will interfere very materially with the proper handling of the piece.' Despite such reservations, many individual companies were happy to wear it. These included the Perote Guards, Pioneer Guards, Alabama Rifles, Camden Rifles, Tuskegee Light Infantry, Montgomery Mounted Rifles,

and the Independent Blues. At regimental level, the 1st Regiment of Volunteer Infantry was presented with a uniform of blue 'frock shirts' buttoned down the front, blue jean pants, and wide-brimmed black hats by 'the ladies of Alabama' in July 1861. Meanwhile, T. C. DeLeon, a clerk in the Confederate topographical office in Richmond, had noted in late June, 'the Alabamians from the coast [the 8th and 9th Volunteer Infantry] nearly all in blue of a cleaner hue and neater cut' than troops from other states.

The influence of the Alabama Volunteer Corps uniform lasted well into the conflict. The 4th Volunteer Infantry were described as wearing 'dark blue jean Frock coats at Island No. 10' in 1862. During July 1863, Sergeant Crawford Jackson of the 6th Volunteer Infantry reported he was wearing 'a black broad cloth coat, Alabama staff buttons, cut and trimmed in regulation style, a pair of gray trousers and slouch hat . . .'

Another uniform issuance, known as the 'Alabama State Uniform', was also prescribed by Governor Moore during February 1861 for those units not called into Confederate service. This was described as follows: 'The coat, pants and cap of regimental officers and enlisted men called into service of the State of Alabama . . . will be cadet gray. The trimmings, badges of rank and pattern of uniform will be the same as that of the United States Army, conforming to same colors to distinguished corps.' A report from Mobile shortly thereafter, describing 'Alabama volunteers in homespun coarse gray suits, with blue and yellow facings and stripes,' may be a reference to this uniform.

Not all Alabamian companies adopted these prescribed uniforms. One officer informed the Governor that his company had bought uniforms which he feared might 'differ

Although the unit Private John T. Davis served in is not known, he probably wears the uniform adopted by Alabama in August 1861. (U.S. Army Military History Institute/Jim Enos)

Right: Brothers in the Billy Gilmer Grays, Co. F, 14th Alabama Infantry, raised at Hickory Flat on 31 July 1861 by Captain M. P. Ferrell. This unit added extensive trim and unusual external pockets to their version of the uniform adopted by the state in August 1861. Corporal Jefferson Strickland (left) has taken his small brass-framed pistol from its leather holster and placed it in his pocket. Sergeant Madison Strickland (right) has a Colt Navy Revolver pushed in his waist belt, a smaller calibre revolver in his pocket, and a sheathed bowie knife on his right hip. Both men hold Enfield rifled muskets. Margaret P. Milford via U.S. Army Military History Institute/Jim Enos)

from the State Uniform'. He went on to explain that it was 'like the Dutchman's Wife: not much for pretty, but Hell for strong.' A report from Montgomery on 28 April 1861 mentioned encountering 'uniforms of every variety and every stripe'. This was particularly the case with the older volunteer militia who continued to wear elements of their dress uniforms supplemented by items of service wear. That of the Mobile Cadets consisted of a gray forage cap with black band, nine-button gray jacket with collar, cuffs and shoulder straps faced black with white piping, and gray pants with light-colored (possibly gold) seam stripes. Setting aside their 'Continental uniform', the State Artillery wore a 'handsome service uniform of indigo blue trimmed with red, and brown gaiters' in May 1861. The Perote Guards adopted a fatigue dress including a coat of 'very dark cassimere, heavy weight, trimmed with light gray, single row of buttons and frock skirts.' The Emerald Guards of Mobile initially wore green frock coats, but later adopted an eight-button gray satinette or broadcloth shell jacket with dark (possibly green) facings on collar and cuffs, and very light-colored pants.

Some of the newly-formed companies also adopted very individual, locally-made garb. A reporter in Montgomery noted that many Alabama volunteers wore: '. . . old flannel bags, closed and drawn to a point at one end, with tassel dependent. This style of fatigue head-dress was introduced by one of the Mobile Companies, and in an incredibly short space of time the fever for possessing them spread from rank to rank, and Company to Company, until nearly everyone now is supplied.'

This head-dress was the 'Sicilian' cap, made famous by the Sicilian revolutionaries led by Giuseppe Garibaldi in 1860. The Raccoon Roughs, Co. I, 6th Alabama Infantry, proudly sported rough fur caps made of raccoon skins when they marched off in May 1861. The Dale County Beauregards, Co. E, 15th Alabama Infantry, wore a uniform of white osnaburg with 'blue stripes on the trousers and jackets'. The Henry Pioneers, Co. G of the same regiment, went to war in red flannel shirts. Hardaway's Artillery acquired 'coarse gray tunics with yellow facings, & French caps'.

Although the state supplied some of the clothing for these uniforms, by mid-April 1861 it found itself unable to cope with the growing number of companies rapidly forming. It therefore handed over responsibility to the Confederate government which was in no position to supply clothing, but promised

This unidentified member of the Clark County Rangers, Co. D, 2nd Alabama Infantry ('The Magnolia Regiment') has 'Fight with us and end it' inscribed on his sabre, which may have been a photographer's prop. (David Wynn Vaughan collection)

financial support via the commutation system. Three months later, it became apparent that the Alabama troops in Confederate service were being poorly outfitted, and that little provision was being made for the coming winter. Once again the state assumed responsibility for clothing and equipping its men in the field, as well as the new companies being formed, by collecting commutation money from the Confederacy or from the men themselves. Hence Governor Moore issued a circular on 26 August 1861 emphasizing that the items most needed were: 'Uniform jackets, great coats and pantaloons of good strong cloth, of gray color . . . shirts of flannel, or checked or striped cotton; draws of woolen, or cotton flannel or stout osnaburgs; woolen socks; gloves, shoes and blankets.'

On 31 August, the Quartermaster General, Brigadier General Duff C. Green, announced in the *Montgomery Weekly Advertiser* that the proposed uniform was to consist of a single-breasted seven-button jacket with low standing collar and pocket inside the left breast. Straps were attached to the shoulders, and 5-inch-long belt loops sewn on the bottom of the jacket on the side seams. Pantaloons were to be cut full. The great coat also had a standing collar, and was fastened by seven large brass military buttons. The cape reached to the elbow with five small buttons on the right, and was removable and fastened to the collar with six hooks and eyes.

Because these uniforms were to be made by numerous soldiers' aid societies, as well as large textile companies, an attempt was made to ensure that a reasonable level of uniformity was achieved by sending out clothing patterns together with available samples. To obtain cloth, buttons and other materials, the state entered into contracts with firms including the Eagle Manufacturing Company of Columbus, Georgia; the Prattville Manufacturing Company of Prattville, Alabama; Philips, Fariss and Company of Montgomery, Alabama; and Barnett Micon and Company of Tallassee, Alabama. The first three firms supplied 56,300 yards of hickory shirting, linsey, kersey and drilling, while the last mentioned provided 1010 gray and white blankets, and 14,000 military buttons.

The collective response to Governor Moore's appeal was considerable. By the end of 1861 the following had been furnished: 7416 complete uniforms, 2974 great coats, 2412 blankets and 3000 pairs of shoes. During the first quarter of 1862, 90 soldiers' aid societies and suppliers had contributed over 1532 uniforms, 900 great coats, 1644 pairs of pants, 3810 flannel, cotton and hickory shirts, and 1082 pairs of shoes. Each piece of completed uniform was marked according to its size by a numbered card firmly sewn to the garment. Each item was boxed and shipped to either Huntsville or Montgomery at the expense of the state. They were then directed to Governor Moore for distribution. Typical of issuance via this source was that of the Calhoun Guards, Co. A, 2nd Alabama Infantry, who, whilst camped at fort Morgan, Alabama, received from 'the state of Alabama before being mustered into the service of the Confederate States of America . . .: 72 common caps, 72 uniform coats, 72 overalls, 144 flannel shirts, 144 pairs of drawers, 144 pairs of socks, 72 blankets, [and] 144 undershirts.'

A member of Captain A. M. Moore's Company, Co. F (Sumter Shorter Guards), 4th Regiment Militia, was photographed during the Spring of 1862 wearing a uniform of this pattern, which consisted of a seven-button gray wool jacket with dark standing collar, shoulder straps and pointed cuffs. His pants were plain gray without seam stripes.

Other styles of uniform were also issued at this time. Whilst encamped near Centreville, Virginia, during November 1861, the 12th Alabama Infantry received 'gray dress uniforms' which consisted of 'scissor tailed coats' and caps that 'fell over in front with a place for letters.' Similarly, members of the Cherokee Rangers, Co. I, 19th Alabama Infantry, were photographed wearing plain gray eight-button wool and cotton coats with swallow tails; and gray pants. By 22 January 1862, Alabama had spent $375,000 supplying their troops in Virginia with uniforms. This clothing was distributed via a state depot situated at Richmond.

Georgia

The enrolled militia system of Georgia possessed little tangible reality during the decade before the civil war. Nonetheless, on paper it consisted of 13 divisions, each with two brigades. Each brigade embraced from 2 to 12 counties, dependent on the population. The Volunteer Militia, on the other hand, was thriving if ill-controlled, particularly after John Brown's raid in 1859. By February 1861 there was 173 companies on the rolls, with some 35 more in the process of organization. In that year, the adjutant general sent out Special Order No. 24 to all volunteer militia companies instructing them to report on their arms, equipment and uniform. The collective response shows units in swallow-tail coatees, frock coats and jackets, with shakoes, forage caps, slouch hats and kepis, in all styles and colors. Many had an undress, as well as

The Sumter Light Guards became Company K, 4th Georgia Infantry. In this image, probably taken by Tucker and Perkins, of Broad Street, Augusta, during March 1861, they parade in their dark blue jackets, pants, and caps, trimmed with buff. Their First National flag is held high by the color sergeant, with color guard either side. (Georgia Department of Archives and History)

These members of the Clinch Rifles, Co. A, 5th Georgia, were photographed in camp at Macon on 10 May 1861, the day before they were mustered in. Generally relaxing in civilian clothing, several wear their dark green uniform caps and trousers. Note the company initials painted on tent and camp equipage, and their stacked Model 1841 Rifles and sword bayonets. (U.S. Army Military History Institute/Jim Enos)

The uniform worn by Private James Greet of the West Point Guards, Co. D, 4th Georgia Infantry, was described thus by the Augusta Daily Constitutional and Sentinel on May 1861 – 'Their suit is gray, of Roswell manufacture, black stripe on pants, gray cloth caps'. (Alabama State Archives)

M. H. Cutter enlisted in the Floyd Rifles, Co. C, 2nd Battalion, Georgia Infantry on 20 April 1861. He wears a double-breasted black frock coat. (David Wynn Vaughan collection)

full dress, uniform. Although Georgia seceded from the Union on 19 January 1861, preparations for secession, and for raising a state military force, began in early November 1860.

Governor Joseph E. Brown urged the legislature to raise a million dollars, and accept 10,000 troops, for state defense. The office of adjutant general was revived, and the volunteer companies collectively offered their services to the state. Consequently, Fort Pulaski, near Savannah, was occupied by

the 1st Regiment Georgia Volunteers, a volunteer militia unit commanded by Colonel Alexander R. Lawton, on 3 January 1861. The Augusta Independent Volunteer Battalion seized the Augusta Arsenal 20 days later. The companies involved in these actions wore a variety of distinctive fatigue uniforms. The Republican Blues, Co. C, 1st Regiment, wore dark blue shell jackets trimmed with white cord on collar, shoulder straps and pointed cuffs; sky-blue pants with broad white seam stripes; and dark blue forage caps. The Irish Volunteers, Co. E, wore 'service hats, jackets, dark pantaloons and waist belts.' Within the Augusta Battalion, the Clinch Rifles donned their 'dark green cloth' shell jackets, possibly with yellow lace trim around collar and on cuffs; black pants, and green Model 1856 caps with stiffening removed. The Richmond Hussars wore an army blue shirt trimmed with yellow, a black Hardee hat with black feather plumes, and sky-blue pants with broad seam stripes.

It was not until 15 February 1861 that Adjutant General Henry C. Wayne prescribed state uniform regulations via General Orders No. 4 which referred solely to the two infantry regiments and two battalions of artillery and cavalry which made up the Georgia Army, organized that month. Accordingly, officers were to wear frock coat and trousers of dark blue cloth, the latter 'to be made loose, and to spread well over the foot'. For full dress, general and staff officers wore the U.S. Army dress (Hardee) hat, looped up on the right side with a large gilt Georgia state seal button, with gold cord and three black ostrich feathers. A *chapeau bras*, or cocked hat, could also be worn if preferred. Captains and other subordinate officers wore the same, with two black feathers, and the regimental number embroidered in 1-inch-high numerals on a black velvet ground. Officers were also permitted to wear a blue chasseur cap for fatigue. Commissioned rank was indicated by either epaulettes or shoulder straps.

Non-commissioned officers and enlisted mens' frock coats and pants were of 'Georgia Cadet gray', with black 'cord or welt' trim on collar and pointed cuffs for infantry, and orange for artillery. The cavalry battalion probably wore a gray jacket. Headgear consisted of the Hardee hat looped up on the left, without feather, and with a worsted gold cord and gilt company letter in front. A blue flannel sack coat was prescribed for fatigue. Non-commissioned officers' chevrons corresponded to those of the U.S. Army.

Although this uniform was meant only to apply to the small Georgia Army, the same clothing was furnished to the 1st Regiment Georgia Regulars, a three-year infantry unit, on 17 July 1861. Furthermore, according to contemporary newspaper

Unidentified soldier, probably a Georgian, wearing a very elaborate 'Sicilian' stocking cap, tinted red, along with his waist sash, in the original image. (David Wynn Vaughan collection)

Orderly Sergeant Marmaduke H. Marshall of the Webster Confederate Guards, Co. K, 17th Georgia Infantry, wears a version of the distinctive Georgia-pattern jacket with black three-pointed sleeve patches as issued by the state during the Fall of 1861. Note the unusual lozenge and single chevron on one sleeve only. His sword belt plate curiously bears the Palmetto Tree device associated with South Carolina. He holds an elaborate militia officer's sword, which suggests that this image was taken shortly after his promotion to 2nd Lieutenant in August 1862. (Georgia Department of Archives and History)

Captain Dilmus L. Jarrett commanded the Jackson County Volunteers, Co. C, 18th Georgia Infantry, in June 1861. He holds a militia officer's sword. Rank is indicated by Federal-style shoulder straps. Note the single button sewn on the point of his cuff facings. (U.S. Army Military History Institute/Jim Enos)

reports during 1861, many infantry companies either adopted or changed to gray uniforms trimmed with black, whilst most officers wore blue. A typical account is held within the memoirs of Captain James C. Nesbet who commanded the Silver Grays, Co. H, 21st Georgia Infantry: 'The uniforms of gray, made to order, had to be shipped by E. Winship, Macon, Georgia, for which I paid . . . The men, uniformed in gray, presented a good appearance. The lieutenants were uniformed in home-made blue jeans. My uniform was of regular U.S. Army blue, tailor-made, a present (with my sword and belt) from my sister . . .'

To assist in uniforming its state forces, the Georgia legislature appropriated $648,780, which was used to pay local manufacturers, plus Northern military suppliers in New York and

Three soldiers in examples of frock coats supplied between 1862 63. Private James Anderson Scruggs, Gibson Volunteers, Co. A, (left); and Private Thomas C. Mobley, Burke Volunteers, Co. D, 48th Georgia Infantry (centre), wear coats of possible South Carolina provenance, as their regiment was stationed at Camp Donaldson, near Grahamville, from 4 March until 1 May 1862. Private William Henry Witcher (right) enlisted in the 3rd Battalion, Georgia Sharpshooters, organized on 8 June 1863. His coat may well have been one of the 7272 coats the Georgia Quartermaster Department had 'on hand' in March 1863. (U.S. Army Military History Institute/Jim Enos; Woodruff Library, Emory University; U.S. Army Military History Institute/Jim Enos)

Philadelphia from Georgia agents had actively purchased goods up to April 1861. On the 10th of that month, Governor Brown requisitioned his state for 3000 military companies, and required them all to have a plain service uniform and 'change of underclothing'. After numerous enquiries regarding the type of service uniform needed, he announced on 28 May that the volunteers should have a coat or jacket; two pairs of trousers; one forage or fatigue cap; two flannel shirts, preferably gray or blue (not red as they presented 'an excellent mark for the enemy'); and one light, black necktie. In response, a wide variety of uniforms was adopted. These reported being worn by companies passing through Augusta by the *Daily Chronicle and Sentinel* during this period are quite typical, e.g. Burke Guards (Co. A, 3rd Georgia) – 'Their uniform is dark gray, trimmed with green; officers with coats, privates with jackets, slouched hats'; Brown Rifles (Co. B, 3rd Georgia) – 'gray, with red trimmings'; Dawson Grays (Co. C, 3rd Georgia) – 'Georgia gray, trimmed with black'; Home Guard (Co. D, 3rd Georgia) – 'Georgia gray': Home Guard (Co. D, 3rd Georgia) – 'Georgia gray': Governor's Guards (Co. E, 3rd Georgia) – 'a red jacket, blue-black pants, with white stripe, and German fatigue cap': Wilkinson Rifles (Co. F, 3rd Georgia) – 'Georgia kersey, buff-colored': Southern Rifles (Co. A, 4th Georgia) – 'Georgia gray, trimmed with black velvet': LeGrange Light Guard (Co. B, 4th Georgia) – '"Rosswell gray" jackets and pants trimmed with black. Georgia buttons': Twiggs Volunteers (Co. C, 4th Georgia) – 'a durable cassimere, manufactured at the Eagle Factory, Columbus; the pants with dark stripe. A portion of the company wear red shirts with both cloth and glazed caps': Baldwin Blues (Co. H, 4th Georgia) – 'a dark blue; very neat and serviceable'.

The 'flannel shirts' worn also varied greatly, prompting Governor Brown's instructions. A letter from 'Camp Oglethorpe', near Macon, dated 5 April 1861, describes troops wearing: 'red shirts, blue shirts, gray shirts, and shirts without order and indescribable to an unpractised eye . . .' Those worn by the Clinch Rifles encamped at the same place the following month included polka-dots and patterned bib fronts.

The Zouave fashion was represented in Georgia by a boys' company commanded by Captain Speillers called the Young Zouaves, formed in Augusta in 1860, who wore 'bright blue jackets and fiery red trousers'. About 30 members of the Macon Volunteers, led by Captain R. A. Smith, wore a version of the Zouave uniform. The *Macon Telegraph* reported: 'a group of gentlemen surrounding a figure, who, from his fantastic dress . . . was either a Japanese, a Chinese, a Sioux Indian, or one of the latest importation from Africa. We drew near, and discovered the fantastic figure to be that of our fellow-citizen, Mr. D. B. W., Orderly of the Volunteers, and was dressed in the uniform of the Macon Volunteer Zouaves. This uniform is made of bright cloth, and in a strange fashion, and presents a picturesque and graceful appearance.'

The 'Sicilian'-style stocking cap, complete with tassels and havelock, was also popular amongst Georgia troops early in the war. The Thompson Guards, Co. F, 10th Georgia Infantry, wore 'cap covers . . . parti-colored, or plaid, long and pointed, and so arranged that they may be thrown back on the neck or over the visor'. Other companies photographed wearing this item include the Gardner Volunteers, Co. H, and the Henry Volunteers, Co. K, of the 22nd Georgia Infantry. It was fashionable to wear these caps either over, or under, slouch hats and forage caps.

Numerous small firms throughout the state were involved in clothing the growing number of Georgia units in 1861. Henry Lathrop and Co. in Savannah employed 75 women to make uniforms of different kinds. The Belville Factory of Augusta, owned by George Schley, produced 'a handsome and durable assortment of solid colored and striped twilled cotton goods for soldiers' wear'. By June 1861, they had furnished several companies with serviceable uniforms – among them the Independent Blues, who became Co. D, 10th Georgia Infantry. Other important suppliers included the Eagle Factory at Columbus, the Milledgeville Manufacturing Co., and the Ivy Woollen Mill at Roswell. The latter, established by Connecticut Yankee Roswell King in 1839, produced cloth of a dark bluish-gray cast called 'Roswell gray'. These efforts were supplemented by the numerous aid societies established in every county in the state. Typical of these was the Ladies Aid Society of Clarke County which bought cloth with money raised by taxes, issuing bonds, or soliciting subscriptions. Local tailors measured and cut out the uniforms, which were sewn together by the ladies of the Society and friends. Some counties, like Clarke, continued to supply their menfolk throughout the entire conflict.

During the autumn of 1861, Governor Brown began to realize that Georgia troops in Virginia would not be adequately

(Continued on page 201)

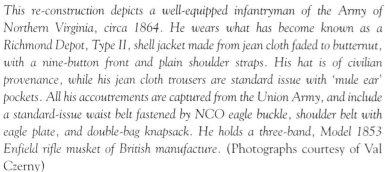

This re-construction depicts a well-equipped infantryman of the Army of Northern Virginia, circa 1864. He wears what has become known as a Richmond Depot, Type II, shell jacket made from jean cloth faded to butternut, with a nine-button front and plain shoulder straps. His hat is of civilian provenance, while his jean cloth trousers are standard issue with 'mule ear' pockets. All his accoutrements are captured from the Union Army, and include a standard-issue waist belt fastened by NCO eagle buckle, shoulder belt with eagle plate, and double-bag knapsack. He holds a three-band, Model 1853 Enfield rifle musket of British manufacture. (Photographs courtesy of Val Czerny)

This beautiful daguerreotype shows Private Bartos Jeffcoat, from Lexington, South Carolina, who enlisted in the Congaree Cavaliers, a unit that became Company B, cavalry battalion of the Holcombe Legion. After reorganization into Company D, 7th South Carolina Cavalry, he died from disease in the Federal prison camp at Elmira. He wears an example of the Type III jacket issued by the Richmond Clothing Depot. (S.C. Confederate Relic Room & Museum, courtesy of W. C. Smith)

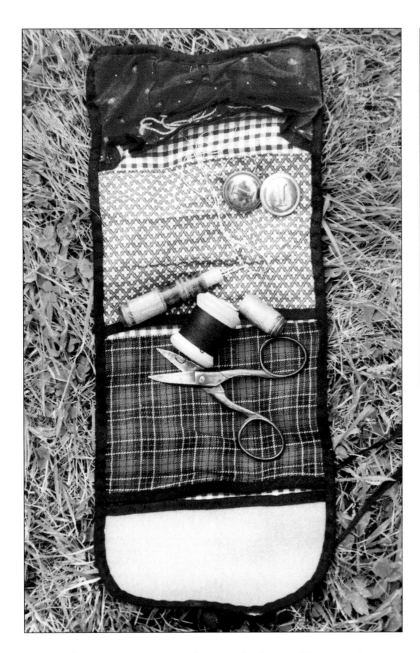

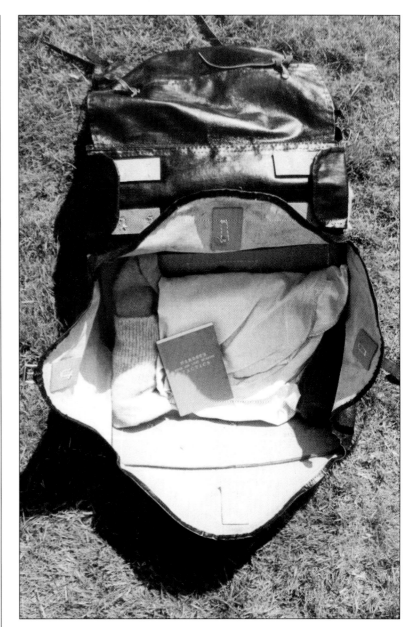

Every well organized Civil War soldier carried a 'housewife' or repair kit, which was usually made from scraps of cloth . This example contains a needle case, cotton or thread reel, scissors, plus two spare 'block I' Confederate buttons. (Photograph courtesy of Richard O'Sullivan)

Above right: This reconstruction shows a U.S. Army-type double-bag knapsack, of the kind often commandeered by Confederate soldiers in the field. It consisted of two bags of black painted or enamelled cotton cloth, attached together by a flexible strip. The front section partially enclosed a leather fitting to contain small objects. The rear section, seen open at the bottom, carried clothing and larger possessions, and had four triangular flaps that buckled together when closed. Many Confederate troops discarded knapsacks entirely, preferring to carry a blanket roll over their shoulder. (Photograph courtesy of Richard O'Sullivan)

Right (top): This reconstruction shows details of a typical Confederate camp scene. The captured Union black-tarred haversack holds much of the soldier's personal belongings. These are set out to the left, and include a tin plate, knife, spoon, and three-pronged carbonated steel knife. The skillet to the rear was made out of half a smooth-sided Union canteen. (Photograph courtesy of Richard O'Sullivan)

Right (bottom): Many Confederate soldiers carried wooden drum canteens, which were not popular as their sharp edges dug into the waist or ribs, especially if fallen upon. They preferred the cloth-covered, smooth-sided Union canteen seen in the rear, which was often captured or picked up off the battlefield. (Photograph courtesy of Richard O'Sullivan)

Musicians were an essential part of the Confederate Army, being able to convey orders to the men of their unit above the din of battle. The forage cap and frock coat, complete with musician's trim, belonged to a North Carolinian. Bugles were often used by rifle regiments and companies, as well as cavalry units, while heavy infantry employed drummer boys. The snare drum at centre was carried by a member of the 13th Virginia Infantry. Regimental bands often entertained the troops in camp, and sometimes lifted the spirits of the men in battle. A clarinet is seen at bottom left, while several fifes are at bottom right. (Courtesy of The Museum of the Confederacy)

Details of a jacket worn by Private Alfred M. Goodwin of Sturdivant's Virginia Battery. Made of dark cadet gray kersey by Peter Tait of Limerick, Ireland, and run through the blockade, the red collar and cuffs are post-war additions. (top left) Back of same. (bottom left) The photograph shows a detail of Virginia state seal buttons. (Courtesy of Alan Thrower)

Right: Confederate headgear and epaulettes. (top left) Model 1858 Hardee hat of Colonel Francis S. Bartow, of the 7th and 8th Georgia Regiments; (top right) cotton havelock worn by W. H. Kirkpatrick of Georgia; (middle left) forage cap of Brigadier General George Wythe Randolph; (middle right) captain's epaulettes of Major General H. D. Clayton; (bottom left) full dress beaver skin chapeau worn by Captain A. J. Grayson, Co. B (F), 45th Virginia Infantry. (Artifacts courtesy of The Museum of the Confederacy)

Overleaf: The Stonewall Brigade at First Manassas, 1861. The 1st Brigade of the Army of the Shenandoah, commanded by Brigadier-General Thomas J. Jackson, earned their legendary nickname at First Manassas on 21 July 1861. Arriving on the battlefield in time to stem the Federal tide sweeping back the Confederate left flank, they gained immortality when General Barnard E. Bee declared: 'Look at Jackson's Brigade! It stands there like a stone wall'.

Liberty Hall Volunteers, Co. 1, 4th Virginia Infantry (left) were largely composed of students at Washington College in Lexington. They wore collarless light blue-gray hunting shirts with dark blue trim, on top of white cotton shirts with collars showing; light gray trousers with 1-inch-wide dark

blue seam stripes; and plain blue forage caps with black leather chin strap and visor. Waist belts appear to have been non regulation and probably home-made, with various buckle styles. They were armed with the U.S. Model 1822 Musket, .69 cal. originally a flintlock but altered to percussion by the thousands between 1843 and 1861. This ungainly weapon weighed more than 10 pounds and measured 57 inches long. Members of this company also provided themselves with short bowie knives.

Marion Rifles, Co. A, 5th Virginia Infantry (centre). Raised in Frederick County, Virginia, this company adopted a nine-button gray frock coat with solid black collar, and three horizontal bands of black braid around the slashed cuffs, which were fastened by three small buttons. Trousers were also gray with black seam stripes. Headgear consisted of plain black felt hats with narrow brim. The figure in the plate wears his pinned up on both sides. His white webbing waist belt supports a black leather cap pouch made at the Baton Rouge Arsenal. He is also armed with a M1822 altered musket.

West Augusta Guard, Co. 1, 5th Virginia Infantry (right). Organized at Staunton in the Shenandoah Valley in 1858, the West Augusta Guard, nick-named the 'Wags' wore a version of the state regulation uniform adopted during the same year. This consisted of a dark blue frock coat cut after U.S. regulation pattern and fastened with nine gilt buttons bearing the Virginia State Seal. Collar and cuffs were edged with sky-blue piping. Brass shoulder scales were worn for full dress, but these would obviously have been removed for campaign duty, revealing the cloth loop and brass staple by which means they could be attached. Trousers were also dark blue with sky-blue seam stripes. 'Hardee' hats followed M1858 U.S. regulation – with yellow metal bugle insignia in front. The brim was looped up on the left by a brass 'eagle' device, with a sky-blue worsted hat cord and tassels, and single black ostrich feather attached to the right side of the crown. Their ostrich feather was probably not worn at first Manassas, as members of the Potomac Guards, Co. A, 33rd Virginia Infantry, of the 'Stonewall' Brigade, reported removing theirs on the eve of battle because they believed that the 'Yankees 'wore the same. (Painting by Richard Hook)

Privates Daniel, John and Pleasant Chitwood enlisted in the Bartow County Yankee Killers, Co. A, 23rd Georgia Infantry. They all wear 'Checked Cottonade' shirts popular as fatigue wear with many Southern companies. They hold large Bowie knives of identical manufacture, and Colt Model 1849 Pocket Revolvers. (Georgia Department of Archives and History)

clothed for the oncoming winter. Therefore, on 4 September he placed advertisements in state newspapers expressing a need to purchase enough woollen cloth for 30,000 suits of clothing, plus 30,000 pairs of shoes. The success of this appeal may be gauged by a letter from Brown to the new Confederate Secretary of War, Judah P. Benjamin, dated 19 October, enquiring whether clothing for troops in government service had to be uniform, or whether it could be 'any substantial woolen clothing'.

A number of photographs of Georgia infantrymen taken during this period indicate that gray shell jackets of remarkably similar styles were being issued. All were distinguished by black three-pointed sleeve patches with small buttons, set well in from the cuff edge. One version, worn by members of the West Point Guards, Co. D, 4th Georgia Infantry, and the Franklin Volunteers, Co. G, 7th Georgia Infantry, is fastened by six buttons, with solid black collar and shoulder straps, and pockets on each breast, about level with the third button from the top.

A private in the Roswell Guards, Co. H, 7th Georgia, donned a slightly different version fastened by eight buttons, with a black tab or loop with small button attached to a gray collar. Yet another eight-button version with collar edged with black tape was worn by a member of the Ben Hill Volunteers, Co. F, 21st Georgia Infantry. This similarity in jacket design possibly indicates that a standard pattern was being made available to Soldier Aid Societies until at least March 1861. The trousers accompanying these jackets generally seem to be plain, whilst headgear mainly seems to have consisted of black, drab or gray slouch hats.

As the result of a call for 12 additional regiments in February 1862, the Confederate government agreed to furnish all clothing and equipment. By the fall of that year the supply system had broken down, and Governor Brown reported to the legislature on 6 November that 'Georgia troops in Confederate service are almost destitute of clothes and shoes, and must suffer terribly this winter . . .' This led to the passage of 'An Act to appropriate money to procure and furnish clothing, shoes, caps or hats, and blankets for the soldiers from Georgia . . . ,' and the establishment of a state clothing bureau at Augusta under the supervision of Captain George W. Evans, and a shoe manufactory run by Captain E. M. Field at Marietta. Based on the appropriation of $1,500,000, Quartermaster General Ira R. Foster was able to report on 25 March 1863 that the following had been supplied to Georgia troops in 19 regiments and 2 battalions in Confederate service in Virginia, Tennessee, and South Carolina: 4556 coats, 5288 pants, 4646 hats, 5449 shirts and 5744 shoes. These articles were mostly shipped to their destination in the charge of bonded State Agents. In a few cases,

the Quartermasters of Regiments had personally collected them from the storehouses. At that time, Foster stated that manufactured clothing still on hand amounted to 7272 coats, 9257 pants, 129 hats, 10,400 shirts and 5878 shoes. Also available was 12,983 yards of osnaburgs, 18,850 yards of shirting, 6410 yards of kerseys, 970 yards of duck, and 35,063 pounds of leather. Despite the latter, he warned that Georgia troops would 'suffer more the coming winter than they did the past . . .' unless further appropriations were made whilst materials were still available. Consequently, on 26 April 1863 Governor Brown directed that a further $2,000,000 should be expended on the purchase and manufacture of clothes and shoes.

By November 1863, Foster was able to report that his bureau had issued hats, clothing and shoes to 44 regiments, 7 battalions, and 2 companies, as follows: '4719 hats, 7291 jackets, 8828 pants, 9185 shirts, 8036 drawers, 12,294 shoes, 7517 socks'. He also had on hand nearly: 'forty thousand suits of clothes, which are ready for distribution among the troops as their necessities may require'.

Despite increasing problems with shortage of supply and difficulties with labour, especially after the fall of Atlanta, Quartermaster General Foster maintained a supply of clothing to Georgia troops during 1864. A considerable amount of the uniform cloth, and other goods, continued to be run through the blockade, whilst raw wool was acquired in Texas in exchange for 'colored osnaburg'. During the closing months of the war, sufficient clothing remained on hand to ensure that Georgia's contingent in the Confederate army, which totalled between 25,000 and 30,000 men, remained well clad whilst access remained to supply routes.

Louisiana

The only regulations governing the uniform of the Louisiana military prior to 1861 were those of 12 January 1857 which applied purely to the Commanding General and staff. This was based on U.S. regulation dress except for state buttons. Therefore, when the 'Pelican state' seceded from the Union on 26 January 1861 the volunteers who rushed to her standard were uniformed in a multitude of different uniforms which illustrated its large foreign-born population. Military dress ranged in style from French, Irish, Italian, Scottish, and German, to those of the many 'native' American companies of light infantry and riflemen. Several battalion militia uniforms did see some early war service. The Washington Artillery of New Orleans, nicknamed 'The Game Cocks' by President Jefferson Davis, joined Confederate forces in Virginia in June 1861 wearing a uniform made by the leading tailors of the city. This consisted of a dark blue frock coat with red collar and pointed cuffs, white shoulder and waist belts, and sky-blue pants with red seam stripes. A red kepi with blue band and yellow lace, adopted late in 1860, replaced their pre-war Model 1851 dress cap. White canvas gaiters were worn for infantry service. During First Manassas they also placed red flannel stripes on their left arms above the elbow to avoid being mistaken for the enemy, despite General (P.) G. T. Beauregard's orders that all 'wing badges' should be removed on the eve of battle. Later in 1861, this battalion sent their frock coats to Richmond for use on furlough, and adopted a blue-gray shell jacket with red piping on cuffs and shoulder straps, with blue jean pants, and red cap with blue band. The 5th Company, Washington Artillery, organized as a reserve on 27 May 1861, wore a similar uniform except that their shell jackets were dark blue trimmed red on collar and shoulder straps.

The Orleans Battalion of Artillery, which first became involved in the seizure of forts Jackson and St Philip below New Orleans, and later converted to infantry, wore a plain blue jacket and pants of gray-blue Kentucky jean tucked into black leather gaiters, and a blue kepi trimmed with red. The first uniform chosen by the Chasseurs a Pied, or Louisiana Foot Rifles, was described by the New Orleans *Daily Crescent* as being 'finer and much neater fitting than that of the famed French soldiers . . . Their very small caps, perched on top of their heads; their tight fitting, dark colored, short tailed coats, with their slender red

William H. Martin (left) of the 7th Louisiana Infantry wears an example of the uniform issued by the state during the Fall of 1861. His father, James Martin (right), wears the full dress uniform of the Continental Guard, Louisiana Militia, which consisted of a blue cut-away coat faced with buff, buff breeches, and black tricorne hat with red and white feathers. (Confederate Memorial Hall)

The Tiger Rifles, Co. B, 1st Special Battalion. The zouave uniform received by this unit consisted of a light-weight mazarine blue jacket with deep red wool trim, full zouave trousers, or serouel, made from blue and white 'Hamilton' mattress ticking, deep red woollen shirts with placket front fastened by small porcelain buttons, red zouave cap with 'tassel down the back', and white gaiters over 'colored stockings'. (From descriptions and artefacts by Ron Field)

fringes and green epaulettes; their enormous mouse colored breeches, falling in loose folds below their knees, their tight yellow leggins and their white gaiters – all these new things in military dress in this country, combined to give this new company a very novel and picturesque appearance'. By early 1861 this battalion had adopted a blue undress uniform with white gaiters.

The Orleans Guard Battalion, which was designated the 13th Louisiana Battalion, wore a dark blue frock coat and pants, and red forage cap for full dress. By February 1861 they had a fatigue uniform composed of 'dark blue kepis . . . jackets or short coats and pants of the same color, all trimmed with red, black belts and cartouche boxes'. During the battle of Corinth on 3–4 October 1862, the 6th Kentucky, at the sight of this 'blue uniform brought out from New Orleans', mistook the Orleans Guard Battalion for the enemy and fired on them, killing two men! Shortly thereafter, they were ordered to 'turn their uniform wrong side outwards, thus giving them the appearance of going to a masquerade ball'.

The Legion Française, formed among the French citizens of New Orleans, adopted a copy of the French infantry dress which consisted of a horizon-blue coat, and red pants and cap. The Confederate Guards Response Battalion paraded in 'gray frock coats, caps and white pants'. The Garibaldi Legion, expanded from a volunteer militia company called the Garibaldi Guards, wore a 'black cocked hat, with a black plume on the cocked side, the stem of the plume . . . being covered with little feathers of red, green and white, (the colors of Italy) and the whole secured with a pelican button. A red jacket, tight fitting to the waist but spreading out at the hips; a black belt around the waist, with cartouche-box behind, and the jacket buttoned up to the chin with Pelican buttons. Gray trousers, of the largest Zouave style, bulging out as low on the knee; and then buff leather leggins, strapped and buckled the rest of the way down to the gaiters'.

Regarding some of the individual companies of Louisiana volunteer militia in 1861, the Orleans Flying Artillery, commanded by Captain Everitt, formerly of the Bengal cavalry, chose: 'a black navy cap with gold band and seven white stars around, glazed top painted white, and gold chain chin strap; a scarlet flannel or cassimere jacket with epaulettes, navy blue pantaloons, with patent leather bottoms and straps of chain; heavy boots with boxed spurs, a black sword belt, long swords, and shoulder cross belts for cartridge box, with a brace of large navy revolvers.'

The British Guard under Captain Shannon wore a suit of 'white flannel with blue and silver facings'. The Belgian Guards' uniform was composed of 'dark green frock coats, trimmed with yellow, and pants and cap of same'. That worn by the Orleans Rifles was in imitation of '. . . the Kentucky or frontier Riflemen, consisting of broad brimmed black hats cocked on one side, loose hunting shirts of green with black fringes; pants yellow to the knee and below that black in imitation of yellow buckskin and leggins; and small cartouche boxes slung at the side'.

The Louisiana Guerrillas wore 'a velvet hunting jacket, *mi tasses*, or leggins, similar to those worn by Indians, cotton pantaloons and an otter skin cap'.

During the weeks prior to secession, Louisiana began to recruit companies for two 'Regular' regiments, one each of infantry and artillery. After an unsuccessful attempt to contract for cloth for uniforms for these units, a solution was found in having it made at the State Penitentiary at Baton Rouge, where a textile factory had existed since at least 1857. According to a report in the *Charleston Daily Courier*, this institution possessed '5632 spindles, 200 looms, and the necessary carding machines, with the capacity to consume about fifteen bales of cotton, and turn out twelve thousand yards of cloth a day'. The full dress regimental uniform received by the 1st Regular Infantry was to be based on 'the rules and regulations of the U.S. Army', and consisted of a dark blue frock coat and pants, and blue cap. It is doubtful whether this was ever received by the whole unit. A company of regulars involved in the occupation of the New

Second Lieutenant James C. Wilson, of the Bienville Blues, Co. C, 5th Louisiana Infantry, wore this dark blue frock and lighter-colored braided cap when he mustered into Confederate service on 4 June 1861. He holds what appears to be a Virginia Manufactory artillery sabre with an iron guard. (Confederate Memorial Hall, New Orleans, Louisiana)

Orleans barracks during January 1861 wore an undress uniform, issued around the 13th of that month, which consisted of 'a dark blue jacket, coming down to the hip, single-breasted, with five pelican buttons, and dark blue pants, with a stripe of yellow cord'. As yet without headgear, they presented a 'motley array of silk hats, slouched tiles and glazed caps' when drawn up for inspection. According to the *Daily Delta*, they were soon to receive 'a graceful looking Zouave cap, of navy blue cloth'. On 14 January, Company B of this regiment, originally commanded by Captain John A. Jacques, 'adopted a neat gray undress cap with pelican buttons obtained at D'Arcy's Store, the stock of which was disposed of in an hour'.

Regarding uniforms for the Louisiana volunteer regiments and battalions raised for Confederate service, the organizations of which began on 25 April 1861, individual companies began their war experience wearing either what they could provide themselves, or what local aid associations could come up with. The 1st Louisiana Infantry Battalion, commanded by Colonel Charles D. Dreux, arrived at Pensacola in a variety of garb. The Louisiana Guard, Co. A, wore a 'blue roundabout', or shell jacket, trimmed with buff, 'French army pattern' dark blue caps trimmed with gilt braid, and white gaiters. The Crescent City Rifles, Co. B, paraded in a suit of 'light gray, Zouave style, with golden crescents embroidered on their kepis', plus 'newly washed [white] gaiters'.

The Orleans Cadets, Co. F, was the first Louisiana company mustered into Confederate service. Their full dress consisted of a nine-button dark gray frock with solid black trim on the collar, shoulder straps and pointed cuffs; gray chasseur-pattern forage caps with a black band and quartered with thin black piping; black waist belts and gray pants with black seam stripes. For 'camp or fatigue' they arrived on the coast wearing a uniform put together in New Orleans from 'gray tweeds made in Georgia', composed of a seven-button zouave-style jacket trimmed all around, and on cuffs, with black edging and braid respectively. Their very full-cut pants were also trimmed with narrow black seam stripes.

En route through Montgomery, Alabama, members of this battalion were presented with a version of the ubiquitous 'Sicilian' cap of 'sugar loaf shape and of the tri-color red, white and blue, which make the wearers in appearance quite "a la Zouave".'

The 1st Special Battalion, or 2nd Louisiana Infantry Battalion, raised by Chatham Roberdeau Wheat, who had seen military service in Mexico, Cuba, Nicaragua, and Italy, was composed of a mixture of 'Irish roustabouts and riff-raff' of New Orleans, filibusters, and the sons of wealthy planters. Some members of this unit had taken part in the Lopez expedition and, until they acquired uniforms, still wore their 'off-white drill pants or breeches with gaiters or boots, red flannel shirt, and broad-rimmed hat . . .' The Tiger Rifles, Co. B, initially decorated their hats with 'pictures of tigers in attitudes and slogans'. Their zouave uniform was paid for by A. Keene Richards, a wealthy citizen of New Orleans.

Other Louisiana units initially wearing zouave uniform included Coppens' Louisiana Zouaves, or the 1st Confederate States Zouave Battalion; the 2nd Zouave Battalion, commanded by Major St. Leon Dupeire; and the Avegno Zouaves, also known as the Battalion of Governor's Guards. This six-company battalion from New Orleans, commanded by Major Anatole Avegno, wore blue jackets and full red trousers. By 11 September 1861, they formed part of the 13th Louisiana Infantry. John W. Labouisse, an officer in the Southern Celts, Co. A of the same regiment, was photographed early in the war wearing a gray jacket and trousers which also had a zouave appearance. His jacket was fastened by 11 small ball-buttons, with light-colored trim on pointed cuffs. The rank of first lieutenant was indicated by two bars sewn on the turned down collar. His full-cut pants had dark-colored seam stripes.

A number of individual Louisiana volunteer, militia, and cadet companies are believed to have worn full or partial zouave dress. The Hope Guard paraded in 'Zouave jackets and pants of dark blue, nearly trimmed, white belts, and blue kepis . . .' The Young Cadets, also called the Louisiana Cadets, attached to the Orleans Rifle Battalion, wore a 'neat and elegant Zouave uniform of light blue', with black caps. The Home Sentinels, a militia company of Iberville Parish which did not enlist into Confederate service, 'wore a Zouave-like uniform with close-fitting jacket and red-striped pants'. In Monroe, a small North Louisiana town, two boys' companies – the Monroe Zouaves and the Monroe Cadets – combined to form the Ouachita

Right: Private Thomas Taylor, Phoenix Company, 8th Louisiana Infantry, wears an example of the uniform issued by the state during the Fall of 1861, and holds a M1842 Musket. His accoutrements include an Enfield Rifle Musket cartridge box and a U.S. regulation cap pouch. (Eleanor S. Brockenbrough Library, The Museum of the Confederacy, Richmond, Virginia)

Fencibles, and were furnished 'colorful uniforms and armed with double-barrelled shotguns'. Another company from New Orleans, called the Monroe Guards, which later became Co. K, 5th Louisiana, had a vivandiere called Leona Neville who wore a 'nicely-fitting black alpaca uniform'.

Regarding artillery, the Watson Artillery, originally commanded by Captain Allen A. Bursley, wore a steel gray shell jacket, pants and kepi trimmed with crimson facings. After travelling up the Mississippi River via Memphis to report for duty at Columbus, Kentucky, the unit became so dissatisfied with its officers that they 'removed the "W.A." from their caps'. The Donaldsonville Artillery, a volunteer militia company founded in 1837, had a dress uniform similar to that of the Orleans Guard Battalion, but in 1861 adopted a fatigue outfit consisting of a gray shell jacket, with shoulder straps, fastened by nine gilt buttons bearing a flaming bomb over crossed cannon, with the inscription 'Les Canonniers de Donaldsonville'. Pants were plain gray. Caps were also gray with dark, possibly red band, with gilt crossed-cannon insignia in front.

State clothing provision for Louisiana troops came later in the year, with over $600,000 being spent on the task for approximately 20 units. Typical was that received by the 3rd Louisiana Infantry in Missouri during September. Each man was given 'one red flannel shirt, one cotton shirt, one plaid linsey shirt, to be worn over the cotton shirt, one pair of plain linsey or flannel drawers, one pair of heavy woolen jeans pants and a long jacket, lined inside with linsey, and padded on the shoulders to carry the gun with ease'. This was elsewhere described as being 'of substantial material known as jeans, being grayish-blue in color, with the exception of Company K [Pelican Rifles], which is of dark brown'. The cloth for this issuance were also produced at the State Penitentiary, being subsequently made up by the Ladies of Baton Rouge. Uniforms sent to the 1st and 2nd regiments were lost, or delayed. The 4th and 5th regiments also received theirs during September. On 19 August 1861, Lieutenant-colonel Charles de Choiseul wrote: 'I am getting made new fatigue uniforms, for the entire command, of a light blue heavy cloth, a very pretty and serviceable uniform indeed.' A member of the same regiment wrote on 1 October 1861: 'the new uniform is now all here complete, and I can assure you to see 1000 men all dressed alike makes for a different impression on a spectator than a variety of colors, caps, and hats, coats and jackets, and such like mixtures'.

The whole of General Richard Taylor's Louisiana brigade,

composed of the 6th, 7th, 8th and 9th Louisiana regiments, plus Wheat's 1st Special Battalion, were reviewed in this uniform, with white gaiters, during May 1862. That received by the 8th Louisiana revealed the problems the State Penitentiary workshops experienced producing cloth of standard quality and color. Some of the clothing was in appearance as 'absurd as a harlequin dress, the body and sleeves being of diverse colors and materials'.

Excluded from state issuance were the 14th Louisiana, and the 3rd Infantry Battalion. By December 1861, the former were reported to have 'received no clothing of any description from the state . . . they are not in a situation to purchase clothing other than that furnished by their officers from the $25 allowed by the Government for six months clothing'. By 9 March 1862, the 21st Louisiana was 'airing the new clothing so opportunely sent by the Governor of Louisiana'. The uniforms of the 24th Louisiana, 'consisting of strong, substantial gray cloth, and very neatly and handsomely made[,] were furnished in 3 days . . .' during the same month.

As cloth grew scarce these long jackets, or coats, were quickly replaced by shell jackets fastened by a variation of six, eight or nine buttons, usually trimmed around the edges, collar, shoulder straps, and cuffs, with ½-inch-wide black braid. Many volunteers received chasseur-style caps, often quartered with thin black piping and bands of various colors, suggesting that some regimental preference may have existed.

Members of the Confederate States Rangers, Co. K, 10th Louisiana were photographed wearing slouch hats looped up on the left with their state uniform. Trousers were full cut with black seam stripes. The cap style generally worn with this series of issuance may also have been influenced by that of the prestigious Orleans Cadets described above. Likewise, the jackets seem to follow the pattern adopted for fatigue by that company at the beginning of 1861. Alternatively, the choice of the latter may have been dictated by the economics of war.

The full dress of the Orleans Cadets described above may have influenced the pattern of uniform acquired by a number of Louisiana units after receipt of their state issue. Paul Thibodaux, a member of the Lafourche Creoles, Co. G, 18th Louisiana, was photographed after promotion to corporal on 17 December 1861, and before receiving a wound at Shiloh on 6–7 April 1862, wearing a uniform virtually identical to that of the Orleans Cadets. Other photographic examples include that of Private William Y. Dixon of the Hunter Rifles, Co. G, 4th Louisiana, taken on 7 March 1862. Fastened by only five buttons, Dixon's coat has a turned-down black collar, and a small button at the point of his solid black-faced cuffs. Private Edwin F. Jennison, Claiborne Guards, Co. F., 2nd Louisiana, was photographed sometime before his death at Malvern Hill on 1 July 1862 in similar garb. Private William Strong, 2nd Louisiana Cavalry, wore what appears to have been a cavalry version of this uniform, with yellow-faced collar, cuffs and shoulder straps.

This 'Orleans Cadet'-style frock coat may have been issued to Louisiana troops even later in the war. Whilst in winter quarters at Camp Qui Vive at Fausse Point, Louisiana, during the period November 1862 to April 1863, the 18th Louisiana were 'furnished with a lot of Confederate gray cloth [probably still being manufactured at the State Penitentiary for the Confederate States Quartermaster Department], which was distributed among the different camps'. The regimental quartermaster, Major Silas T. Grisamore, recalled: 'Col. [Leopold L.] Armant ordered me to go to St. Martinsville to a tailor'. There follows a long, humorous description of the uniforms, which were almost all cut too small, including: '. . . [we] pulled the garment so high up behind the neck that the buttons [on the coat tails] were right between the shoulders'. The buttons were 'real shining brass beauties', whilst the 'wrist bands', or cuffs, on the coat were described as being 'trimmed with black . . .'.

Texas

On the eve of the Civil War, the militia of Texas consisted of five divisions, with regiments raised on a county-wide basis. As in most other states, the enrolled militia was virtually dormant. Uniformed volunteer militia companies were attached to each battalion and regiment, but only seven of these existed in 1858: the Alamo Rifles of San Antonio; Washington Light Guards, Milam Rifles, and Turner Rifles, of Houston; Galveston Artillery and Lone Star Company, of Galveston; and the Refugio Riflemen. Other units were hastily formed as secession approached, and by 1861 the 1st Regiment Galveston Volunteers was formed which included the Galveston Zouaves, Wigfall Guards and Lone Star Rifles. No state regulations were issued to govern the dress of these companies.

After secession on 1 February 1861 the Committee of Public Safety, appointed by the Secession Convention, elected Ben McCulloch, a Mexican War veteran, colonel of cavalry with orders to raise a force to capture U.S. property, including the arsenal at San Antonio. The force collected by McCulloch included a Volunteer battalion from Gonzales, companies from Lockhart, Sequin and San Antonio; and six companies, or 'castles', of the Knights of the Golden Circle, a southern rights society founded in 1854. An eye-witness described these units 'appearing, two by two, on muleback and horseback, mounted and on foot, a motley though quite orderly crowd, carrying the Lone Star flag before them . . . Some had coats, but others were in their shirt-sleeves, and not a few were wrapped in old shawls and saddle-blankets'. McCulloch's command was subsequently disbanded when it became apparent that General David E. Twiggs, then commanding the Department of Texas, was not going to offer resistance.

During March 1861, the Committee authorized the organization of two state cavalry regiments to operate along the northern and southern frontiers. These regiments were mustered into Confederate service for one year, and were designated the 1st (H. E. McCulloch's) and 2nd (J. S. Ford's) Mounted Riflemen. Neither of these units were uniformed, but the former wore red flannel stripes on the shoulders of their civilian shirts and coats, and were armed with Model 1861 Colt revolvers. Companies of non-uniformed citizens called Minute Men were also formed at this time for frontier defence.

Texas received her first call for 8000 troops from the Confederate Government during April 1861, mainly for coastal defence. This was followed in August by a request for 2000 troops for service in Virginia. A total of 32 companies were sent to Richmond, where they were organized into the 1st, 4th, and 5th Infantry Regiments. These, in turn, were formed into the brigade commanded by John Bell Hood.

By the end of 1861, Texas had raised seven regiments and four battalions of infantry, amounting to approximately 7100 men. About seven companies of artillery were also organized. By contrast, 16 regiments, 3 battalions, and 3 independent companies of cavalry were in the saddle, totalling around 17,338 troopers. These figures illustrate the strong preference of Texans for mounted service, and a natural aversion to foot-slogging! Consequently, a number of cavalry units later had to be dismounted in order to relieve the shortage of infantry.

As with other Confederate states, Texas was burdened with the task of clothing her volunteers. In the absence of a large-scale textiles industry, she initially had large stocks of imported cloth and garments which could be turned into uniforms, but there were difficulties making this available. Governor Edward Clark urged companies to come prepared with clothing. Others purchased it on route to war. By September 1861, each county

The hat of Private Clement Newton Bassett, Co. H, 8th Texas Cavalry, in the Museum of the Confederacy, displays a broken red star with the letter R in the centre, around the whole of which is arranged the letters TEXAS. (Ron Field, from an original artefact)

had been made responsible for the acquisition of cloth through private societies, and clothing depots were established in 11 centres. Based on the successful results of this system, the central government requested that Texas continue to clothe her troops and accept the commutation allowance in payment. It was not until late 1862 that Confederate quartermasters took over the task of supplying Texas troops.

Probably the largest source of private supply were the innumerable 'ladies' aid societies'. In Marshall, Texas, four committees were established on 31 July 1861 to collect blankets, hats, socks and shoes for the Lane Rangers on their way for duty on the Texas frontier. By November, the 'Society' in the vicinity of Lancaster had collected and sent to the 2nd Regiment, Texas Partisan Rangers, commanded by B. Warren

Surrender of ex-General Twiggs, late of the United States Army, to the Texan Troops in the Gran Plaza, San Antonio, Texas, 16 February 1861. A Harper's Weekly *artist depicted the mounted troops present as being uniformly dressed in broad brimmed hats, long duster-style coats, and trousers tucked into boots. An accompanying report generally described this force as being 'plainly dressed, some in Kersey, a fine-looking body of men, with a determined air'.* (Harper's Weekly, *23 March 1861)*

Stone, coats, jeans pants, flannel and linsey shirts, boots and shoes. William D. Cater, member of the Lone Star Defenders, Co. C, 3rd Texas Cavalry, recalled that his uniform consisted of: 'Black coats, with vests to march, brown (Huntsville made) jeans pants, black hats and black boots made of calfskin tanned leather. It looked well enough but was very hot to wear in the summer; however, we wore them when ready to start. Nothing was said about the color of the shirt or cravat. Mine . . . was white and the neckwear was a black silk string tie. This, of course, was soon a thing of the past. Our company started without guns or pistols. I had a knife made in a blacksmith shop with a blade about six inches long, which I carried in a scabbard in the leather belt I added to my uniform.'

The 8th Texas Cavalry, also known as Terry's Texas Rangers, wore a great variety of dress during initial months of service. En route east with the first battalion of the regiment, R. C. Hilliard observed of their appearance in a letter home from New Iberia, dated 19 September 1861: 'Some in Red, some in Blue – Brow [sic], Greene yellow – some in broad sombreros, some in caps, some without either, as daring a set as ever marched to battle.' After reaching New Orleans, the Daily Picayune of 30

September described the Tom Lubbock Rangers, Co. K, as being: '. . . all athletic men and dress[ed] fantastically in hunting shirts of different materials, with large boots worn on the outside, coming over the knee, with Mexican spurs attached. Some wore fancy Mexican pants trimmed down the side with little brass buttons [conchos], and silk sashes around their waists. Others had the Confederate flag, worked in

The Lone Star Rifles, Co. L, 1st Texas Infantry, in front of their quarters at Camp Quantico during the winter of 1861/62. The two men on the left wear the distinctive company fatigue uniform consisting of a plain gray overshirt of a double-breasted fireman's style, with a front 'plastron' fastened by two rows of five buttons. The collar was cut in a broad falling style, while the cuffs, rather than being gathered, appear quite plain, like a jacket, rather than a shirt. (Austin History Centre, Austin Public Library)

different colored leathers to represent it, on the legs of their boots.'

Captain John G. Walker, commander of the above company, was further described as wearing a buckskin hunting shirt that hugged his large form, 'immense' boots, large Mexican spurs, sombrero and a 'beautifully worked' Mexican blanket across his shoulders. By late February 1862, the clothing of this company was described as being 'shabby, ragged, and dirty', the only element of uniformity being a red star on their hats and caps. Later in the war, the 8th Texas Cavalry attempted to introduce a hint of uniformity in their clothing by the addition of red trimmings to jackets, shirts and trousers.

Photographic evidence bears further witness to the great variety of dress worn by the Texas mounted units throughout most of the war. Private Wady Williams of the Grimes County Rangers wore a multi-colored shirt and gray trousers with ball buttons running the length of his leg when he was mustered into the 5th Texas Cavalry on 31 August 1861. The only semblance of military garb worn by Private Japhet Collins of the Bastrop County Rawhides, Co. D, 12th Texas Cavalry, was his Mexican War-style forage cap, and a plain gray woollen overshirt. Private William Burgess, Co. D, 27th Texas Cavalry, volunteered in a homemade uniform coat with solid facing on turned-back front, collar, cuffs and breast pocket top.

Although Texas infantry units were generally clothed in an equally haphazard fashion, those within Hood's Brigade – the only troops from the state to see service in the Eastern theatre of the war – were well supplied with uniforms of various cut and style. Within the 1st Texas Infantry, the Star Rifles, Co. D, wore gray jacket and pants, faced in a dark color on collars, pointed cuffs and trousers stripes. The jackets bore three rows of seven large buttons on the front, linked by a doubled darker cord, with trefoils under the outer buttons, an imitation of military academy dress coats. Headgear consisted of high crowned Hardee hats with brim pinned up on the wearer's left with metal

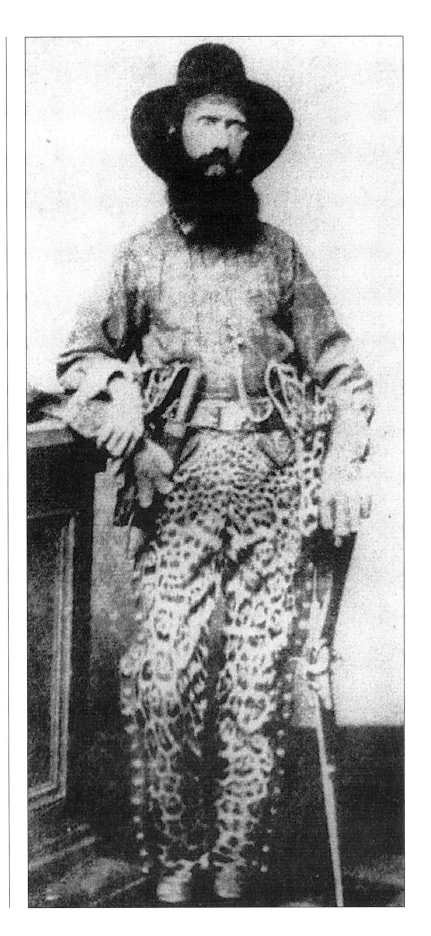

The most unusual dress in Texas mounted service must have been that of Captain Samuel J. Richardson, who commanded an independent company of cavalry. Although his wide-brimmed black slouch hat and plain shirt may be considered normal wear, his jaguar-skin trousers, with conchos down the side seams, and matching revolver holsters, were certainly not! Members of the 8th Texas Cavalry were also reported to have clothed themselves in bearskin pants. One even had an entire bearskin suit! (U.S. Army Military History Institute/Jim Enos)

stars. The Reagan Guards, Co. G, wore 'dark suits with bright red stripes'.

Captain Edward Currie of the Crockett Southrons, Co. I, posed for a photograph before he resigned in late December 1861 wearing a gray overshirt with a broad band of black facing color, edged with light trim down the front opening edge. Two large patch pockets were also edged with ½-inch black tape. Shoulder straps and cuffs were also probably faced black. Rank insignia consisted of C.S. regulation bars sewn to the standing collar, the latter being an unusual feature on such a shirt. His light-colored narrow-brimmed hat was pinned up one side.

According to a memoir written by Private O. T. Hanks, the Texas Invincibles, Co. K, 1st Texas Infantry, left home in uniforms of 'good gray woolen goods cut and fitted by W. A. McClanahan and his helpers, and trimmed with blue collars

and cuffs'. The Invincibles' accoutrements were similarly of local manufacture. One member recalled that their 'cartridge boxes were made of leather by our home saddlers and harness workmen', while another confirmed that he and a local saddler

Men of the 1st Texas Infantry wearing uniforms received whilst at Camp Quantico. Their single-breasted frock coats were fastened with nine large buttons. The collar and pointed cuffs were faced a dark color, perhaps black, and the cuffs bore a single button on the point. Trousers were also gray with dark seam stripes. Forage caps, with flat tops tilted forward, may have been plain gray, and were ornamented with a small star in the centre, with TEXAS in brass letters curved around the bottom edge. The latter feature was a popular fad throughout the whole army during this winter period, and were more than likely purchased from a sutler than representing any kind of general issue. (Rosenburg Library, Galveston, Texas)

had 'made each of the boys a leather built pistol and knife scabbard and cap box'. These knives, rather than being merely side knives, were intended for use as improvised bayonets, and were made by local blacksmiths from old saw mill blades: 'Some were about twelve inches long [and] one and one half inches wide. Every fellow ground and polished his own . . . The scabbards were made of good leather, were sewed and riveted with lead rivets. They were arranged to carry . . . on the cartridge belt. Our bayonets were fitted to the muzzle of the guns by Uncle Ranse Horne, who was an ingenious workman . . .'.

By the winter of 1861/62, the Lone Star Rifles, Co. L, and possibly the whole of the 1st Texas, were well clothed in uniforms probably purchased under the commutation system, and made up by tailors in Virginia. Photographic evidence points to the fact that an officers' uniform was adopted by the 1st Texas at the same time. Unusually this consisted of a double-breasted coat for company grade officers, following Confederate rather than U.S. regulations. Insignia combined the two influences, with Federal shoulder straps and Confederate collar bars.

Regarding the 4th Texas Infantry, the best evidence for the first uniform of the Tom Green Rifles, Co. B, is provided by the ambrotype and recollections of Private Valerius C. Giles. Shortly after enlistment, Giles wrote: 'We were a motley looking set but as a rule, comfortably dressed. In my company we had about four different shades of gray, but all the trimmings were of black braid . . . The citizens of Austin and the surrounding neighborhood bought the cloth. An old tailor took our measurements and cut the uniforms[,] then the ladies made them up. Oh, we were fine!'

In his ambrotype, Giles wears a single-breasted frock coat of gray, a little shorter in the skirts than many of the period, and slightly darker gray trousers with black seam stripes. The coat is trimmed around the collar and down the front edge with black tape. The same braid edges the shoulder straps and cuffs, the latter with a parallel band no more than 2 inches in from the edge. This garment fastened with seven large buttons.

Private John S. Pickle, Co. B, 18th Texas Cavalry, wears an example of the uniform manufactured at the State Penitentiary at Huntsville during 1862. He holds what seems to be a Whitney Navy Revolver. The butt of another weapon is pushed into his waist belt. (Austin History Centre, Austin Public Library)

The Tom Green Rifles wore fatigue caps, but Giles' father insisted that his son purchase for himself 'the best hat on the house', which he wore in his photo, one brim pinned up with a star bought at the photographer's studio. This impressively large hat, waterproofed with goose grease, lasted Giles until Gaines' Mill in 1862!

The first uniform of the Lone Star Guards, Co. E, was made of 'imported gray cloth', tailored to individual measurements and sewn by the Ladies Aid Society of the First Methodist Church at Waco. These uniforms were trimmed in dark blue. Based on an image of the Taylor brothers who enlisted in the company, photographic evidence indicates that this uniform consisted of a gray jacket with either eight or nine buttons, trimmed around all the collar, edges and cuffs with ½-inch-wide braid. Gray trousers were also trimmed with a seam stripe of the same material. Black slouch hats were pinned up on one side, probably by metal stars. Both Taylor brothers wore narrow civilian leather belts without accoutrements. Over their shoulders were slung straps of light color probably supporting haversacks and canteens.

Evidence suggests that one, if not more, of the companies comprising the 4th Texas originally wore dark blue U.S. Army sack coats, and possibly also trousers of the same provenance. Although the Sandy Point Mounted Rifles, also known as the Henderson Guards, enlisted in civilian dress, each man was issued a 'blue sack coat, very full, almost in the shape of a gown', together with blue trousers, a pair of shoes, two pairs of socks, and two shirts, whilst at Camp Van Dorn near Houston. It would seem reasonable to assume that these were large size coats taken over by the state with the capture of Federal military property. Similarly, members of the Grimes County Grays, Co. G, and the Porter Guards, Co. H, were photographed wearing sack coats of dark color.

Two members of the Grimes County Grays were also photographed between July/August 1861 wearing plain gray frock coats, with darker-colored slough hats and trousers. Musician Richard Pinckney wore a single-breasted seven-button coat, whilst that worn by his brother, Private John M. Pinckney, was double breasted with two rows of seven buttons.

While the 1st Texas evidently adopted a regimental-style uniform for officers, those in the 4th Texas appear to have chosen a version of the Confederate regulation uniform. An interesting variation appears in a photo of 3rd Lieutenant William D. Rounsavall of the Sandy Point Mounted Rifles,

This hispanic Confederate from Houston Texas has solid facing color on his collar and cuffs. (David Wynn Vaughan)

who is shown wearing a plain double-breasted gray frock coat of regulation style with a single gold collar bar and sleeve knot of a single gold braid. Rounsavall's forage cap is also gray, apparently with a gold braid around the top of the band. On the flat crown, brass letters spell out TEXAS.

The dress of the 4th Texas' chaplain, Presbyterian minister Nicholas A. Davis is unusually well documented. A correspondent to the *Daily Richmond Enquirer* of 25 September 1861 noted: 'I observed a chaplain (Rev. Nicholas A. Davis, of Texas) in uniform on yesterday, which . . . I admired above anything I have yet seen. A suit of black clothing strait (sic) breasted, with one row of brass buttons, and simple pointed cuff with a small olive branch about six inches long, running up the sleeve. We learn that it was made by C. Wendlinger, No. 146, Main St. No stripes on the pants.'

Davis himself complained of the 'exorbitant charges' of Mr. Wendlinger for the 'coat and pants – $45.00 which is a little more than contracted for . . .' A photograph of this uniform shows the coat to have had eight buttons, with two small ones on each cuff. The 'olive branch', consisting of a single narrow gold braid, was formed of nine 'leaves' or loops, becoming progressively smaller towards the top. Davis was noted by an eyewitness as wearing a slouch hat.

Gray overshirts of various patterns seem to have been very popular with the 5th Texas. B. Hugh Fuller of the Bayou City Guard, Co. A, was photographed wearing a light gray double-breasted version with falling collar and plastron front secured by two rows of small buttons. The collars, cuffs and plastron were all edged with narrow dark trim, whilst a small five-pointed star also decorated the former. Private James J. Smith of the Dixie Blues, Co. E, was photographed, probably upon enlistment, also wearing a long, gray blouse-shaped hunting shirt which buttoned down the front, with long black patches sewn along the shoulders in imitation of shoulder straps. He also wore a plain black felt hat. Private Andrew Jackson Read wore a plain gray pullover shirt with three buttons down the front, and light gray forage cap with brass letters spelling out his name A J READ on top, when he joined Company F in July 1861. Two soldiers believed to have belonged to the Milam County Grays, Co. G, were photographed wearing similarly-patterned light gray overshirts and trousers with dark seam stripes. To confuse things, the Felder brothers of the Dixie Blues wore single-breasted frock coats and pants of an unmatched shade of gray wool when they were mustered in on 8 August 1861. Their headgear also differed, that of Rufus King Felder being a Model 1861-pattern forage cap, whilst Myers Martindale Felder's was basically a Model 1851 dress cap with stiffening removed. The possible lack of matching clothing in this regiment is best illustrated by the fact that Private John W.

Stevens was advised upon enlistment in the Texas Polk Rifles, Co. H, to 'get just what suited his fancy and have it made up in any style he chose – Jes so it was a uniform'!

A member of the 4th Texas wrote of being issued 'tolerably good' overcoats 'with capes on them' in late October 1861. It would seem likely that the whole of Hood's brigade was furnished with winter overcoats at the same time. About this time it was described as being a '. . . long line of gray. Three thousand bright Texas boys . . . with Enfield rifles and bayonets glittering.'

The Texas troops remaining in the Western theatre of the war were far less well served with clothing. The companies and regiments of volunteers assembling in camps of instruction went through a long hot summer not only without receiving arms and uniforms, but without wagons, tents, medicines, and many other necessities. Rip Ford's 2nd Mounted Riflemen were deplorably short of clothing. Since being stationed on the Texas frontier, it had received no contributions from the people of the state. By the fall of 1861 President Lincoln's blockade, though not highly effective, had cut off direct trade through Galveston and other regular ports. One of the first moves of the Military Board established by the legislature in January 1862 was to utilize the State Penitentiary at Huntsville for the manufacture of cloth. Eventually, a tannery and workshops for making shoes and hats were also established. This operation thus became one of the largest cotton and woollen mills in the Confederate southwest. Once produced, this cloth seems to have been cut and tailored into uniforms by local tailor shops working under state contract. A Dallas *Herald* article reported that Company B, 18th Texas Cavalry, was dressed in a 'yellowish-gray tunic coat and pantaloons made of Penitentiary Jeans, with two rows of brass buttons on the front of the coat and a yellow stripe down the side of the pantaloons', when they arrived in that city on 22 January 1862. Penitentiary records show that this company, commanded by Captain H. S. Morgan, was furnished Kersey wool, cotton osnaburg and cotton jeans in December 1861.

Colonel John C. Moore of the 2nd Texas Infantry (also known as the 2nd Texas Sharpshooters) was noted for caring for the welfare of his troops. As a last resort he also took advantage of captured Federal clothing, and issued his 'rag-tag regiment' with dark blue U.S. Army sack coats like those worn within Hood's Brigade in Virginia. The 2nd Texas later received uniforms of undyed wool a few days before leaving Corinth for Shiloh in March 1862. After the battle, a Federal prisoner is reputed to have inquired: 'Who were them hell cats that went into battle dressed in their graveclothes?'

Private Henry D. Hart of Bate's Battalion (Brazoria Coast Regiment), Texas Volunteers, reorganized into the 13th Texas Infantry, was photographed sometime during 1862 wearing another possible example of a uniform made from Penitentiary cloth. Fastened by a single row of eight large buttons, the coat was gray with solid faced collar and cuffs, the latter bearing at least two small buttons sewn along the top seam. One-inch-wide braid of the same color was also sewn diagonally from the collar to the shoulder seams, and also along the coat front and around the tails. His cap and pants were made from the same cloth and trimmings. The 16th Texas Infantry was described as being clad in 'wool, and straw hats, homespun pants, and faded penitentiary jackets' in 1863.

Towards the end of 1862 the machinery at the Penitentiary began to wear out and efforts to replace it met with little success. Hence, Texas troops were again without a reliable supply of clothing. The agent for Darnell's 18th Texas Cavalry, dismounted and stationed in northwestern Arkansas, returned to Dallas on 13 September, where he placed in the *Herald* an urgent request for clothes. Items specified were flannel, linsey, shoes, hats, leather, or additional clothing of 'any description whatever'. He would pay for delivery. Despite such shortages, the British diarist, Lieutenant Colonel Arthur Freemantle, observed a dress parade of the 3rd Texas Infantry on 8 April 1863, and recorded: 'The men were well clothed, though great variety existed in their uniforms. Some companies wore blue, some gray, some had French kepis, others wideawakes and Mexican hats . . . During all my travels in the South I never saw a regiment so well clothed or so well drilled as this one, which has never been in action, or exposed to much hardship.'

Six days earlier, Freemantle had found the 14th Cavalry Battalion Partisan Rangers wearing 'flannel shirts, very ancient trousers, jack-boots with enormous spurs, and black felt hats, ornamented with the "lone star of Texas".' The dismounted 2nd Cavalry Regiment (Pyron's) was described during the same period as being 'dressed in every variety of costume, and armed with every variety of weapon.'

The rank of Third Lieutenant James C. Bates, 9th Texas Cavalry, may be indicated by his very long shoulder straps. (U.S. Army Military History Institute/Jim Enos)

Virginia

On the eve of secession, the militia of Virginia was organized territorially into 5 divisions, 28 brigades, and 185 regiments of the line. Each brigade embraced two or more counties and contained four or more regiments. On average during the years 1851– 1860, there were between 125 and 150 active volunteer militia companies of light infantry or riflemen. These belonged either to distinctive Volunteer Militia regiments or battalions, or were formed into a 'Volunteer Battalion' of a line militia regiment. John Brown's Raid on Harper's Ferry, plus rumours of attempts to free the prisoners at Charlestown, prompted a call for approximately 50 Volunteer companies into active state service for various periods of duty during October/ November of 1859.

Essentially, the volunteer militia companies of Virginia adopted uniforms of their own choosing during the period prior to the Civil War, despite the fact that a state uniform was prescribed by the militia law of 1858. Detailed in general orders dated May of that year, it was based on 'the regulations of the army of the United States, except that the buttons shall have the Virginia coat of arms thereon'. Other significant differences for cavalry included frock coats, trimmed with yellow, instead of jackets as worn by the regular service. The influence of this state uniform was widespread, as the companies formed after its creation were in theory expected to adopt it. However, plans for a state-wide uniform were further thwarted by the act of 30 March 1860, which once again permitted companies to choose their own style of dress.

Only two Volunteer organizations in the state adopted anything like a regimental uniform. These were the 1st Regiment of Virginia Volunteers, originally organized in 1851, and the 2nd Battalion Virginia Volunteers, established in 1860.

On 5 July 1858 the 7th New York Regiment had visited Richmond, and their smart black-trimmed gray jackets, caps and pants, with white waist and shoulder belts, left a marked impression on their Virginian counterparts who wore a mixture of blue, green and gray. Efforts to prescribe a regimental uniform for the 1st Regiment in the wake of the 7th's visit initially came to naught; but by July 1859 the *Daily Richmond Enquirer* was able to report: 'The different Companies attached to the First Regiment of Virginia Volunteers . . . are almost all adopting the gray uniform. Even the Irish and German companies are throwing off their characteristic styles of national dress, and are adopting the American gray . . .'

Although a detailed description of the regimental full dress chosen by the 1st Regiment has not survived, a reconstruction

Three members of the Richmond Grays, Co. A, 1st Regiment of Virginia Volunteers, photographed at Charles Town, Virginia, at the time of the hanging of John Brown in December 1859. The sergeant at centre wears the short-skirted frock coat adopted by this company around 1851. The officer at left, and the enlisted man at right, both wear the fatigue jacket adopted in 1859. (Russell Hicks Jr)

of it is possible based on the changes which occurred in company dress during the period prior to the Civil War. From available evidence it seems that most of these companies adopted a black cloth, of beaverskin, 'National Guard'-style dress cap with pompon; gray cloth fatigue cap with black band; gray frock coat trimmed according to company preference; gray shirt and black overcoat. With the exception of the Virginia Rifles and the Howitzers, all companies wore white webbing cross belts. The former retained their black cross belts, whilst the Howitzer Company preferred only a white waist belt for their sabres.

The Richmond Grays, Co. A, of this regiment had been wearing a gray uniform based on that of the 7th New York since their organization in 1844. About 1851, the short-skirted frock coat replaced the coatee. Also the National Guard-style dress cap, as worn by the 7th New York, with black felt body and black patent leather strap strips at top and bottom, with white pompon, was adopted. By 1859, the Grays also had items of undress uniform including a nine-button gray fatigue jacket with belt loops, and black edging on a low collar, black shoulder straps; gray forage cap with black oilskin covers, and RG in brass letters on the front. New gray frock coats of the long-skirted pattern were procured in early 1861.

The Richmond City Guard, Co. B (originally called the Fireside Protectors, and also later known as Lee's Riflemen, after their second commanding officer), adopted a plain gray frock coat with 'gold braid rectangles' on the collar and gold epaulette keeps, after their organization in December 1860.

The Montgomery Guard, Co. C, paraded for the first time in their 'newly adopted gray uniform' on 4 July 1859, on which occasion the *Richmond Enquirer* reported that it 'looks neat, fits well, and though it is gray, is more preferable to the eye, than the marked abundance of vivid green that formerly character-ized the style of the gallant Montgomeries'. The latter is a reference to the full dress worn by this unit before 1859, which consisted of a green coatee with three rows of buttons, trimmed with gold lace and faced with buff collar, cuffs and coat tails; sky-blue pants with 1½-inch buff seam stripe; and green M1851 dress cap with buff band. This uniform continued in use for special occasions throughout 1860. Organized on 23 June 1859 under Richmond attorney Randolph Milton Cary, the great aim of F Company was 'to build up a regiment in imitation of the "National Guard" of New York'. Hence, they chose a full dress consisting of a long-skirted 'cadet gray' frock coat with collar

Private John Werth, Richmond Howitzers, Co. H, 1st Regiment of Virginia Volunteers, wearing the dark gray fatigue jacket adopted by this company in 1861. Werth probably left the Howitzers in May of that year to form a Home Guard unit called the Richmond Mounted City Guard. (Eleanor S. Brockenbrough Library, The Museum of the Confederacy, Richmond, Virginia)

F Company, 1st Regiment of Virginia Volunteers, wearing the uniform adopted in 1861. (From photographs and descriptions by Richard Warren)

edged black, and black worsted epaulettes with white fringe, and white cord inside the crescent. Pants were also gray with 2-inch wide black seam stripes. Headgear consisted of the National Guard-style dress cap. This company also adopted a fatigue jacket, cap and trousers similar to that of the Grays.

By 1861 the dress uniform of F Company had been revised somewhat. As later described by John H. Worsham, who joined the unit that year: 'This company had a fine cadet gray uniform. It consisted first of a frock coat which had a row of virginia fire-gilt buttons on its front. Around the cuff of the sleeve was a band of gold braid and two small fire-gilt buttons. On the collar the same gold braid was so arranged that it looked very much

like the mark of rank for a first lieutenant which was afterwards adopted by the Confederacy. The pants had a black stripe about one and a quarter inches wide along the outer seams. The cap was made of the same cadet gray cloth, trimmed with black braid and two small fire-gilt buttons. On its front was the letter F. The non-commissioned officers had their mark of rank worked on the sleeves of their coats with black braid.'

The Richmond Light Infantry Blues, Co. E, were normally resplendent in their dark blue coatee with white cassimere collar, cuffs and plastron front; blue trousers with white seam stripe; and blue cloth cap with pompon – but by February 1861 had adopted their gray regimental uniform with long-skirted frock coat.

Company G, commanded by Captain William Gordon, was originally organized in July 1859, and by February 1860 paraded in 'full uniform and undress cap', consisting of a nine-button gray frock coat, with collar edged with black braid and decorated with a gold loop; gray trousers with broad black seam stripes; and a gray forage cap with black band and brass letter G on the front. By August 1860 this company had also acquired an 'undress uniform' which included a 'Fatigue Jacket'.

Formed on 9 November 1859, the Howitzer Company, which later expanded into a battalion known as the Richmond Howitzers, initially assembled during January 1860 in 'red shirt, gray pants, [and miscellaneous] fatigue cap'. During the following month, they acquired a 'full dress uniform' from 'Stagg's', and 'dress caps from Ellet & Weisiger'. The former consisted of a gray frock coat with 'wings', whilst the latter was presumably a version of the 'National Guard' dress cap. Gray fatigue caps with red band and gilt letter H, their company designation within the 1st Regiment, on the front, were being worn by October 1860. By the beginning of the Civil War, the Howitzer Battalion had a dark gray fatigue jacket with belt loops, and red wool piping around collar and shoulder straps.

The Virginia Rifles, Co. K, laid their blue and green dress uniforms aside, and appeared on parade in 'new gray uniforms, with black cross belts and shoulder straps' on 12 April 1860.

The Armory Band, under the leadership of James B. Smith, became the regimental band of the First in April 1860, and members were photographed wearing long-skirted plain gray frock coats, gray chasseur-pattern forage caps with dark bands, and darker, possibly blue trousers with narrow, light-colored seams stripes.

It seems that most companies received 'new Regimental

Private Henry A. Tarrall, Woodis Riflemen. Organized at Norfolk, Virginia, in 1858, this company wore a dark green frock coat with black velvet front, collar, and shoulder patches, trimmed with gold cord. Pants were also green with black stripes edged with gold. A red pompon is pinned to his black Hardee hat. (From a private collection. The Museum of the Confederacy, Richmond, Virginia)

overcoats' during January 1860. According to J. H. Worsham, F Company 'had black cloth overcoats – the skirt reaching a little below the knees, the capes a little below the elbow – and the buttons were Virginia-gilt'.

The 2nd Battalion Virginia Volunteers was formed in Spotsylvania County during the spring of 1860, when the Fredericksburg Rifle Grays, Washington Guards, and the Coleman Guards – all of Fredericksburg – were detached from the 16th Regiment, Virginia Militia. On 23 April of that year the Richmond *Daily Dispatch* announced: 'The Fredericksburg (Va.) volunteer companies have adopted the gray uniform of the Richmond Regiment'.

Charles A. Pace of the Danville Blues, a light infantry volunteer company organized in 1841. This unit became Company A, 18th Virginia Infantry. Probably photographed in 1861, Pace wears full dress which includes fountain plume, tail-coat, and white gloves. (Eleanor S. Brockenbrough Library, The Museum of the Confederacy, Richmond, Virginia)

With the secession of Virginia on 7 April, the older Volunteer Militia companies, including the 1st Regiment of Volunteers, were enrolled for active state service. By late July 1861, the uniforms of the First, which presumably included a mixture of gray frock coats and fatigue jackets, had seen hard wear on the 'plains of Manassas' and, according to regimental historian Charles T. Loehr, were 'somewhat in need of repairs'. Even the Drums Corps was in need of new jackets and pants. On 9 September 1861 the Richmond City Council appropriated $50,000 in order to supply volunteers from the city with winter clothing. The First was probably in receipt of new uniforms via this source by late October. An ambrotype of Hampden Pleasants Hay of the Richmond City Guard, and L. R. Wingfield of the Old Dominion Guard, taken sometime before the former was sent on detached service, shows two men from different companies in the regiment wearing an identical uniform, possibly based on the fatigue dress adopted before the war by the Richmond Grays and F Company. Hay and Wingfield wear an eight-button gray fatigue jacket with black tape trim around the edges of the collar, and black shoulder flaps. Their trousers are plain gray, and tucked into boots, possibly indicating winter wear. Hay holds a dark-colored forage cap with a gilt letter B on top.

The pattern of fatigue jackets issued to the 1st Regiment of Virginia Volunteers in October 1861 may well have influenced the Confederate Clothing Bureau, established in Richmond earlier during August of that year, in its decision to produce the short-waisted 'shell jacket' as part of the uniform supplied by the Quartermaster Department to troops in Confederate service throughout the remainder of the Civil War.

Regarding the countless other Virginia companies which volunteered for Confederate service during the summer of 1861, their uniforms were generally composed of a mixture of frock coats, jackets, tail-coats, and 'hunting shirts', varying in color from gray, blue, green, black and red. Headgear variously consisted of dress caps, forage caps, 'Sicilian' caps, slouch hats, and Mexican War hats.

Drum Major Charles Rudolph M. von Pohle, of the 1st Regiment of Virginia Volunteers. He wore a gray frock coat with black plastron front and gold lace braid linking three rows of ten gilt buttons; gray trousers with gold lace seam stripe; red sash trimmed with blue; and tall bearskin cap topped with a large red, white and blue pompon. His Drum Corps, consisting of 16 boys over the age of 16, was organized during April 1860 and paraded at the head of the 1st Regiment 'attired in red jackets and white pants' on 31 May 1860. (From a photograph by Ron Field)

Lynchburg Rifles, Co. E, 11th Virginia Infantry, with plastron fronts removed. (From photographs by Ron Field)

Much of the cloth for these uniforms was procured from the Crenshaw Woollen Company of Richmond, which had been converted from a flour mill in 1860 by Lewis D. Crenshaw. This firm produced 'Fine Cassimeres and Cloths of every variety, from Fine Virginia Merino and Mestizo wool'. It began by producing 'Army Cloths, . . . at first expressly for the Virginia Military Academy' in 1861. Kelly, Tackett & Ford of Manchester, Virginia, produced a variety of goods, including red flannel and some light blue cloth. The Scotsville Manufacturing Company, and Bonsack & Whitmore, both produced large quantities of woollen jeans. Material of various colors was also obtained from a Staunton mill, whilst the Swartz Woollen Mills at Waterloo supplied cloth for the troops from Culpeper County and vicinity.

Typical of the goods available for military companies to purchase on the eve of secession was that advertised for sale in 1860 by Kent, Paine & Co., of Richmond: '60 pieces Medium and fine Blue Cloths, 250 pieces Blue and Gray Satinets; Army Clothes; Green Clothes, for Rifle Corps; medium and Extra Military Buttons; Gauntlets; Gilt and Worsted Braids and Cords . . .' By April 1861, this firm was offering 'Gray Cassimeres, manufactured in Maryland, Virginia and Georgia'.

Early in the war, hunting shirts were particularly popular among the companies which made up the 11th Virginia Infantry, raised mainly in Lynchburg. Commonly referred to today as a 'fireman's shirt', this garment consisted of an overshirt with falling collar, pointed cuff facings, and a double-breasted front panel, or removable plastron. The Home Guard, raised by Samuel Garland, Jr during November 1850 in response to John Brown's Raid on Harper's Ferry, originally chose a dark blue frock coat and pants based on the 1858 state regulations, 'substituting the cap for the Hungarian [Hardee] hat'. However, by April 1860 they wore a 'fatigue uniform' composed of a 'blue flannel hunting shirt, with red breast and collar, trimmed with light blue, black pants and blue cap'. The Home Guard volunteered under Captain Kirkwood Otey as Co. G, 11th Virginia, in May 1861.

The Lynchburg Rifles were raised among the faculty and students of Lynchburg College during the spring of 1861. On 1 May the *Lynchburg Daily Virginian* reported: 'The Lynchburg Rifles are progressing well in their drills. They promise to make a fine company. Their uniforms are being made and will soon be completed. They are of gray goods trimmed with blue and will look well.' Based on photographic evidence, this uniform consisted of a gray hunting shirt with dark blue collar, plastron, and cuffs with a single small button sewn at the point. When unbuttoned and removed, the plastron front revealed three broad, vertical, possibly light blue, bands of silk or polished cotton trim. On some shirts a small patch of the same material appears to have been sewn along the top of the shoulders, in imitation of a shoulder strap. The shirt front could, in turn, be unbuttoned and fastened back forming two wide lapels. The forage cap worn by the Lynchburg Rifles was gray with a dark, probably blue, band. Their trousers were also gray with dark 1-inch seam stripes. Commanded by Captain James E. Blankenship, this unit became Co. E of the 11th Virginia.

The Lynchburg Rifle Grays, Co. A of this regiment, were organized on 23 January 1860, and elected Maurice Langhorne as their captain. The following day, the *Daily Virginian* announced: 'The uniform of the company will be made in Virginia of Virginia goods, the cloth being manufactured at Staunton; the suit made by our tailors; and the caps by Sinzer.' Members of this company were photographed wearing a gray hunting shirt similar to that of the Lynchburg Rifles. The collar, plastron and cuffs were possibly dark blue or black. Once the plastron was removed, the shirt probably had narrow bands of dark braid running vertically up the front, parallel with, and outside, the two rows of buttons. The Rifle Grays also wore gray forage caps with dark bands, with the letters RG on the front. Their pants were gray with broad seam stripes.

The Southern Guards from Yellow Branch, Campbell County were reported by the Petersburg *Daily Express* of 4 May 1861 to be wearing 'black jackets; [and] gray pants with black stripes'. According to surviving photographs, this may be interpreted as meaning a gray hunting shirt faced with black collar, plastron, and cuffs. Caps were gray with black bands, and the letters SG in front. At least four members of this company were photographed wearing large 'secession cockades' pinned to their plastron fronts.

The Fincastle Rifles, Co. D, 11th Virginia, were formed during December 1859, and hastily donned a 'fanciful uniform'

Right: Thomas B. Horton enlisted as a sergeant in the Southern Guards, Co. B, 11th Virginia Infantry, and was promoted to captain in April 1861. The fact that he carries a sword here would indicate that he received his dark gray hunting shirt with satinette plastron front around that time. Note the patches on his shoulders, and white dress gloves. (Eleanor S. Brockenbrough Library, the Museum of the Confederacy, Richmond, Virginia)

James Henry Woodson, Appomattox Rangers, Co. H, 2nd Virginia Cavalry, wears a uniform similar to that of the Lynchburg companies. Woodson's unit was raised in Appomattox County but was mustered into state service at Lynchburg. Hence he was probably outfitted there. (Russell Hicks Jr)

described in the Alexandria *Gazette* as being 'a plain linsey hunting shirt – black and red'. This was subsequently described by the *Frank Leslie's Illustrated Newspaper* correspondent reporting the execution of John Brown's accomplices at Charlestown as being 'a most picturesque uniform, being half Scotch' in style. The artist accompanying him illustrated this as a plaid, or tartan hunting shirt, together with 'green baise cape', plumed slouch hat, and knee-high stockings!

Other Lynchburg companies wearing hunting shirts made by the tailors and ladies of the city included the Lynchburg Artillery and the Beauregard Rifles, temporarily known as 'the Zouaves'. Regarding the former, artilleryman James McCanna was photographed sometime between late April and May 1861 wearing a gray shirt with plastron front removed showing herring bone-pattern trim, possibly red in color. Cuffs and collar were also in the same facing color. The Beauregard Rifles, also known as the Lynchburg Beauregards, who later re-organized as

Captain Marcellus N. Moorman's Company, Virginia Horse Artillery, were described as wearing 'gray pantaloons, gray shirts with green front, trimmed with black, and navy caps' soon after organization in April 1861. Upon their arrival in Richmond, the *Dispatch* reported them as having 'a peculiar red cap', which may bear witness to a continued 'zouave' influence. An unknown member of this unit was photographed with his green plastron removed revealing four narrow, vertical bands of black trim running from neck to waist. Collar and pointed cuffs were also faced with the same material.

Elsewhere in the state, the Appomatox Invincibles, who enlisted as Co. A, 44th Virginia Infantry on 26 April 1861, adopted a uniform of cloth made by the Crenshaw Woollen Mills, designed by company member First Lieutenant John M. Steptoe, consisting of 'gray pants with black stripes one inch-wide, a gray shirt with collar to turn down or throw open and trimmed with black cord. The cap also will be gray with a black band. The pants and shirt to be held to the waist with a patent lether [sic] belt with brass plate in front.'

During the Fall of 1860, two military companies were formed by the students of the University of Virginia. The Southern Guards, under Captain E. S. Hutter, wore a light blue pullover shirt fastened with three small buttons, and trimmed with dark blue around a low standing collar, pocket, buttoned front and cuffs. Their high-crowned forage caps were gray and quartered with black piping. Trousers were originally to be black, but an ambrotype of company member Henry Mitchie and friend shows gray pants with wide black seam stripes. The Sons of Liberty, commanded by Captain J. T. Toch, wore 'red shirts'.

In Richmond, the 179th Regiment Virginia Militia, embracing all of the city east of 10th Street, had taken steps to arm and clothe some of its companies for possible active service during February 1861. On the 4th of that month, it was recommended that the uniform of the regiment should consist of a 'Blue flannel cloth hunting shirt with blue fringe and Virginia buttons: pants, dark (civilian)'. It is not known how far this recommendation was acted upon, or how many of its companies were thus clothed. However, the Fireside Protectors, raised during January 1861 and subsequently known as the Virginia Life Guard, were attached to the 179th as 'a uniformed company of the line', and later volunteered for state service as Co. B, 15th Virginia Infantry wearing a uniform of this description, also manufactured at the Crenshaw Woollen Mills.

Virginia cavalry companies were particularly fond of wearing

hunting shirts. That worn by James Henry Woodson of the Appomatox Rangers, Co. H, 2nd Virginia Cavalry, was gray with light-colored plastron, collar and cuffs. William Worsley Mead of the Loudon Cavalry, Co. K, 6th Virginia Cavalry, wore a plain gray shirt trimmed with narrow braid around edges, collar and pockets. That worn by Bladen Dulany Lake of the Mountain Rangers, Co. A, 7th Virginia Cavalry, was gray faced with black in a broad band of facing color running down its buttoned front, and on collar, cuffs, and pocket tops.

Other Virginia cavalry units seem to have clung to their pre-war dress when they entered Confederate service. The Amelia Light Dragoons (Co. G) and the Loudon Light Horse (Co. H), 1st Virginia Cavalry, continued to wear their dark blue 1858 state regulation uniforms well into the summer of 1861. The latter took part in the charge on the 11th New York (Ellsworth's

The Sussex Light Dragoons, Co. H, 13th Virginia Cavalry, adopted a plain gray woollen shirt with small, rectangular plastron secured by four buttons on each side. Headgear consisted of a high-crowned dark blue forage cap, quartered with yellow piping, with the gilt letters SLD over crossed sabres in front. The man at centre has a light-colored seam stripe just visible on his trousers. (Eleanor S. Brockenbrough Library, The Museum of the Confederacy, Richmond, Virginia)

Fire Zouaves) at First Manassas. The Wise Troop, of Lynchburg, named after ex-Governor Henry A. Wise, was formed during November 1859, and adopted 'red coats', 'bright blue pants with a gold cord down the sides', and helmets with 'the brightest scarlet horsehair tufts hanging down behind them'. Later, during July 1861, and after this unit had entered war

Private Richard Henry Toler (right) of the Lynchburg Home Guard received his hunting shirt, possibly from the same source as Captain Horton, before being detailed on signal telegraph duty with E. P. Alexander in November 1861. Murray Forbes Taylor (left) also served under Alexander as an adjutant. (Russell Hicks Jr)

scarce in "the land of cotton", it was patched up with common bolting cloth.'

The Botetourt Dragoons, raised at Fincastle during January 1861 under Captain Andrew L. Pitzer, adopted a 'blue cloth suit, trimmed with yellow', which may be a further reference to the 1858 state uniform. During July 1861, the Boston *Courier* reported the seizure of 'a coat and cap belonging to the Old Dominion Dragoons [Co. B, 3rd Virginia Cavalry].' Taken by members of the Wightman Rifles, 4th Regiment Massachusetts Militia, near Fortress Monroe, they were described as follows: 'The material from which they are manufactured is heavy blue satinet, far superior in quality to the material of the clothing of our troops. The coat is strongly, though not handsomely, made. The cap, or ordinary army pattern, was made at Norfolk by W. H. C. Lovitt, and, judging from this specimen, the Massachusetts volunteers, when they capture that city, will find him a good man to patronize. It is ornamented with cross sabres in front, and bears in large brass letters, the initials of the company's name, "O.D.D." The coat appears to have seen some service, but is almost as good as new. A mischevious contemporary suggested that the coat be shown to the contractors for clothing for our volunteers.'

The Prince William Cavalry, who became Co. A, 4th Virginia Cavalry, proudly enlisted on 17 April 1861 in a uniform of gray cloth made at Kelly's Mills in Culpeper County, which consisted of 'a frock coat with one row of buttons up the front and one each side; connecting at the top with a gold lace V'. They also wore gray pants with 'yellow stripes, black hats with black plumes on the left side held up with crossed sabers and a shield with the letters PWC in front – a neat uniform in which the most insignificant must look his best . . .'

The first uniform of the Little Fork Rangers, also of Culpeper County, was: 'beautiful and conspicuous – red, white, blue and yellow. They would have furnished a splendid target for Yankee bullets, had they worn them into battle, but fortunately they did not. Blue caps, red cut-away jackets with yellow stripes designated their branch of service – cavalry. This was their uniform during the summer and fall of 1860. During the winter and early spring of 1861, they wore black trousers with a red stripe down the seam.'

After the secession of Virginia on 7 April 1861, the Rangers purchased gray cloth from the Swartz Mills at Waterloo, which was cut by a tailor at Warrenton and put together into uniforms by the ladies of the neighbourhood. They went on to become Co. D of the 4th Virginia Cavalry.

service as Co. B, 2nd Virginia Cavalry, the *New York Times* reported that 'a uniform coat taken from a secession captain [John S. Langhorne] of the "Wise Cavalry" was on exhibition in Philadelphia. It was further described as being 'scarlet faced with black velvet, on which are two rows of bell buttons, on the face of which are the Virginia arms with the motto "Sic semper tyrannis". It was a curious looking uniform, and as lining was

Regarding early war artillery uniforms, the Bedford Light Artillery made 'a fine appearance' in their uniform made 'of dark blue material, the coat buttoning straight up the front, fastened at the waist by a belt, with a short skirt below it'. The pants and coat were trimmed with red with 'a cap to match, mounted with two brass cannon crossed obliquely'.

The zouave influence was represented in Virginia by the Richmond Zouaves, who organized under Captain Edward McConnell Jr during May 1861. Their uniforms were made by the ladies of the Monumental Episcopal Church, and were probably based on a typical colorful zouave pattern, consisting of a blue jacket and orange baggy trousers. On 10 June, the Richmond *Daily Whig* published the following by 'Le Zouave', an anonymous member of the unit: 'At drill hours our Armory [Corinthian Hall] presents quite an animated scene, and uniforms other than the blue and orange, mingle cum toga civile. Tonight, two of the Zouaves Francais were present and expressed themselves well pleased at our appearance and movements. All thanks to the courteous Frenchmen, whether we deserve the compliments or not.'

Presumably the latter is a reference to members of Coppen's Battalion of Louisiana Zouaves who had arrived in the city three days earlier. A complete zouave uniform, which possibly belonged to an officer of the Richmond Zouaves, survives in the collection of the Chicago Historical Society. The navy blue jacket is edged with interwoven gold braid, and is fastened together at the neck by two small buttons or studs secured through a small gold edged tab. The sleeves are decorated with a white clover-leaf design outlined with gold braid, and are slashed and buttoned at the underseam by six small brass buttons bearing the Virginia State seal. The scarlet pants with gold braid seam stripes are in the chasseur-style, being gathered at the waist with pleats, and below the knee into narrow cuffs fastened by buckles or buttons. The chasseur-pattern forage cap is scarlet with gold piping and Hungarian knot on the crown. The blue wool cummerbund has a short scarlet fringe.

A Richmond Zouave, Co. E, 44th Virginia Infantry. (From artefacts and descriptions by Ron Field)

The Richmond Zouaves also adopted leggings of white ducking which F. Thomas of Richmond undertook to make for 75 cents a pair. However when Captain McConnel called to collect them, Thomas refused to hand the goods over claiming that he had charged $1.50 a pair. McConnell handed over the extra cash, but subsequently hauled Thomas through the Mayor's Court on charges of fraudulently obtaining '$5.00, one roll of ducking, and one gross of buckles'!

By 6 September 1861, a C.S. Quartermaster Department Clothing Bureau had been set up in Richmond, and Virginians became some of the first troops in Confederate service to receive supplies of clothing from the central government. This source of clothing continued to be supplemented by the efforts of various ladies aid societies across the state. A supply of state manufactured clothing was particularly essential for those troops not in Confederate service. Units making up the Virginia State Line, established on 15 May 1862, were clothed purely on this basis. A Quartermaster Depot established at Wytheville under Captain J. B. Goodloe had, by 27 December 1862, manufactured the following articles: '6,912 shirts, 6,708 drawers, 3,368 jackets, 3,960 pants, 1,897 overcoats, 1,764 military caps.' In his 1862 report, Quartermaster General L. R. Smoots remarked: 'No efforts or expense have been spared on the part of this office, to supply the wants of the state line troops.'

Arkansas

Throughout the decade prior to the Civil War, the enrolled, or non-uniformed, militia of Arkansas was divided into two divisions: the First being designated to the western portion of the state with its Indian frontier, while the Second embraced the remainder. Within each country, the militia laws authorized the formation of four uniformed volunteer militia companies: one each of artillery, cavalry, infantry and light infantry. Most counties were devoid of such

Company H, 3rd Regiment State Infantry, photographed at Arkadephia in June 1861. No two men are dressed alike. They wear pullover shirts of various cuts and shades, some with trim of different colors around the pockets, cuffs and collars. All wear slouch hats, and at least 30 hold D-guard Bowie knives or large side knives. Many have tin cups attached to their belts, and wear what appear to be canvas packs on their backs. The man second row from the front wears sunglasses, whilst a black confederate volunteer stands in the fourth row, fourth from the right!
(General Sweeny's Museum, Republic, Missouri)

Second Lieutenant, Fort Smith Rifles, Co. A or D, 3rd Arkansas State Infantry (left); Color Sergeant, Belle Point Guards, 5th Arkansas State Infantry (centre); Sergeant, Davis Blues, Co. F, 5th Arkansas State Infantry (right). (From photographs by Ron Field)

commands, but by 1860 a few, like Phillips and Pulaski, had one or more volunteer companies of reasonably long standing. In Pulaski County these included the Capital Guards, established around 1840; the Pulaski Lancers, a mounted company under Captain Thomas J. Churchill; and the Totten Artillery commanded by Captain W. E. Woodruff Jr. These companies were permitted to select and procure their own uniforms in whatever style and color they saw fit to choose.

In addition to this, the Arkansas Military Institute had existed at Tulip, in Dallas County, since 1850. Modelled on the

Virginia Military Institute, it apparently adopted the gray dress and fatigue uniforms of that revered establishment. Its doors were closed in 1861 as the cadets under Captain James B. Williamson formed Co. I, 4th Arkansas Infantry.

On 21 January 1861, Governor Henry M. Rector approved

These two Arkansians wear a variety of fatigue and civilian shirts. Private James McDavid Flynt (left), 2nd Arkansas Infantry, was killed at Murfreesboro. Private William Martin Flynt (centre), 2nd Arkansas Infantry, died 25 July 1865.

two acts of the legislature which reorganized the militia, and placed Arkansas in a more defensible position. The raising of further volunteer companies was encouraged, and moves were made to arm them, especially those units being formed along the western borders of the state. At the same time the legislature ruled that militia officers were to wear the same uniform as the U.S. Army, 'except commissioned officers of companies, who shall be allowed to adopt any uniform which they may see proper'.

Arkansas was largely unprepared to manufacture uniforms when secession took place on 6 May 1861. The only clothing factory was situated at Nashville in the far southwest corner of the state. Hence, virtually all the clothing supplied to regiments raised in 1861 was improvised and largely homemade. The Military Board established on 15 May, with Governor Rector as president, created the Army of Arkansas, a force comprising the 1st through 5th State Regiments enlisted for six months state defense. These regiments embraced most of the former volunteer militia, who mostly enlisted in their various pre-War uniforms. Second Lieutenant Decatur McDonald of the Fort Smith Rifles, Co. D, 3rd Regiment State Infantry, was photographed in a short-skirted gray frock coat, darker gray trousers, and plumed hat pinned up on the right. Others in his company wore gray coats and pants trimmed with buff braid. Private Clem McCulloch of the Van Buren Frontier Guards, in the same regiment, was pictured on 18 May 1861, wearing a nine-button dark gray, or blue, sack coat with turned-down collar, and rectangular U.S. 'eagle' plate fastening his waist belt.

Private John Harrison Raleigh, 11th Arkansas Infantry, was captured at Island No. 10. Note the small heart-shaped patch sewn on his breast. (General Sweeny's Museum, Republic, Missouri)

Judging by the uniform worn by Sergeant Simeon McCown when he posed for an ambrotype during the summer of 1861, the Davis Blues, raised in Nashville, Arkansas, by Captain A. S. Cabell, were particularly well clothed. Designated Co. F of the 5th State Infantry, this company's uniform was probably made at the factory at that place. His gray woollen frock coat was trimmed with either dark blue or black braid across the chest, collar and sleeves.

Color Sergeant Paul Richard Krone, of the Belle Point Guards, a company of the 5th State Infantry raised among the German population of Fort Smith, was photographed wearing a dark blue frock coat, mid-blue trousers, and holding a M1851

dark blue dress cap with brass letters BPG topped with feather plume. His rank was indicated by three inverted chevrons on each upper arm. John H. Rivers of the Centrepoint Riflemen, also of the Fifth, recalled: 'We had Uniforms made at home, all alike, the shirts were made of hickory checks, and had red stripes across the breast, five in number: And the pants were out of some thin goods: They were blue, and had red stripes on the outside of each leg, about an inch wide: We were proud of Our Uniforms.'

The 1st Arkansas Volunteer Infantry (Fagan's), raised for 12 months Confederate service at the same time as the State Regiments, wore uniforms of equally great variety. The Eldorado Sentinels, Co. A, were 'well uniformed' in neat gray caps and frock coats, with black cap band, collar and cuffs. Twenty-four men from this unit left home without these items, and were 'uniformed in Virginia at [their] own expense'. Taking advantage of earlier state legislature permitting company grade officers to choose their own uniforms, Captain Charles S. Stark, commanding the Clark County Volunteers, Co. B, chose to wear a light gray coat trimmed, apparently, in light blue, while his light blue pants carried a gold stripe. His coat had three rows of nine buttons, with three small buttons up the front of the cuffs. His company possibly wore a similar uniform. The Camden Knights, Co. C, wore dark blue caps, pants and hunting shirts, the latter cut in varying styles, either plain or with light blue trim. The letters CK occasionally embroidered on their cap fronts were a personalized touch. The Jacksonport Guards, Co. G, adopted light gray caps and trousers, with black cap bands and seam stripes. Their dark gray blouses had the company initials JG appliqued on either side of the breast in black cloth capital letters. In line with state legislature regarding officers above company grade, Colonel James F. Fagan wore a dark blue frock coat with two rows of five buttons and federal style shoulder straps, and a French-style forage cap with gold rank braid.

The 6th Arkansas Infantry, raised at Little Rock by Colonel Richard Lyon during June 1861, spent most of its time in the Western theatre of the war. The City Guard, Co. H, from Camden, enlisted in 'gray roundabout and pants trimmed with red', and 'glazed caps'. William Shores, of this company, was photographed wearing a black Mexican War-pattern cap. The Ouchita Grays, Co. K, wore 'gray roundabouts and pants trimmed with green', with glazed caps.

An attempt to overcome the lack of uniformity within these

The Totten Battery, later renamed the Pulaski Battery, was organized by William E. Woodruff, Jr, in 1860. Lieutenant Omar Weaver (left) was killed at Wilson's Creek. (General Sweeny's Museum, Republic, Missouri)

Private C. F. Wrenfrey, 1st Arkansas State Cavalry, enlisted in May 1861. He wears a nine-button 'roundabout', or shell jacket, with shoulder straps, and holds a Smith and Wesson revolver, a weapon popular with Confederates early in the war. (General Sweeny's Museum, Republic, Missouri)

regiments, and probably even within some companies, was observed by a correspondent of the *Register* of Rock Island, Illinois, on 11 September 1861: 'The uniform of the Confederate army [of the West] is multiform. They are not uniformed at all, and generally speaking, it is impossible to distinguish a Colonel from a private. The only mark of distinction about them, except for their arms, is a piece of flannel stitched to the left shoulder. I was told that white

flannel was the distinguishing mark of the troops, yellow that of Arkansas, red that of Louisiana, and so on. Of course this only applies to the Southwest.'

On 15 July 1861, the Military Board agreed to transfer Arkansas commands to the Confederacy. On this occasion it was also agreed that the state should furnish its men with clothing, in return for which it would be recompensed by the War Department at commutation rates. During the following month, the Military Board sent circular letters to all counties asking for citizens to collect clothing for the soldiers and turn it over to the county judge, clerk or sheriff. The Board proposed to pay citizens for the clothing received with Arkansas or Confederate bonds. The Crockett Rifles, Co. H, 1st Arkansas (Fagan's), named after their original commander Captain Robert H. Crockett, left home without arms or uniforms. Company member Wiley A. Washburn, recalled: 'We immediately proceed[ed] to Va. Stoped [sic] at Lynchburg[,] recd our uniforms and guns. The cloth was bou[g]ht by funds recd from the State.'

Various volunteer aid societies throughout the state supplemented the efforts of the Military Board. Organizations such as the Randolph County Central Committee raised funds and purchased 'equipment for volunteers', which was sent on to Governor Rector. Sometimes, committees devoted their labours to one particular company. The Union County Central Committee purchased 'provisions, clothing, [and] arms' specifically for the Lisbon Invincibles, a unit which became Co. I, 6th Arkansas Volunteer Infantry. The citizens of Hempstead supplied the Southern Defenders, a Home Guard company, with 'one coat; two pairs of pants; two pairs of socks; and two pairs of drawers'. Gold medals were awarded to encourage the state's womenfolk to make cloth. During a period of four months, Mrs. Sallie Bangs, a widow of Sulphur Springs, wove 'a hundred and eight yards of jeans and seventy-eight yards of plain cloth . . . also she made cloth for her son who was in the army'.

Possibly following the lead of other states in the Confederacy, the Board also established workshops for the manufacture of uniforms and equipage at the state penitentiary on the outskirts of Little Rock, where the capitol building now stands. By 18 November 1861, a committee was able to report to the legislature that the penitentiary had fabricated for the army 3000 uniforms, 8000 pairs of shoes, 250 wagons, 100 sets of wagon and artillery harness, 500 drums, 200 tents, 600 knapsacks and 500 cartridge boxes. Virtually every member of Fagan's 1st Arkansas were in receipt of 'a new uniform, coarse but serviceable', possibly supplied via this source, by November 1861. The usual clothing provided seems to have been frock coats and pants of jean, with gray forage caps. The former usually had either eight- or nine-button fronts, and collars and cuffs faced with either dark blue or black. Private L. Yates of Co. B, 18th Arkansas Infantry, mustered into Confederate service

Private Thomas Bolding, 24th Arkansas Infantry (Portlock's), wears an unusual shell jacket. Fastened by five large gilt buttons, it has buttoned-down pockets on each breast – reminiscent of jackets issued to some Georgia troops. (General Sweeny's Museum, Republic, Missouri)

on 12 march 1862 in an eight-button version of this garment. During the same month, two members of the 23rd Arkansas Infantry were photographed wearing nine-button coats. An officers' version of this uniform, with two rows of five buttons, collar and cuffs faced black, or other branch service color, and three small buttons on cuff front, may also have existed.

Regarding mounted units, a tinted image of Mark Noble, a trooper in the 2nd Arkansas Cavalry, raised during February 1862 under Colonel Charles W. Phifer, indicates that he wore a nine-button gray frock coat with black collar and plain sleeves; light blue trousers; and a black hat pinned up on the left, with a large black plume held by a yellow metal pin or socket. His shoulder and waist belts were white leather. This may represent an early war uniform, as many members of this regiment were originally part of Phifer's Battalion of Cavalry.

Later in the war, this state uniform issuance largely changed to shell jackets and felt hats. A description of the brigade commanded by General St John R. Liddell (Cleburne's division of Hardee's corps, Army of Tennessee), which consisted of the 2nd, 5th, 6th, 7th, and 8th Arkansas Infantry regiments, were described in June 1863 as being 'well clothed, though without any attempt at uniformity in color or cut, but nearly all were dressed either in gray or brown coats and felt hats . . . many of the soldiers had taken off their coats and marched past the general in their shirt sleeves'.

Photographic evidence indicates that various styles of jackets and coats were issued to Arkansas troops during the second year of the war, and it is difficult to ascertain whether these garments were of state, or C.S. Quartermaster, provenance. Private Francis Warford was issued a gray sack coat with four bone buttons, and open pocket on the left breast, some time after his enlistment in the 19th Arkansas Infantry on 1 March 1862. Second Lieutenant William W. Crump wore a plain, tight-fitting gray coat devoid of rank insignia, with single rows of eight small gilt buttons, some time after beginning his service with Co. D, 27th Arkansas Infantry, in February 1862. Private Steven K. Porter enlisted in Co. C, 1st Arkansas Cavalry, raised and commanded by Colonel Archibald S. Dobbin in July 1863, wearing a light gray pullover shirt. In a late war image taken in Mobile, Alabama, Joseph V. Bogy, of the Appeal Battery, Arkansas Light Artillery, wore a long gray frock coat with two rows of seven wooden buttons, plain gray pants, forage cap with dark, possibly red, band, and gilt crossed canon insignia on the front.

Tennessee

The uniform regulations in force for Volunteer companies in Tennessee on the eve of the Civil War were based on the 'Militia Laws' of 1840. That for 'Generals and general staff' was to be: 'of the same grade as in the United States army'. Light infantry were to wear: 'long blue hunting shirts, blue pantaloons, round black hat and red plumes'; Riflemen: 'long black hunting shirts, black pantaloons, hats as infantry, and white plumes'; Cavalry: 'Each regiment of cavalry may choose the quality of the uniform for their officers and privates, and they are authorized to use domestic manufactures for the same: Provided, nevertheless, that the coats and pantaloons of each officer and private . . . shall be of a deep blue color.' This law also stated that it was permissible for a 'company to choose its own uniform and uniform themselves'. Hence a wide variety of military dress was evident within the states.

The militia system these regulations applied to consisted theoretically of four 'divisions' embracing about 160 'regiments' which were scattered throughout the state. A small number of companies of Volunteer Militia were attached to those regiments located in the regions of Nashville and Memphis. By July 1858, those in Memphis had formed into a battalion which, on 22 March 1860, was organized under Colonel W. H. Carroll into the 154th Regiment of Tennessee Volunteers, using a number in the old militia series. The companies in this regiment included the Memphis Light Guard, the Bluff City Grays, the Jackson Guards, the Harris Zouave Cadets, the Hickory Rifles, the Henry Guards, the Beauregards, the Crockett Rangers, the McNairy Guards, and the Sons of Liberty. Of these, the Harris Zouave Cadets is the most interesting. Originally to be called the Harris Cadets, in honour of Governor Isham G. Harris, the company was organized in June 1860, under the command of Captain C. Sherwin. By August, their name had been changed to the Harris Zouave Cadets, or Memphis Zouaves, having clearly been influenced by the drill tour of Ellsworth's zouave Cadets that year. Later the same month, they were reported to be wearing 'the Zouave "fatigue" dress consisting of flowing pants with a scarlet stripe, blue roundabout, bound with the same color and plain blue cap'. During a 'Secession Demonstration' which took place by torch-light on the night of 8 February 1861, they paraded

Captain Alexander E. Patton, Co. A, 1st Tennessee Infantry (Turney's), initially wore a dark shirt with polka-dotted band sewn down the front, over which was slung a broad webbing-type shoulder belt. (Stephen E. Lister)

'dressed in their gorgeous scarlet costumes', which suggests they may also have adopted a full zouave uniform. Another company worthy of note being formed in Memphis during this period was the Highland Guard, raised among the 'Scotch' citizens, who were to be dressed in 'the picturesque uniform of the Highlands of Scotland, plaid, kilt and trews'. It is not known whether the Garibaldi Guards, recruited amongst the Italian population of the city ever adopted a distinctive uniform.

In Nashville a Volunteer Battalion of three companies

evolved out of the Rock City Guard, a unit formed in 1860 and named after the ancient nickname of the capital city of Tennessee.

The people of the state were seriously divided in their views on secession from the Union during the early months of 1861. Nonetheless, Governor Harris held extreme pro-slavery tendencies and was in close liaison with Southern leaders. In the wake of success which accompanied the first wave of 'secession fever' to sweep the South, the legislature of the 'Volunteer State' was sufficiently impressed, and determined to enter into a military league with the Confederacy on 6 May 1861. At the same time an act was passed 'to raise, organize and equip a provisional force' to consist of 25,000 men with 30,000 in reserve.

The 'Regulations adopted for the provisional force of the

Tennessee Riflemen entering Winchester from Stratsburg. Published in Harper's Weekly on 6 July 1861, the only unit this could represent is Turney's 1st Tennessee Volunteers who arrived in Virginia about two months prior to this date. Described as being 'mostly hunters and men used to outdoor life', they were armed with 'tomahawk, bowie-knife, and revolver', as well as shoulder arms. The uniform of these men is reminiscent of the hats, hunting shirts and black pants prescribed for Tennessee volunteer militia. Note the officers wear darker, possibly blue, Federal-style frock coats and trousers.

Tennessee volunteers', which accompanied this act, were based on the U.S. regulations of 1857/58. Accordingly, infantry wore dark blue frock coats with sky-blue edging. The number of the regiment was worn on the collar. Cavalry, dragoons and mounted rifles wore jackets. Artillery, infantry, mounted rifles and dragoons wore dress caps. Cavalry wore hats. All branches of service wore sky-blue pants.

At the same time, 'A Digest of the Militia Laws of Tennessee' stated: 'Tennessee having separated herself from the Federal Union, of course the officers will discontinue that uniform.'

Even before these events, Harris had commenced to raise a state army. The first unit to be formed was the 1st Tennessee Volunteer Infantry (also known as the 1st Confederate Infantry), hastily recruited in the mountain counties of the Middle Tennessee by Colonel Peter Turney. Fully organized by 21 April 1861, this regiment went straight into Confederate service, and was encamped in Virginia by 5 May. Most of the companies of Turney's First marched off to war in their civilian clothes and were uniformed in the vicinity of Richmond by the Confederate Government. The Tullahoma Guards, Co. I, acquired distinctive blue caps with long bills. Once these troops had arrived in Virginia, the central government presumably placed orders with local clothiers for uniforms.

Possibly adopting a very liberal interpretation of the antiquated Tennessee state militia uniform regulations, two officers of the Boon's Creek Minute Men, Co. K, – Captain Newton C. Davis and Lieutenant T. J. Sugg – were subsequently photographed wearing nine-button dark blue, cassimere frock coats, and trousers of the same cloth with broad light-colored seam stripes. Rank was indicated by Federal-style shoulder straps and waist sashes. Captain Davis wore a Hardee hat looped up on the left after Federal-style shoulder straps and waist sashes. Captain Davis wore a Hardee hat looped up on the left after Federal regulations for infantry, whilst Lieutenant Sugg wore a dark blue forage cap with light-colored band, which may have represented part of the fatigue dress of this company.

A similar, if not identical, style of officers' uniform was in use in regiments including the 11th, 12th and 16th Tennessee Infantry, during June 1861. This consisted of a dark blue frock coat with light-colored trim around the bottom of the collar only, plain sleeves, and collar rank consisting of stars and bars, based on Confederate States regulations unofficially published in the New Orleans press in May 1861.

Two unidentified Tennessee infantrymen were photographed by C. Rees of Richmond wearing seven-button gray frock coats with collars and shoulder straps edged with dark-colored trim. Trousers were also gray with black seam stripes. Another unidentified member of the Fayetteville Guard, Co. G, wore a

Private Hershel Bel Wilson, Co. G, 23rd Tennessee Infantry (left) and Captain Samuel B. Wilson, Co. A, 45th Tennessee Infantry (right). Captain Wilson's dark blue uniform is based on the Tennessee state militia uniform regulations, which in turn were loosely based on those of the U.S. Army as prescribed in 1840. Private Wilson's shoulder and waist belts are of white webbing. His cap pouch is of the type manufactured at the Baton Rouge Arsenal in New Orleans, whilst he holds a M1842 Musket in the 'Shoulder Arms' position. (U.S. Army Military History Institute/Jim Enos)

nine-button gray shell jacket with black facing on collar and cuffs; gray pants with narrow light-colored seam stripes; and a gray forage cap with black band bearing the brass letters FG in front. The latter may represent later war quartermaster issue.

Other early war units included the Rock City Guard, who wore a chasseur-style uniform consisting of red caps, red flannel trousers and brass-buttoned blue coats in January 1861. Expanded

Private Samuel H. Dunscomb, Co. E, 3rd Battalion Tennessee Infantry, also known as the Memphis Battalion. The letters WR on his hat may indicate that he was a member of the Washington Rifles, a well-established volunteer militia company in Memphis, when this tintype was taken. (David Wynn Vaughan collection)

First Sergeant Elbert Monroe Snipes, 37th Tennessee Infantry. His neck tie almost obscures the solid facing on his collar. (Dan Snipes, descendant)

to a battalion of three companies by April, they joined the ranks of the 1st Tennessee Infantry (Maney's) wearing a service uniform consisting of a nine-button gray shell jacket with light-colored facing on collar and cuffs; light gray, or pale blue pants, with dark seam stripes; and forage caps bearing company letters A, B and C in front. Sam Watkins of the Maury Grays, Co. H, wore a gray frock coat with dark blue collar, five small buttons on slash sleeves, and black broad-brimmed hat bearing the letter H. Another member of this company wore the same uniform, with a white feather plume in his hat.

The 3rd Tennessee Infantry, under Colonel John C. Brown,

was organized at Lynnville on 16 May, and mustered into Confederate service on 7 August 1861. Private James F. Walker of Company D wore a gray fatigue shirt with light-colored facing edged with black on buttoned front, cuffs and probably collar. His tall-crowned forage cap quartered with yellow piping was in exactly the same style as that worn by members of the Bate's 2nd Tennessee Infantry. Private John W. McCown of Company C, 3rd (Memphis) Tennessee Battalion, wore a light gray fatigue shirt with turned down collar, pants of the same material with broad dark seam stripes, and gray cap with dark band. John Johnston recalled receiving 'a gray flannel shirt, gray pants with a dark stripe down each leg and gray coats', when he enlisted in The Danes, Co. K, 6th Tennessee Infantry. The Jackson Grays, of the same regiment, wore a gray coat with black collar, and gray cap with company letter G on its dark band.

Prior to the war, the 1st Company, Tennessee Artillery Corps, commanded by Captain Arthur M. Rutledge, wore blue frock coats, pants and forage cap, with havelock. During May 1861, this unit changed to a short gray coat, gray pants with red seam stripes, and gray felt hat with brass cross cannon insignia. Sergeant Burr Bannister of the 2nd Tennessee Field Battery, commanded by Captain Thomas K. Porter, wore a dark blue M1847 forage cap with light band, and gray frock coat with solid red collar.

Many of the uniforms worn by these early war troops were supplied by the Military and Financial Board of the State of Tennessee, which had been established by 6 May 1861. This Board was composed of three businessmen: Nashville attorney and former governor, Neil S. Brown; influential owner of Belle Meade plantation, William Giles Harding; and Clarksville attorney, James E. Bailey. At the beginning of May, regimental commanders were instructed to 'draw from the military store cloth, lining, trimmings, buttons & threads for uniforming'. Assistant Quartermaster General E. Foster Cheatham was given a six-step set of instructions outlining how to purchase the cloth, turn it over to contractors, specify the sizes to be made, and deliver the packaged uniforms to the captains of companies.

Some of the first cloth acquired was 'blue jeans'. Other types available on a commercial basis included 'Cadet Gray Satinets, Blue Satinets, Gray Wool Tweeds, Gray Wool Flannels'. Irby, Morgan & Co., of Nashville, advertised: 'Gray Wool Overshirts' throughout the South. In Memphis, Southworth, Nance & Co., on Main Street, stocked 'Gray and Cadet Cassimeres and Jeans [and] Army Blue Broadcloths'. Among other things, Strauss, Lehman & Co., supplied 'Jeans Pants, Check & Hickory Shirts, Gold Lace and Trimmings, [and] Drab Hats'. Miller & Dunn sold black, brown, gray, and pearl 'wide brim hats'. The 'Southern Cap Manufactory' owned by J. D. Blumenthal, guaranteed that military companies would be 'furnished with any style of Caps desired'. Francisco & Co., were making 'the Zouave Military Cap' by the end of May 1861.

Much of the cloth supplied to the Military and Financial Board was made by the womenfolk of Tennessee. On 8 August 1861, a notice was published in all the newspapers of the state appealing to 'the wives, mothers & daughters of Tennessee to manufacture woolen goods & stockings for those who are defending their homes . . .' It was suggested that 'each lady . . . shall prepare goods for one suit of clothing & knit two pairs of stockings. If this shall be done, every soldier will be amply clothed & provided against the suffering of a winter campaign.' Organizations such as the 'South Memphis Ladies' Sewing Society' not only provided cloth for the Board, but made up uniforms for the military companies of the city.

Several men from different Tennessee regiments were photographed during the second year of the war wearing remarkably similar uniforms, which suggests a common source of state supply. A hand-tinted image of Private Robert Patterson of Company F, 55th Tennessee Infantry, a unit raised in February 1862 and commanded originally by Colonel Alexander J. Brown, shows a nine-button dark blue/gray frock coat, and pants, with light blue solid collar and cuffs. Presumably before he became an adjutant of the same regiment, Robert B. Hurt Jr, was photographed wearing a seven-button coat of the same shade, collar and cuff facings. Also, Private John W. Branch, Co. D, 12th Tennessee Infantry, a regiment reorganized in 1862, wore a coat of exactly the same pattern as Patterson. Towards the end of that year, Tennessee troops began to receive some clothing via the Confederate Quartermaster department.

M1847 forage cap worn by an officer in the Hardeman Avengers, Co. B, 6th Battalion Tennessee Cavalry. (From a photograph by Ron Field)

North Carolina

The first troops to enter active duty from the 'Old North State' were 10 uniformed volunteer companies organized for six months service on 13 May 1861 into the 1st Regiment North Carolina Infantry. This regiment went on to take part in the first large-scale land battle of the Civil War, which took place at Big Bethel on 10 June 1861. The companies which made up this command were some of the oldest in the state. They arrived at the capital wearing their ante-bellum uniforms, probably combined with elements of service dress. Some time prior to the conflict, Second Lieutenant William S. Long of the Edgecombe Guards, was photographed wearing a dark blue frock coat with a lighter facing color on collar, epaulette keeps, and cuffs. His sash sleeves were ornamented with eight buttons each. Rank was indicated by gold lace collar loops, and brass epaulettes with narrow gold-bullion fringe. His trousers were also dark blue with broad light-colored seam stripes. Presumably the NCOs and enlisted men of this company wore a similar uniform with facing color appropriate to their rank.

Captain Egbert A. Ross, commanding the Charlotte Grays, of Mecklenburg County, wore a gray pullover shirt with full sleeves, narrow cuffs, and dark facing color on turned down collar and buttoned front. Rank was indicated by Federal-style shoulder straps sewn to the shoulders of his shirt. His pants were also gray with black seam stripes edged with gold. Ross probably wore this uniform at the head of his company at Big Bethel.

John Thomas Jones, of the Orange Light Infantry, was twice photographed wearing a single-breasted nine-button gray frock coat with dark piping on collar and pointed cuffs. The collar was also decorated with a dark lace loop terminating in a single small button. The cuff had a small button sewn at its point. His headgear consisted of a Model 1839 U.S. forage cap with light-colored band, and the letters OLI on the front. He wore plain white cotton summer pants.

The Buncombe Rifles were organized at Asheville during December 1850. According to the Charleston *Daily Courier* of 9 January 1860, this company adopted a 'uniform of steel-mixed Rock Island cassimere, made in Mecklenburg County'. Some time prior to the war, the unit commander, Captain William W. McDowell, was photographed wearing his full dress uniform, which consisted of a single-breasted, seven-button dark steel-gray, frock coat with collar and cuffs edged with light-colored lace, and double row of piping down front edge and around coat

The Iredell Blues, a volunteer militia company, parade in their full dress uniforms, with white summer pants, in front of Stockton Hall in Statesville, ca. 1860. Note the feather plumes fastened to their Mexican War-style caps, and tail coats. Most carry muskets with bayonets, but six men on the left next to the musicians have carbine-like weapons with shortened forestocks. (North Carolina Division of Archives and History)

skirts. Rank was indicted by epaulettes and four chevrons on each upper sleeve. His trousers were the same color, trimmed with broad light-colored seam stripes. Headgear consisted of a tall-crowned black hat pinned up on the left with a star insignia, while the front bore the letters BR set within a metal wreath. The uniform for enlisted men seems to have been much simpler, and consisted of a single-breasted, seven-button plain, steel-gray frock coat with three large buttons sewn at wide intervals vertically on the front of each sleeve. Coat skirts may have had a broad band of trim, similar in style to many South Carolina companies.

According to an image of an unidentified officer, the LaFayette Light Infantry wore dark blue frock coats, light blue trousers, and Model 1851 dress caps with tall feather plume, before the war. Doubtless, a service dress would have replaced much of this by 1861.

The Enfield Rifles, of Halifax Company, wore 'shiny-visored' forage caps, and a 'bright blue tunic' with light-colored trim around collar and on epaulette keeps. Pantaloons were the same color. The Southern Stars, who hastily changed their name from Lincoln Guards, in 1861, volunteered in nine-button gray frock coats. One member, and possibly the whole company, wore a large five-pointed star embroidered on his left breast. Their slouch hats were also decorated with a star-shaped brass pin.

Other volunteer militia companies called into service during the first weeks of conflict included the Thomasville Rifles, who later became Co. B, 14th Regiment North Carolina Troops (4th Regiment N.C. Volunteers). Formed in 1859, they adopted Hardee hats with stamped brass bugle horn insignia for riflemen, and dark blue frock coats and pants probably faced with green collar, cuffs and epaulettes. This company appears to have quickly acquired a new issue of gray coats faced green after the beginning of the war. The Guilford Grays, organized in Greensboro during 1860, wore a 'frock coat, single-breasted . . . pants to match, with black stripe, waist belt of black leather'.

With little knowledge of the regulations prescribed by the Confederate Government, many of the newly forming companies in North Carolina adopted uniforms of their own choice. The Moore's Creek Rifle Guards acquired light blue forage caps, and dark blue nine-button frock coats with red cuffs. The Mountain Tigers volunteered in six-button plain gray frock coats, with very large outside pockets on their right breasts. The Caldwell Rough and Ready Boys chose plain, possibly red, overshirts and light-colored kepis. The Poplar Spring Grays

Second Lieutenant Charles Betts Cook wears the dark blue full dress uniform of the Fayetteville Independent Light Infantry. One of the oldest volunteer militia companies in North Carolina, it became Company H, 1st Regiment N.C. Volunteers in 1861. (North Carolina Division of Archives and History)

Right: John Lawson Wrenn, may be the same man as the 'John A. Wren' who served as a private in the Buncombe Rangers, Co. G, 1st Regiment N.C. Cavalry. His unusual shell jacket, worn over a chequered civilian shirt, may be trimmed yellow in branch service color. Likewise his pants. He clearly enjoyed a cigar. (North Carolina Division of Archives and History)

wore very substantial seven-button gray frock coats with light-colored edging around collar, cuffs, and across their shoulders. The Montgomery Grays adopted nine-button gray frock coats with bars of dark tape-trim across their chests.

One of the most reputable sources for cloth in North Carolina

Private William C. Steele, Company D, 33rd Regiment, N.C. Troops, wears the six-button gray sack with sewn-down black epaulettes specified in uniform regulations issued by the North Carolina adjutant general in 1861. His cap appears to be dark blue. Accoutrements are black leather, whilst his hand rests on a tin drum canteen. (North Carolina Division of Archives and History)

situated in Iredell County. Cotton factories were also operating in Yadkin, Surry, Catawba, Cumberland, and elsewhere.

Troops organizing for war in 1861 found a great variety of clothing available for purchase in cities such as Raleigh and Wilmington. E. L. Harding, in the capital, advertised 'Military Goods just received from Richmond, Virginia', which included 'Gray Flannel shirts for soldiers'. These were also available in red, 'Checked Gingham', and 'Mixed Cassimere'. O. S. Baldwin, of Wilmington, advised that he was 'Contracting for Making and Trimming Uniforms', for those companies with their own cloth.

An anonymous letter to the editor of the Raleigh *North Carolina Standard*, published on 1 May 1861, urged the units organizing for war to buy uniforms of North Carolina gray cassimere. 'Its advantages', it was argued, were that it '. . . is cheap, that it will last well, and the experiments made by the French Emperor prove that gray is the most difficult color to take sight upon, hence is less often hit. Again, it is the product of our own soil. I have lately seen a company uniformed in blue broadcloth and Northern blue cassimere. Now, that is just the uniform of the regular U.S. troops, further it is of northern make and very expensive. If a man expects to go into service there is no sense in his wearing his ball-room clothes, no more than there is in his going into a pig-pen with them.'

The first attempt by state authorities to regulate the clothing of its military forces was partial and makeshift. In a general order of 20 April 1861, Adjutant General John F. Hoke directed that volunteers were to wear 'blue or gray blouses'. A much more substantial effort was made on 23 May, when Governor John W. Ellis appointed a board of officers to determine a uniform for the new regiments of State Troops and volunteers being rapidly formed. Their findings were formalized in General Orders No. 1 on 27 May, which created a uniform which hereafter will be called the state 1861 pattern. In its several varieties, this uniform was worn by most of North Carolina's soldiers throughout the remainder of the conflict. Details of it were prescribed by

and, indeed, throughout the South during the years before the war, was the Rock Island Manufacturing Company of Charlotte, in Mecklenburg County. Run by Young & Wriston, they produced 'a very superior article of goods for uniforms', and their 'Cassimeres' won several awards at State Fairs during 1860. Other antebellum firms producing 'yarn and cotton osnaburgs' included the Eagle Mills, owned by Messrs. Colvert & Co.; and the mills owned by W. Turner, at Turnersburg – both

Right: The Cathey brothers, of Jackson County, served in the Jackson Rangers, or Jackson Volunteers, a unit which became Company A, 6th Regiment N.C. Troops. All three brothers, and possibly the whole company, wore light-colored slouch hats with their state uniforms. Benjamin Hamilton Cathey stands with his musket at 'Support Arms' at centre. William Hillman Cathey also holds a small pocket revolver at left. Francis Marion Cathey sits at right. (North Carolina Division of Archives and History).

published regulations, printed shortly after at the 'N.C. Inst. for the Deaf & Dumb & the Blind'. Essentially, these regulations called for dark blue frock coats and trousers for general officers and staff, the same in gray for regimental officers, and gray sack coats and pantaloons 'of North Carolina Manufacture' for all enlisted men, with branch of service colors of buff, red, yellow and black for general officers and staff, artillery, cavalry and infantry respectively.

In anticipation of this move, a notice appeared in the newspapers, dated 18 May, advising that: 'Tailors and others wishing to contract for making Uniform Clothing for the North Carolina Troops are requested to make immediate application at the Quarter Master's General's Office in Raleigh. The material will be delivered to the contractors at any railroad depot in the state.' The distinctive enlisted men's six-button sack coat, with falling collar and shoulder trim, produced via this source, was provided by the state to a considerable number of companies that decided to purchase it with their commutation money, rather than fending for themselves.

By September 1861 the current stocks of state uniforms were exhausted, and it became very apparent that the Confederate government would be unable to provide clothing before the winter. Hence, on the 21st of that month the legislature reorganized the military departments, which resulted in the hasty establishment of a clothing manufactory at Raleigh under Captain I. W. Garrett. Every mill in the state was urged to furnish every possible yard of cloth, whilst further contracts were let for caps, shoes and accoutrements. Agents were also sent into several other Southern states to purchase everything that could be used for clothing.

On 10 February 1862, Assistant Quartermaster Major John Deveraux wrote to a firm with which the state had contracts, 'I will be obliged . . . if you will cut no more coats but cut all jackets, a sample will be sent you in a few days.' Hence the sack coat was modified by removing the skirts and turning it into a

This unidentified 'Tar Heel' wears the state regulation gray cap, trousers, and sack coat with black epaulettes. He is armed with a M1842 U.S. musket, a holstered revolver (possibly the Volt M1849 revolver) and has what appears to be a Smith and Wesson 'Model No. 1' rimfire revolver, calibre .22, pushed into his belt. His waist belt is secured by a rectangular brass plate, and supports a cap pouch under his arm. He also carries a tin drum canteen, and black rubberised cloth haversack. (North Carolina Division of Archives and History)

six-button jacket. The falling collar and shoulder trim were retained on this garment. The next stage in the modification of the state jacket occurred during the summer of 1862 with the elimination of the colored shoulder trim and the replacement of the falling collar by a more orthodox standing collar, making a 'second pattern' plain six-button jacket. This type was issued till the end of the war. Thus, between 30 September 1861 and 30 September 1862 Garrett had manufactured for the Quartermaster's Department, the following: '5,979 overcoats, 49,093 jackets, 5,954 coats, 68,364 pants, 61,275 shirts . . .'

Regarding headgear, General Officers and Staff were originally prescribed black felt hats, whilst Commissioned Officers and other ranks were to acquire gray felt hats, with branch of service insignia. Also, forage caps were to be worn by all ranks 'when off duty or on fatigue duty'. Those for officers were to be of the 'French'-pattern, whilst enlisted men's were 'gray'. During the year ending 30 September 1862 slightly fewer than 9000 hats were issued, compared with 60,000 caps. Supply problems inevitably affected the type and color of both hats and caps available. Some blue caps were supplied via Marshall Parks, North Carolina's purchasing agent in Norfolk, Virginia, under the state's first cap contract. On 1 June 1861, Quartermaster General Lawrence O'Bryan Branch wrote to parks: 'If gray can he had, please require the maker to furnish only that color. I will not object to different shades of gray, provided they are packed in different cases so that my assts. can put an entire Regiment in the same shade.' Whatever the color, Parks acquired the caps from W. H. S. Lovitt, of Virginia. Some brown caps may have been issued in early 1862, since Devereaux wrote to a supplier on 17 January, instructing him to 'cut no more caps out of the brown kerseys sent you. Genl. Martin objects to a variegated color'. While infantry were supplied with gray caps with black bands, and plain gray caps, red and yellow bands were put on the caps supplied, probably, to the 1st Artillery and Second Cavalry, judging by Devereaux's instructions to another contractor in December 1861 to 'bind 1000 caps with red for artillery', and, in February 1862, to send '1000 caps bound with yellow for cavalry'.

When in October 1862 the Confederate Government abandoned the commutation system, and took over the responsibility for clothing the state troops in her service, North Carolina insisted, in a fine display of state's rights defiance, on continuing to furnish her own, taking payment for supplies turned over by her to the Confederate quartermaster to issue to North Carolina troops. With the approach of another winter of war, the situation was becoming critical. Short term measures saw the state troops through the worst, but as a long-term solution, the state turned to blockade-running. Agent John White was mainly responsible for purchases in England, principally through middlemen Alexander Collie & Co. Initially White was instructed to buy '400,000 yards woollen cloth for soldiers' uniforms, 25,000 yards gray cloth for officers' uniforms, 150,000 yards blue flannel for shirts, 60,000 pairs shoes . . .'

From June 1863, when the first shipment arrived, to January 1865, when Fort Fisher fell, North Carolina is believed to have imported, at an approximate total, gray wool cloth sufficient for 250,000 suits of uniforms, and 12,000 overcoats; 50,000 blankets; and leather and shoes for 250,000 pairs. The cloth imported is believed to have been a dark bluish-gray shade which was quite distinct from the drab grays of the Confederate-made jeans cloth of the period, and is sometimes referred to as 'blue', or 'English blue'. In a much-quoted recollection Governor Zebulon B. Vance later estimated that the state had on hand '92,000 suits of uniforms' at the war's end.

Missouri

On the eve of the Civil War, the old enrolled militia system of Missouri had been all but abandoned, and the state's sole military force consisted of uniformed Volunteer Militia companies, the majority of which resided in St Louis and Jefferson City, the state capital. An act of state legislature passed in 1859 authorized these companies, some of which were organized into regiments and battalions along the lines of the defunct enrolled militia, to choose their own uniforms, and for general officers to do likewise. The dress chosen by some of these companies may have been influenced by the uniforms of their grandfathers, as prescribed by the state legislature on 22 June 1821, which called for: 'Officers in – Blue hunting shirts trimmed with red, white pantaloons and vest, black hat with a black cockade and red plume – noncoms to be uniformed as above, except hunting shirts trimmed with white, [and] white plumes –.'

The slavery issue, and the Kansas/Missouri Border War of 1856, had already sharply divided the state, but when governor Claiborne F. Jackson, a strong Southern sympathiser, was inaugurated in 1861, he made it clear that he intended to stand by the South in the approaching conflict. The military companies which also avowed that cause tended to be of older American, or Irish stock and filled the ranks of the 1st Missouri Brigade, Volunteer Militia, based at St Louis. Generally these companies were distinctively garbed, but regimental uniforms were adopted by several units by 1861. The 1st Missouri Infantry Regiment wore a uniform consisting of blue frock coats, sky-blue pants, and M1851 cloth dress cap, based on the State Regulations of 1858, which in turn were largely based on U.S. Army regulations, with the exception of the eagle and wreath cap insignia and white worsted epaulettes, instead of shoulder scales.

The Pioneer Corps attached to this regiment also wore a blue frock coat, trimmed with red and gold lace; dark gray pants with wide red seam stripes; bearskin hats with red bag, cord and tassels, red, white and blue plume; and high black leather boots. They also wore full beards and carried axes! The Engineer Corps wore blue frock coats edged with yellow lace, with gilt engineer castle insignia on collar and dress cap.

Emmitt MacDonald was captain of the St Louis Artillery, a company of the 1st Regiment, Missouri Volunteer Militia, at the beginning of the Civil War. He went on to command the 3rd Battery, Light Artillery, C.S.A., and fought at Wilson's Creek, Lexington and Pea Ridge. He wears a well-lined gray jacket of zouave style, trimmed on collar, cuffs and edges. Note the small, light-colored trefoil braid underneath the collar. His Model 1851 gray dress cap, with lighter-colored band, has the cardboard stiffening removed to give the appearance of a fatigue cap. (General Sweeny's Museum, Republic, Missouri)

The Duval brothers: Private Thomas Duval (left), and Lieutenant William Duval (right), served originally in the Missouri State Guard, before joining the 3rd Missouri Infantry. They both wear homemade fatigue shirts with light-colored trimming, reminiscent of the 1821 regulations. Note the secession cockade pinning up Private Duval's hat brim. (General Sweeny's Museum, Republic, Missouri)

The individual companies within this regiment reserved distinctive uniforms for special occasions. The Emmet Guard wore blue tail coats faced with buff; and sky-blue pants with buff seam stripes. The Washington Blues had a similar coat with light blue facings, and dark blue pants with light blue stripes. Both of these companies adopted

bearskin caps in 1857. The St Louis Grays, Co. D of this regiment in 1861, wore a light gray tail coat with sky-blue facings and epaulettes; black dress cap; light gray pants with wide blue seam stripe.

The Missouri Light Artillery chose a blue frock coat with red collar and cuffs edged with gold lace; brass shoulder scales; sky-blue pants with double red seam stripes; and a sky-blue felt cap with patent leather top, brass flaming shell device, and red horsehair plume hanging on the right side.

Zouave 'fever' began in St Louis with the visit of the celebrated United States Zouave Cadets on 10 August 1860. Influenced by their drill and showy uniforms, the 2nd Missouri Regiment, a pro-slavery unit organized in the city during February 1861, adopted as a regimental uniform a dark gray zouave jacket and full pants, trimmed with black cord; gray shirt; and gray cap with black top. At least one company of the 1st Regiment, the St Louis Artillery, may also have worn this, or a similar, zouave uniform.

On 3 May 1861 the 1st and 2nd Regiments, Missouri Volunteer Militia, gathered at Camp Jackson outside St Louis intent on taking over the U.S. Arsenal in the city. Captured by pro-Unionist forces under Captain Nathaniel Lyon seven days later, they were subsequently demobilized, but many of them made for Memphis, Tennessee, where they formed the 1st Missouri Volunteer Infantry and fought for the Confederacy.

In response to the Federal capture of Camp Jackson, the Confederate government of Governor Jackson, at Jefferson City, passed legislature on 14 May readying the state of defense, and establishing the State Guard, which was to be formed out of the rural elements of the Volunteer Militia. Led by Major General Sterling Price, this force was forced to retire to the southwestern corner of the state. At its height, the State Guard amounted to about 7000 men formed into some 62 poorly organized battalions, drawn from geographical divisions of the state, each division representing a congressional district. Without uniforms, and in some cases without weapons, they repelled the Union columns sent to destroy them. Captain Otto C. Lademann, of the Union 3rd Infantry, recalled the State Guard at the battle of Carthage, 5 July 1861: 'The enemy had no uniforms being entirely clad in homespun butternut jeans worn by every farmer in those days.' Acting Adjutant General of the Missouri State Guard, Colonel Thomas L.

Snead, observed of his comrades: 'In all their motley array there was hardly a uniform to be seen, and then, and throughout all the brilliant campaign on which they were about to enter[,] there was nothing to distinguish their officers, even a general, from the men in the ranks, save a bit of red flannel, or a piece of cotton cloth, fastened to the shoulder, or to the arm, of the former.'

Entries found in an account book for the Missouri State Guard indicate that their Quartermaster must have literally cleaned out every store encountered in an attempt to supply the troops. When clothing was not available, bolts of cloth were purchased and issued to the men, from which they made their own. One of the more unusual purchases, made on 3 July 1861 of Hyatt & Allen, included '24 Buffalo robes at $4.50'! By 2 December 1861, the Missouri State Guard began to break up, and many of its units were transferred as volunteers into Confederate service, and at various points thereafter were in receipt of clothing from the central government. Other elements of the State Guard joined guerrilla bands which continued to operate in Missouri. The most notable of these was that led by William Clarke Quantrill who, in time: '. . . developed a dress peculiar to themselves which became known up and down the border. Its distinguishing item was a "guerrilla shirt". This shirt, patterned after the hunting coat of the Western plainsmen, was cut low in front, the slit narrowing to a point above the belt and ending in a rosette. The garment had four big pockets, two in the breast, and ranged in color from brilliant red to homespun butternut. They were made by the mothers, wives, and sweethearts of the guerrillas, and many were elaborately decorated with colored needlework.'

Quantrill's Guerrilla's also fought in captured blue Federal uniforms, prompting General Orders No. 100 from the U.S. Adjutant General's office, dated 24 April 1863, which stipulated: 'Troops who fight in the uniform of their enemies, without any plain, striking and uniform mark of distinction of their own, can expect no quarter.'

Henderson Duval, also of the Missouri State Guard, wears a plain civilian shirt tucked into military trousers with light, possibly gold, colored seam stripe. He appears to be holding a Tucker and Sherrod & Co., .44-calibre revolver, whilst a horse pistol is pushed into the waistband of his pants. (General Sweeny's Museum, Republic, Missouri)

Left: Private S. W. Stone, California Guards, and Private P. S. Alexander, Moniteau County Rangers, Missouri State Guard. Taken at Jefferson City in May 1861, soon after the formation of the Missouri State Guard, the only sign of possible military dress on these men is the cap worn by Private Stone, who is armed with a musket, and wears a fancy tooled leather holster and double buckle accoutrement belt which also supports a bowie knife. Alexander holds a double-barrel shotgun, and has a wide leather shoulder belt which probably supports a cartridge box. A large knife is stuck in his belt, and a bouquet of wild flowers adorns his hat. (General Sweeny's Museum, Republic, Missouri)

Kentucky

With the approach of Civil War, and opinion divided on State's Rights, it became apparent to military experts in Kentucky that the militia system of that state was in need of total reform. Its enrolled militia was defunct, and only a few Volunteer Militia companies existed within its borders. Simon Bolivar Buckner, was a West Pointer of the Class of 1844, who had distinguished himself in the Mexican War. Resigning from the U.S. Army in 1855, he continued his military career as captain of the Citizen's Guard of Louisville. Under instructions from Governor Beriah Magoffin he drew up plans for an entirely new militia system for Kentucky which included the 'State Guard', a corps of uniformed volunteer militia created via act of legislature on 5 March 1860. Subsequently appointed Adjutant General and Commander of this new force, Buckner re-visited West Point to obtain ideas for the uniform to be worn by the state board. After several days of discussion with instructor of artillery Rufus Saxton, a uniform of gray trimmed with black and gold was decided upon – which happened to be the main colors worn by both West Point Cadets, and the Citizen's Guard of Louisville.

It is difficult to ascertain exactly when it was adopted but, by August 1860, Buckner and other officers of the Kentucky State Guard began to appear in the new uniform. Made of cadet gray cloth, generals and field officers wore a double-breasted frock coat, with collar and cuffs faced with black velvet based on 1857 U.S. Army regulations. That worn by Buckner survives in the collection of the Museum of the Confederacy. Made from gray wool broadcloth, his general officer's rank insignia consisted of an embroidered silver shield flanked by two five-pointed stars; and a silver eagle on black velvet shoulder straps bordered with two rows of silver lace edged with thin gold cord.

Other Kentuckian general officers photographed in this uniform include George B. Crittenden, Humphrey Marshall, and Benjamin H. Helm, Abraham Lincoln's brother-in-law. Photographed officers of lesser grade in this uniform indicate that a complicated collar and shoulder strap rank insignia system was in use throughout the short period of existence of

Simon Boliver Buckner in the Kentucky State Guard uniform he designed in 1860. Two rows of Kentucky State buttons are arranged in groups of three in line with 1857 U.S. Army regulations for a Major General. His slash cuffs are fastened by three small buttons.

the Kentucky State Guard. At some point in early 1861, the general officer's version of this uniform was misconstrued as the regulation dress of the new Confederacy, and convenient photographs were altered to show these distinctive collar and shoulder devices on a variety of persons.

Company-grade officers wore a single-breasted version of this uniform with black cloth collar, cuffs, and shoulder straps. Officers caps of chasseur pattern were cadet gray with a black band quartered by gold lace trim. Trousers were also cadet gray with a light-colored, possibly gold, seam stripe.

Staff N.C.O.s of the Kentucky State Guard wore a single-breasted coat with plain collar and cuffs, and plain black cotton shoulder straps. Rank insignia consisted of black inverted chevrons. Short brown buttoned gaiters were worn by both officers and men.

According to Buckner's wife, a 'Hunting shirt', in imitation of 'the clothes of the pioneers of the state', was encouraged as a fatigue dress of the Kentucky State Guard. That worn by General Buckner is held today in the collection of the Museum of the Confederacy. The Jefferson Rifles, a volunteer militia company organized by John Hunt Morgan, wore a similar style of shirt.

With the outbreak of hostilities in 1861, Kentucky adopted a neutral position, and many Kentuckians with southern sympathies made their way to the newly formed Confederate States to offer their services. Colonel Blanton Duncan formed a battalion at Harper's Ferry during April–May 1861, and uniformed them in hunting shirts possibly based on those worn by the Kentucky State Guard. This unit became part of the 1st Kentucky Infantry. Numerous Kentuckians entering Tennessee during June 1861 led to the organization of the 2nd and 3rd Kentucky Infantry regiments at Camp Boone, Montgomery County. These two units were supplied by the wealthy citizens of Louisville, and many appear to have worn their State Guard uniform. As further regiments were formed in southern Kentucky and northern Tennessee, volunteers provided their own uniforms.

However, by October 1861 a clothing shortage became evident. At Bowling Green, Kentucky, Quartermaster V. K. Stevenson, unable to supply adequate uniforms to Colonel Thomas H. Hunt's 5th Kentucky Infantry, advised that company captains supply only those men in most need. At Clarksville, near Camp Boone, 200 women were put to work making clothing for the 2nd, 3rd and 4th Kentucky Infantry

regiments. Meanwhile, at Camp Alcorn, near Hopkinsville, Kentucky, the Quartermaster admitted that he was 'entirely deficient'.

Nonetheless, the lack of heavy campaigning, and large amount of clothing that volunteers brought with them, probably enabled Kentuckians to stay well uniformed into late 1861. Private Thomas W. Blandford, 8th Kentucky Mounted Infantry, wore a double-breasted mid-gray frock coat with two rows of seven Kentucky State buttons, an outside pocket set at an angle level on the left breast, and black collar and pointed cuffs. Held by the Museum of the Confederacy, a small pin is still attached to it, which consists of a dull silver star, with KY engraved on it, attached to which is a crescent engraved with the motto 'Nil Desperandum'. A red silk ribbon, probably the remains of a cockade, hangs from the pin.

In his recollections of service as an officer in the 4th Kentucky Cavalry, George D. Musgrove remarked that as a rule he was: '. . . fond of gray attire, his style being regulation cavalry boots, a red sash, a large black felt hat, of the slouch variety, with the brim of one side turned up and pinned to the side of the crown with a silver crescent or star, the whole surmounted by a huge, black ostrich plume.'

As the 2nd Kentucky Cavalry, commanded by John Hunt Morgan, set out from Knoxville in 1862 on its first major raid, they were described as lacking 'general uniforms', although some were in 'new regulation gray, others in butternut jeans'. Members of Co. E and Co. F were photographed wearing light gray, seven- and eight-button shell jackets with solid, possibly yellow, facings on collars and cuffs. The latter appear to have been slashed and unusually fastened by a row of six small buttons along the back seam. This feature also appears on a plain, nine-button jacket worn by Thomas Bronston Collins, Co. F, 11th Kentucky Cavalry. Eighteen small buttons were sewn on each of Collins' cuffs! Most of these cavalrymen appear to have worn narrow-brimmed black felt hats. That worn by T. B. Collins was looped up on one side by a small, five-pointed metal star.

The 1st Kentucky Brigade (known today as the 'Orphan Brigade' because its members left home to fight for the Confederacy), composed of the 2nd, 3rd, 4th, 6th, and 9th Kentucky Infantry regiments, were in receipt of Confederate quartermaster-issue clothing, probably from the Columbus Depot, from late 1862 until the end of 1864.

The uniform of the Kentucky State Guard, 1860–61. Brigadier-General (left); Sergeant-Major (centre); Brigadier-General's shoulder strap (right). (From photographs and descriptions by Richard Warren)

Maryland

As a border slave state, Maryland was in a very difficult position at the outbreak of the Civil War. Secessionists both inside and outside her borders had struggled for many years to align her with the South, whilst others sought to keep her in the Union. This divided allegiance was reflected in her Volunteer Militia, particularly in Baltimore, where certain commands such as the 5th and 53rd Infantry Regiments, strongly avowed the Southern cause. Consequently, when Federal forces under General Benjamin Butler occupied the state capital in April 1861, these militia units were forbidden to assemble, and ceased to function. However, many of its members – singly, in small groups, and on a few occasions even by companies – stole out of Baltimore and made for Virginia. By early May, six companies of Maryland infantry had coalesced at Harpers Ferry and four more in Richmond. Those in the Confederate capital were temporarily designated Weston's Battalion. Nine of these companies would shortly join the ranks of the fledgling Virginia army as the 1st Maryland Infantry.

The tenth company (one of the three at Richmond), under Captain J. Lyle Clarke, and composed of 109 ex-members of the Maryland Guard Battalion, became Co. B, 21st Virginia Infantry and served in the Army of Northern Virginia until May 1862. The uniforms received by Clarke's company were made by the Richmond firm of Kent, Paine and Co. Described as being of 'coarse gray, but very durable', that worn by Private E. Courtney Jenkins survives at the Museum of the Confederacy, and consists of a six-button shell jacket and trousers made of heavy satinette. The six-button jacket collar, shoulder straps, and trouser outer seams, are bound in ½-inch black tape. Thin gray tape belt loops are attached near the jacket's side seams. Two of the other Maryland companies in Richmond also appear to have received this type of uniform.

The six Harpers Ferry companies remained un-uniformed and poorly clad until they amalgamated with the three from Weston's Battalion at Winchester, Virginia, on 25 June 1861. At this point, Jane Claudia Johnson, wife of the major of the consolidated 1st Maryland Infantry, 'secured cloth . . . by purchasing it from the mills where it was manufactured for the State of Virginia, and she paid for making it up into uniforms'.

Robert G. Harper wearing the uniform of the Maryland Guard Battalion. He would later serve the Confederacy as a lieutenant on the staff of General Richard Ewell. Dave Mark Collection.

Thus the remaining companies of the 1st Maryland were supplied with uniforms consisting of 'a French kepi (a little gray cap), a natty gray roundabout, collar and sleeves bound with black braid, and a similar stripe down the gray trousers'. This uniform was in all probability patterned on those made by Kent, Paine and Co. for the three Richmond-based companies earlier in the year. Non-commissioned officers wore their black chevrons point down on their right sleeves only.

A zouave unit was raised in Maryland by Richard Thomas, of St Mary's County. Born in 1833, Thomas was educated at Charlotte Hall and Oxford, Maryland, and briefly at the U.S. Military Academy. At first as a surveyor and later as a soldier of fortune, he spent years on the western frontier and in fighting river pirates in China. He also fought with Garibaldi in Italy. There he adopted the title and name of 'Colonel Richard Thomas Zarvona', by which he called himself thereafter. An ardent secessionist, he joined with others, including G. W. Alexander and William Walters, to form two infantry companies in St Mary's and Calvert counties, Maryland, to 'be drilled as Zouaves for the Confederate service'. Members of these companies, led by 'Colonel Zarvona', captured a Chesapeake Bay steamer, the *St. Nicholas*, on 28 June 1861, and went on to take three Federal merchant vessels. At Fredericksburg Confederate authorities honoured the action, and Governor Letcher of Virginia commissioned Zarvona a colonel in the state forces.

Zarvona was subsequently described in the Richmond press as presenting 'a picturesque appearance, attired in his blue Zouave costume, white gaiters, red cap with gold tassel and light elegant sword'. A red fez with a dark blue tassel, believed to have belonged to Zarvona, survives today in the collection of the Maryland Historical Society.

By early July 1861, plans were underway to organize the Maryland Zouaves, 1st Regiment, with William Walters in command of the 'first company', and G. W. Alexander as adjutant. Meanwhile, Zarvona became involved in further naval escapades on the Chesapeake Bay, was captured and imprisoned for two years in a Federal prison, and finally freed in April 1863 on the understanding that he would live abroad until the war was over.

Left: Captain James Thomas Bussey led Co. H, 2nd Maryland Infantry. His double-breasted gray jacket has been created by either cutting the skirts off his frock coat or, more likely, simply tucking them into his pants. (Dave Mark Collection)

The Maryland Zouaves, 1st Regiment, failed to materialize, and the Zouave company led by Walters was designated Co. H, 47th Virginia Infantry. After service on the Peninsula, this unit was transferred to the 2nd Arkansas Battalion, and was mustered out of service on 10 June 1862.

Corporal Francis Higdon, Robertson's Company, 1st Maryland Infantry. Higdon's company received their uniforms in August 1861. His Corsican-style cap with black band is made of the same material as the jacket, and may indicate that the whole of his company received head gear of this type. On the other hand this may have been a personalized item specific to Higdon. Note the corporal's chevrons are on the right sleeve only. (U.S. Army Military History Institute/Jim Enos)

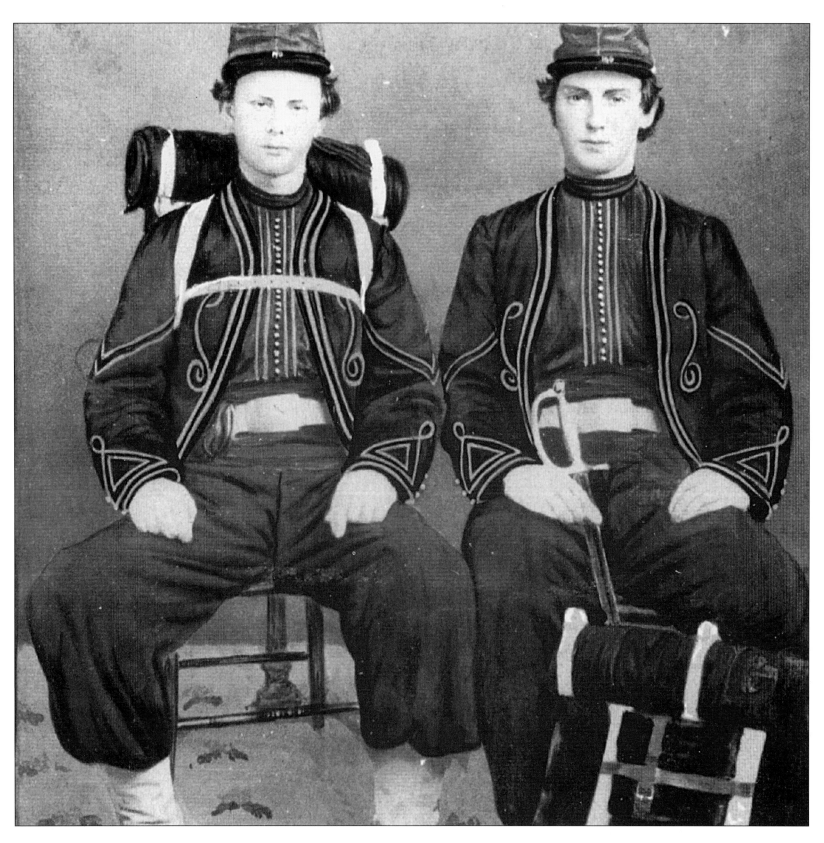

Two corporals of the pre-war Maryland Guard Battalion, a volunteer militia unit organized in 1859. John Eager Howard Post (left) enlisted as a private in the 1st Maryland Infantry and was later commissioned lieutenant in the 1st Maryland Cavalry. Charles R. Thompson (right) served as a private in the same cavalry regiment. Both men wear the full dress ('Class A') chasseur uniform of the Maryland Guard Battalion, which consisted of a dark blue jacket and pantaloons trimmed with yellow; a blue flannel shirt trimmed yellow down the front, and red around the neck; light blue cap with dark blue band, quartered and trimmed with yellow lace; wide red sash; and 'drab' gaiters. The numerals 53 on their rigid militia knapsack denotes the number of the militia regiment to which this battalion was attached. Note the letters M and G just visible on the blue blanket roll. (Dave Mark Collection)

Confederate Quartermaster Issue

The bulk of uniforms supplied by the Quartermaster's Department during the Civil War had little to do with the official Confederate dress regulations produced in June 1861, the design of which was possibly based on the Austrian jaeger uniform, generally believed to have been suggested by Nicola Marschall, a German artist who emigrated to the U.S. in 1849. These regulations called for double-breasted frock coats, or tunics, of medium gray with a bluish cast, known as 'cadet gray'. Also specified was a system of branch color on collar and cuffs, with blue for infantry, red for artillery, yellow for cavalry. Trousers were full cut and sky blue. Forage caps were gray with a band of branch color. Overcoats were cadet gray, and cut like those issued to the U.S. Army. Officer's rank insignia consisted of bars and stars on the collar, and an 'Austrian knot' on each sleeve.

The tardiness in publication of these regulations, the expensive composition of the uniforms prescribed, and

Plate from the Confederate dress regulations of 6 June 1861. (Author's collection)

Private Alexander Murray served in Company A, 2nd Maryland Infantry, and was wounded at Culp's Hill. He wears a Richmond Depot, second pattern shell jacket. (Dave Mark Collection)

Left: An unidentified Confederate enlisted man wearing the uniform coat specified in the Confederate regulations published in June 1861. (Michael J. McAfee)

difficulties experienced by the general government in taking over any serious issue of clothing until late 1861, led to very few of these uniforms being produced and worn. However, the 1861 regulations did accomplish several important things. They set the style of dress of the Confederate officer. They established a branch color system, and pattern of buttons. Most importantly, they did much to establish gray as the official color of the upper garment of the Confederate Army, in contrast with the dark blue being specified during the same period by their Northern counterparts. This choice of color was further influenced by a popular belief in the U.S. that gray uniforms should be worn by volunteers, as opposed to the dark blue of the regular army.

As a result of the commutation system established by the Confederate Government in February 1861, volunteers of the Provisional Army were originally to provide their own clothing, for which they would receive $21 every six months. This was supplemented until at least 1862 by uniform supplies from state government, and local volunteer aid societies. Organized in hundreds of Southern towns and hamlets, the latter raised funds, bought materials, and made frock coats, trousers, shirts, hats, overcoats, shoes, etc. for the troops in the front line.

The first Confederate Clothing Bureau was established on Pearl Street in Richmond, Virginia, by the end of August 1861. Run by Major J. W. Ferguson, it was described as follows shortly after it began manufacture: 'Every portion of the work has its appropriate department. In the upper story of the building is the cutting room, under the direction of superintendents, and lively with the noise of shears. Lower down is the trimming room. Then the department for letting out the making of the clothes, the work being given out to the wives and relatives of the soldiers, and to poor and deserving needlewomen. Lastly comes the packing department, where the clothing, blankets, &c., are packed and forwarded to the camps.' Other bureaus were eventually established at Nashville, Tennessee; Montgomery, Tuscaloosa and Marion, Alabama; Jackson and Enterprise, Mississippi; Athens, Atlanta and Columbus, Georgia and elsewhere. By 8 October 1861 the quartermaster issue system was considered to be strong enough to supply the Confederate fighting forces with uniforms directly, and the commutation system was officially ended. This is not to suggest that all Confederate units now began to receive government clothing. Some of the very needy regiments had been on the issue system as early as the summer of 1861. Others did not get on it until

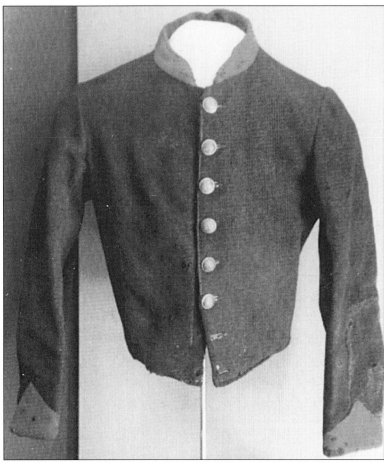

Jacket worn by Private Alfred M. Goodwin of Sturdivant's Virginia Battery. Made of dark cadet gray kersey by Peter Tait of Limerick, Ireland, the red collar and cuffs are post-war additions. Detail (right) showing Virginia state seal buttons. (Alan Thrower)

late 1862 or early 1863, and had meanwhile to make do with whatever clothing the folks back home could make up for them. Evidence suggests that some troops in the West did not get off the commutation system until 1864. However, the issue system was largely in place and functioning by 1864 within the main Confederate armies.

Part of the full clothing allowance for enlisted men for a three-year period of service, established in December 1862, consisted of two jackets in the first year and one a year thereafter. They also received three pairs of trousers in the first year and two per year thereafter. Caps were issued at the rate of two for the first year, and one per year thereafter. It has been

Left: Richmond Depot Jackets. First pattern (top) cadet gray Richmond Bureau jacket. Second pattern (centre) – minus trim. Third pattern (bottom) – minus shoulder straps, which were sometimes used as belt loops.

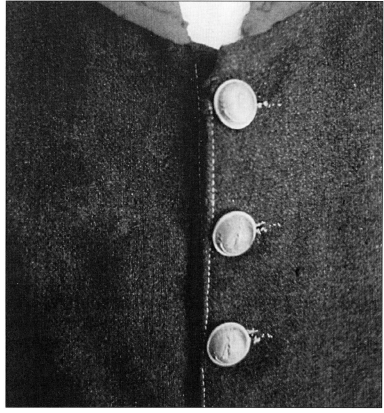

Cap worn by Private Robert W. Royall, 1st Company, Richmond Howitzers, with dark blue-gray kersey sides, and red wool band and crown. (Author's collection)

Left: Private J. P. Sellman, Company K, 1st Virginia Cavalry, wears another example of a Richmond Depot, second pattern uniform. (U.S. Army Military History Institute/Jim Enos)

estimated that the average Confederate soldier on campaign would wear out a jacket in three months, whilst trousers lasted only a month. Hence, despite what would appear to be a generous clothing allowance, the Confederate army in the field was often in a sorry and ragged state.

The pattern and color of the uniforms supplied varied from the outset. Despite the fact that 'tunics' were called for in the 1861 regulations, the uniform supplied from 1862 onwards always included the 'roundabout' or 'shell jacket', which was a much cheaper garment to produce than the frock coat or tunic. Although no Quartermaster Department examples survive, photographic evidence suggests that the first pattern jacket produced by the Richmond Bureau was made of a very fine-quality cadet gray cloth, and had a nine-button front. The collar, shoulder straps and cuffs were trimmed with either tape or piping, which was often in branch color. Belt loops were probably attached, and lining was of a coarse homespun cotton cloth inaccurately called 'osnaberg' in the South during the Civil War. The first trousers supplied were probably made from the same material as the jackets, and usually had only two front pockets. Some had a watch pocket, and either a belt or holes for laces over a vent at the back to adjust for size. There were no belt loops, and many had buttons for braces. Most had a small slit at the bottom of each leg seam. Members of the South Carolinian brigade, commanded by General Joseph Brevard Kershaw, had been the beneficiary of uniforms supplied by the Richmond Depot by July 1862, as Colonel D. Wyatt Aiken, commander of the 7th South Carolina Volunteers, remarked: 'One of the Regiments of this Brigade is dressed in a remarkably neat and comfortable uniform which cost (for roundabout and pants) only eleven dollars to the man. A private could not buy the jacket for that in Richmond. The other two regiments are now being uniformed by the Government in the same way.' During these early stages of issuance some regimental commanders requested and received uniforms for their commands which featured trim on jackets and/or trousers which were unique to their units, e.g. in 1862 Colonel W. E. Starke required a 'stripe on the pants for his Regt. [60th Regiment Virginia Volunteers] & a bar on the shoulder' of their jackets.

Whilst the dress regulations specified a 'Forage cap for officers . . . similar in form to that known as the French kepi,' the pattern of 'uniform cap' to be worn by enlisted men in 1861

Columbus Depot jacket, worn by Elijah Woodward, 9th Kentucky Infantry, ca. November 1862. (Kentucky Military History Museum/ courtesy of Geoff Walden)

was not given but, according to E. Crehen's accompanying lithographs, appears also to have been based on the French chasseur pattern. This consisted of a low, countersunk crown, with a straight visor made of two pieces of leather sewn over a cardboard stiffener. A number of enlisted men's caps of probable quartermaster department manufacture survive based on this pattern. Others are of the forage cap pattern, with higher crown and flat top. Many follow 1861 regulations with gray tops and branch colored, or black, bands, whilst others were either based on the revised 1862 pattern with branch color tops, or were simply plain gray. Photographs often feature the black oilskin

cap covers which were formally prescribed in January 1862 for wear in 'bad weather'.

A second pattern jacket was issued by the Richmond Bureau possibly as early as the Spring of 1862. Generally without trim except occasional piping on shoulder straps and/or collar, they were otherwise based on the cut of the first pattern. Surviving examples indicate that cloth being used by this time varied from a coarse wool, dyed cadet gray, called kersey, to a rough, dark greenish gray woollen material. A third type of jacket produced by the Richmond Bureau by the beginning of 1863 was the product of the Confederacy's purchasing operations abroad. Again based on the same basic shell jacket pattern, it was minus trim, shoulder straps and belt loops, and was made of heavy dark blue/gray kersey spun and woven in England, and brought through the Federal blockade. The arrival of this cloth in Richmond caused considerable interest as one Southern newspaper recorded in February 1863: 'Quite an excitement is going on at the Clothing Bureau of the Quartermaster's Department since the arrival of cloth for uniforms of English manufacture. So great is the rush of officers for suits that a guard, with fixed bayonets, is placed at the door to ensure order. Citizens on the sly are trying to rehabilitate themselves from the Government stores. Eight examples of this type of jacket survive. That worn by Corporal E. F. Barnes, 1st Company, Richmond Howitzers, was worn at the surrender of Lee's army at Appomattox Court House in 1865. Jackets of the same English cloth, but with five-button fronts and utilizing shoulder straps as belt loops, are also believed to have been made at a clothing depot established at Charleston, South Carolina, by the end of 1862.

Caps issued later in the war provide further examples of economy measures made by C. S. clothing bureaus. That worn by Private Robert W. Royall, 1st Company, Richmond Howitzers, has dark blue-gray sides, red wool band and crown, and is minus a chin strap, with a visor made from layers of thin card glued together, covered with black painted cloth, and edged with leather binding.

Another pattern of uniform associated with the latter stages of the war, was also run through the boxes Tait, a clothing manufacturer of Limerick in Ireland, who earlier had clothing contracts with the British army in the Crimea, six examples of the jacket supplied with this uniform survive. Three were worn by members of Northern Virginia; one owner unknown, but found in Virginia; one from a member of the fort Fisher garrison, and one from a person guarding Quartermaster Stores in Greensboro, North Carolina. All were made from dark cadet gray English kersey with a strong blue cast, and originally had an eight-button front, and a linen lining. That worn by Private Garrett Gouge of the 58th North Carolina has a blue piped collar and shoulder straps. The trousers supplied with the jacket worn by Sergeant M. Glennan of the 36th North Carolina were

Kepi worn by R. C. Anderson, 2nd Kentucky Infantry, ca. 1863. (Kentucky Military History Museum/courtesy of Geoff Walden)

made of the same cadet gray cloth with red piped seam stripes. Combined with sky-blue trousers, which were often captured from the Federal army, these mid- to late-war dark gray jackets were cause for frequent comment and incident. A Federal infantryman who talked to some pickets of a South Carolina regiment in Tennessee in late September 1863, described them as 'better dressed than we are, their uniforms being apparently new . . . The Carolinians' uniform is bluish gray . . . with sky blue pants.' According to D. Augustus Dickert, who served in Company H, 3rd South Carolina Volunteers, these uniforms consisted of 'a dark-blue round jacket, closely fitting, with light-blue trousers'. Confederate soldiers wearing these uniforms often exposed themselves to the dangers of being mistaken for Federal troops. Later that year, members of the same unit wearing dark gray jackets were fired on by elements of the 7th South Carolina.

At the beginning of the war, Confederate officers were required to wear regulation frock coats with full rank insignia on collar and sleeves, which they paid for at their own expense. This resulted in their being easy targets for Federal sharpshooters. Hence, a circular from the Adjutant & Inspector General's Office, dated 3 June 1862, permitted them to purchase a quartermaster-issue fatigue uniform in the field including a plain gray jacket with rank insignia on collar only. Finally an 1864 General Order allowed them to draw enlisted clothing on the same basis as other ranks, once all the men had been supplied. On 16 November 1863, Lieutenant Elliott Welch of the Hampton Legion of South Carolina wrote to his mother: '. . . our clothing is still in the Qr. master's storehouse. I recently went to town to purchase a pair [of trousers] & was treated with indifference by a few upstart clerks.' This suggests that Welch, like many other officers, preferred by this time to purchase enlisted men's clothing rather than pay the inflated prices of civilian suppliers. After being on picket duty in June 1864, he wrote that he '. . . felt a bullet go thro' my jacket sleeve – close shave'. During this same period, he felt the need to change from blue trousers (presumably sky blue) to gray trousers. 'Having had a gun, or pistol, pointed at me on several occasions by some of our men[,] I procured a pair of nice gray pantaloons . . . While out scouting[,] a pair of blue trousers with one of our dark gray jackets is apt to make a man think a Yank is in front of him.'

In the West, the Confederate Army of Tennessee received uniforms from three general bureaus, established at Columbus, Atlanta and Athens, in Georgia. The Columbus Bureau was described by the Southern press as being 'second only to the chief department at Richmond'. In January 1863, it occupied 'four, or perhaps five, large buildings, all of which are filled from cellar to garret, either by busy operatives or with army supplies. Over 15,000 suits of soldiers' clothing, manufactured in the city and surrounding country, are now stored away in one of the Government warehouses. The material of which this clothing is made was manufactured exclusively in Columbus. Over 40,000 soldiers' caps, manufactured from similar materials, now lie here awaiting requisitions from the proper army officials.' Surviving jackets issued from this source were made from gray wool jean, faded today to a butternut color, and usually have six-button fronts. Made with a slightly longer body than the Richmond Depot pattern, they also have medium blue wool kersey or wool flannel collars and straight cuffs. A member of the 4th Florida Infantry issued with uniforms from the Columbus bureau during this period recalled: 'The coats are dark and light gray (mostly with blue collars and cuffs . . . it is a worsted cross between cassimere and jeans, very warm and desirable . . .)' Later Columbus Depot jackets had exterior pockets sewn into the left breast.

Much of the cloth for these depots came from textile mills like the Sweetwater Factory at Marietta, the Eagle Factory in Columbus, and the Ivy Woolen Mill at Roswell, Georgia. The latter by March 1862 run by Roswell King's grandsons, Thomas Edward and James Roswell King, negotiated a contract with the Confederate Government to produce a specified quota of woollen cloth, in return for which the Confederacy agreed to furnish workmen and materials. Despite wartime shortages of lubricants and spare parts for the machinery, the Kings still managed to produce about 15,000 yards of high-quality woollens every month, and thousands of Confederate volunteers consequently found themselves in receipt of jackets, caps or trousers of a dark bluish-gray cast called 'Roswell gray'.

Surviving jackets believed to have been manufactured at the Atlanta Bureau during 1864 were made from a rough handloomed wool resembling salt-and-pepper burlap which produced a greenish-gray cast. Fastened by six buttons, they were devoid of trim and minus shoulder straps and belt loops. A peculiarity of these jackets was the cut of the collar, which came to within about an inch of the edge of the coat on the right side, and was flush with the edge on the left. Thus, when fastened, the collar came together in the centre.

Clothing bureaus in Alabama were supplied with cloth from mills such as Barnett Micon & Company at Tallassee, and Phillips, Fariss & Company of Montgomery. Jackets produced at Tuscaloosa, Marion and Montgomery were made of woollen jean with dark blue collars of the same material. All surviving examples have five-button fronts, one exterior pocket which varies from one side of the jacket front to the other, and linings of cotton osnaberg. Two surviving jackets have what appear to be original wooden buttons attached, which illustrates the shortage of metal buttons in the South towards the end of the war. That worn by Silas Calmes Buck, Co. D, 12th Mississippi, had collar and cuffs of green wool twill material.

From 1861, brown cloth was supplied to the Confederate Quartermaster Department in great abundance by southern textile mills such as that owned by William Gregg at Graniteville, South Carolina. Although drained of its work force as local men volunteered for Confederate military service, the Graniteville Manufacturing Company began to supply 'BROWN GOODS' to the Richmond quartermaster authorities as early as October of that year. By March 1862, 'brown drilling at nineteen cents per yard' was supplied to Richmond on a regular basis which lasted until at least 1864. A dye made from copperas and walnut hulls, which produced a color popularly known as 'butternut', was used extensively in the South later in the war. A jacket believed to have been worn by Charles A.

Parkins, an Englishman who served in the 3rd Louisiana Infantry, provides an excellent example of later war homespun butternut. Held in the collection of the Royal Artillery Institution at Woolwich until recently, the material is a beige or light brown wool and cotton 'lindsey-woolsey' mixture, flecked with white and light blue, with a texture like hessian. The weft is apparently wool dyed butternut, or marmalade, with a warp of cotton. Based on the third pattern produced by the Richmond Bureau, it was originally fastened by six Louisiana State Seal buttons, had closed cuffs, and an exterior pocket on the left breast. Although a number of surviving garments of this color are believed to have resulted from the oxidation or discoloration of the original gray cloth, the Parkins jacket was apparently originally brown.

The most bizarre cloth used to provide cheap uniforms in the Confederacy was a type of material called 'wool plains', which was undyed, natural colored wool. A member of the 2nd Missouri Infantry, a regiment organized near Springfield in the spring of 1862, recalled that 'the cloth was or rough and coarse texture, and the cutting and style would have produced a sensation in fashionable circles; the stuff was white, never having been colored, with the exception of a small quantity of dirt and a goodly supply of grease – the wool had not been purified by any application of water since it was taken from the back of the sheep.' When members of this regiment captured an enemy picket later that year, the Federals, finding themselves 'surrounded by men dressed IN WHITE . . . seemed bewildered and somewhat frightened'. Similarly, during February 1863 the 3rd Louisiana Infantry, commanded by Colonel Jerome B. Gilmore, received 'a new uniform, which they were ordered to take, much against their express wishes. The material was a very coarse white jeans . . .' Some of the unit suggested 'the propriety of wearing the new white uniforms on the approaching [Steel's Bayou] expedition, which, it was known, would be among the swamps of the Yazoo valley in Mississippi. The suggestion was almost universally adopted, affording a rare opportunity to give the new clothes a thorough initiation into the mysteries of a soldier's life.'

Bibliography

The Union Army

Main Sources

U.S. Army Dress Regulations, William H. Horstmann & Sons, Philadelphia, 1851.

Todd, F. P., *American Military Equipage 1851–1872* Volume I, Volume II, Volume III. The Company of Military Historians, West Brook Connecticut, 1978. Separate Volume on State Forces published 1983.

Andrews, H., Nelson, C., Pohanka, B., Roach, H., *Photographs of American Civil War Cavalry*, Guidon Press, Pennsylvania, 1982.

Carter, S., *The Last Cavaliers*, St Martin's Press, New York, 1979.

Davis, William C., *The Fighting Men of the American Civil War*, Salamander Books, 1989.

Downey, F., *Sound of the Guns*, David McKay Company Inc 1956.

Downey, F., *Clash of Cavalry, The Battle of Brandy Station*, Butternut Press, Gaithersburg, Maryland, 1985.

Echoes of Glory: Arms & Equipment of the Union, TimeLife Books, 1991.

Griffith, P. J., *Rally Once Again*, The Crowood Press, 1987.

Hennessey, James, *Uniforms of the Fifth New York Volunteer Infantry: 'Duryee Zouaves' 1861–1863*.

Herr, J. K., and Wallace, E. S., *The Story of the U.S. Cavalry 1775–1942*, Bonanza Books, New York, 1981.

Military Uniforms in America, Long Endure: The Civil War Period 1852–1867, The Company of Military Historians, Presidio Press, Novato, California, 1982.

Lord, F. A., *Civil War Collector's Encyclopedia*, Castle Books, New York, 1965.

Lord, F. A., *They Fought for the Union*, Bonanza Books.

Naisawald, L. V. Loan, *Grape and Canister, The Story of the Field Artillery of the Army of the Potomac*, Zenger Publishing Co, Washington D.C., 1983.

McAfee M. J., *Zouaves The First and The Bravest*, Thomas Publications, Gettysburg, Pennsylvania, 1991.

The Photographic History of the Civil War, The Cavalry, edited by Theo E. Rodenbough, The Fairfax Press, New York, 1983.

Sylvia, S. W. & O'Donnell, M. J., *The Illustrated History of American Civil War Relics*, Moss Publications, Orange, Virginia, 1978.

Troiani D., Pohanka, B., *Don Troiani's Civil War*, Stackpole Books, Mechanicsburg, Pennsylvania, 1995.

Urwin, G. J. W., *The United States Infantry, an Illustrated History 1775–1918*, Blandford Press, 1988.

Warren, R., Federal Data Series No 1., *1st to 5th New Hampshire Volunteer Infantry 1861–1862*, Confederate Historical Society, 1987.

Warren, R., Federal Data Series No 2., *1st Rhode Island Detached Militia, 2nd Rhode Island Volunteer Infantry, 1st and 2nd Rhode Island Batteries 1861*, Confederate Historical Society Press, 1987.

Warren, R., Federal Data Series No 2. *Uniforms and Flags of the 69th New York State Militia and the Irish Brigade 1859–1865*, Confederate Historical Society Press, 1988.

Windrow M., Embleton, G., *Military Dress of North America 1665–1970*, Ian Allen Ltd, 1973.

Zimmerman, R. J., *Unit Organizations of the American Civil War*, Rafm Co. Inc., Ontario, Canada, 1982.

The Image of War 1861–1865, Vol 1 Shadows of the Storm, editor William C. Davis, National Historical Society, Gettysburg, Pennsylvania, Doubleday & Company, Garden City, New York, 1981.

The Image of War 1861–1865, Vol VI The End of an Era, editor William C. Davis, National Historical Society, Gettysburg, Pennsylvania, Doubleday & Company, Garden City, New York, 1984.
Griffith, P., *Battle in the Civil War*, Fieldbooks, 1986.

Katcher, P., *Fotofax Union Forces of the American Civil War*, Arms & Armour Press, London, 1989.

Kinsley, D. A., *Favor the Bold, Custer the Civil War Years*, Promontory Press, 1967.

Urwin, G. J. W., *Custer Victorious the Civil War Battles of General George Armstrong Custer*, Associated University Presses, East Brunswick, New Jersey, 1983.

Coggins, J., *Arms and Equipment of the Civil War*, Doubleday and Company Inc., Garden City, New York, 1962.

Cunliffe, C., *Soldiers and Civilians the Martial Spirit in America 1775–1865*, Eyre & Spottiswoode, London, 1968.

Wright, S. J., *The Irish Brigade, Combat History Series, The Civil War*, Steven Wright Publishing, Springfield, Pennsylvania, 1992.

Regimental Histories

Brainard, M. G., *Campaigns of the One Hundred and Forty Sixth Regiment New York State Volunteers*, New York, 1915.

Conyngham, D. P., *The Irish Brigade and its Campaigns*, Patrick Donahoe, Boston, 1869. Reprinted by Ron R. Van Sickle Military Books, Gaithersburg, Maryland, 1987.

Cowtan, C. W., *Services of the 10th New York Volunteers (National Zouaves) in the War of the Rebellion*, Charles & Ludwig, New York, 1862.

Davenport A., *Camp and Field Life of the Fifth New York Volunteer Infantry Duryee Zouaves*, Dick and Fitzgerald, New York, 1879. Reprinted by the Butternut Press, Gaithersburg, Maryland, 1984.

Dowley, M. E., *History and Honorary Roll of the Twelfth Regiment*, New York, 1869.

Glover, E. A., *Bucktailed Wildcats, A Regiment of Civil War Volunteers*, Thomas Yosseloff, New York & London, 1960.

Johnson, C. F., *The Long Roll, Impressions of a Civil War Soldier*, Elbert Hubbard, East Aurora, New York, 1911. Reprinted by Carabelle Books, Shepherdstown, West Virginia, 1986.

Jones, P., *The Irish Brigade*, Robert B. Luce Inc., Washington & New York, 1960.

Nash, E. A., *A History of the Forty Fourth Regiment New York Volunteer Infantry*, Chicago, 1911. Reprinted by the Morningside Bookshop, Dayton, Ohio, 1988.

Nolan, A. T., *The Iron Brigade, A Military History*, Indiana University Press, 1994.

Ripley, W. Y. W., *Vermont Riflemen in the War for the Union 1861 to 1865, A History of Company F First United States Sharp Shooters*, Tuttle & Co, 1883. Reprinted by the Grand Army Press, Rochester, Michigan, 1981.

The 155th Regimental Association, *Under the Maltese Cross Antietam to Appomattox*, Pittsburgh, 1910.

Roehrenbeck, W. J., *The Regiment that Saved the Capital*, Thomas Yosselof, London & New York, 1961.

Tevis, W. C., *The History of the Fighting Fourteenth*, New York, 1911.

Magazines Sources

Bender D., Boots and Saddles, 'A Survey of the U.S. Cavalry from the Civil War to the Great War', *Military Images*, West Chester, Pennsylvania, 1985, Volume VIII, No. 1 pp. 2021.

Field R., 'American Lancers', *Military Illustrated*, London, 1995, No. 91, pp. 2429.

Field R., 'American Hussars', *Military Illustrated*, London, 1996, No. 93, pp. 3035.

Karle, T., 'The 83rd Pennsylvania Volunteer Infantry 1861–1862', *Military Images*, West Chester, Pennsylvania, 1990, Volume XII, No. 1, pp. 2729.

Marcot, R. M., 'The Uniforms & Field Equipment of the Berdan U.S. Sharpshooters', *North South Trader's Civil War*, Orange, Virginia, 1990, Volume XVII, No. 6, pp. 2840.

McAfee, M. J., 'The Well Accoutered Soldier, Army Uniforms of the Civil War Part IX', *Military Images*, West Chester, Pennsylvania, 1988, Volume X, No. 1, pp. 1824.

McAfee, M. J., 'Empire State Soldiers, Images From New York's Bureau of Military Statistics', *Military Images*, West Chester, Pennsylvania, 1990, Volume XI, No. 4, pp. 1625.

Osborne, S. R., 'They Wore an Orange Ribbon', *Military Collector & Historian*, Westbrook, Connecticut, 1986, Volume XXXVIII, No. 1, pp. 4042.

Pohanka, B., 'Like Demons with Bayonets, The 5th New York Zouaves at Gaines's Mill', *Military Images*, West Chester, Pennsylvania, 1989, Volume X, No. 6, pp. 1222.

Rossbacher, N., 'Identification Discs & Inscribed Corps Badges', *North South Trader's Civil War*, Orange, Virginia, 1990, Volume XVII, No. 5, pp. 2431.

Smith, R., 'The Magnificent Zouaves, 5th New York Volunteer Infantry 1861–1863', *Military Illustrated*, London, 1994, No. 78, pp. 1417.

Smith, R., 'Red Legged Devils, 14th Brooklyn Regiment', *Military Illustrated*, London, 1995, No. 86, pp. 2528.

Warren, R., '11th New York Volunteer Infantry, Ellsworth's First New York Fire Zouaves 1861–1862, *Military Collector & Historian*, Westbrook, Connecticut, 1987, Volume XXXIX, No. 4, pp. 174177.

Urwin, G. J. W., 'Come On You Wolverines Custer's Michigan Cavalry Brigade', *Military Images*, West Chester, Pennsylvania, Volume VIII, No. 1, pp. 716.

The Confederate Army

General works

Todd, Frederick P., *American Military Equipage 1851–1872*, 3 vols, Providence, R. I., 1974–1978.

Todd, Frederick P., *American Military Equipage 1851–1872*, Vol. II, 'State Forces', New York, 1983.

Editors of Time-Life Books, *Echoes of Glory: Arms and Equipment of the Confederacy*, Alexandria, Virginia, 1991.

The Company of Military Historians, *Military Uniforms in America – Long Endure: The Civil War Period, 1852–1867*, Novato, California, 1982.

Dyer, Frederick H., *A Compendium of the War of the Rebellion*, Des Moines, Iowa, 1903; reprinted, 3 vols, New York, 1959.

Scott, Robert N. (compiler), *The War of the Rebellion: A Compilation of the Official Records of the Union and Confederate Armies*, Washington, 1880–1901.

Dornbusch, Charles E., *Military Bibliography of the Civil War*, 3 vols, New York, 1961–1967.

Amann, William Frayne, *Personnel of the Civil War*, 2 vols, New York, 1961.

Tancig, W. J., *Confederate Military Land Units 1861–1865*, New York, 1967.

Crute Jr, Joseph H., *Units of the Confederate States Army*, Midlothian, Virginia, 1987.

Albaugh III, William, *Confederate Faces*, California, 1970.

Albaugh III, William, *More Confederate Faces*, California, 1972.

Turner, William A., *Even More Confederate Faces*, Orange, Virginia, 1983.

Serrano, D. A., *Still More Confederate Faces*, New York, 1992.

Thomas, Michael R., *A Confederate Sketchbook*, New Jersey, 1981.

Risch, Erna, *Quartermaster Support of the Army: A History of the Corps 1775–1939*, Washington D.C., 1962.

South Carolina

Cauthen, C. E., *South Carolina Goes to War, 1860–1865*, North Carolina, 1950.

Capers, Ellison, 'South Carolina', in *Confederate Military History*, Vol. V, Atlanta, Georgia, 1899.

Salley, A. S. (compiler), *South Carolina Troops in Confederate Service*, 3 vols, Columbia, S. C., 1913–1930.

McCaslin, Richard B., *Portraits of Conflict – A Photographic History of South Carolina in the Civil War*, Fayetteville, 1994.

Caldwell, J. F. J., *The History of the Brigade of South Carolinians*, Dayton, Morningside Press, 1984 (reprint).

Bigham, John Mills (compiler), 'Palmetto Soldiers – An Album of South Carolina Confederate Soldiers', *Military Images*, Vol. XI, No. 6 (May–June 1990).

Mississippi

Hooker, Col. C. E., 'Mississippi', in *Confederate Military History*, Vol. VII, Atlanta, Georgia, 1899.

Rowland, Dunbar (compiler), *Military History of Mississippi 1803–1898*, Jackson, Mississippi, 1908.

Rietti, J. C. (compiler), *Military Annals of Mississippi*, Spartanburg, S.C., 1976.

Moneyhon, Carl, & Roberts, Bobby, *Portraits of Conflict – A Photographic History of Mississippi in the Civil War*, Fayetteville, Arkansas, 1993.

Bearss, Edwin C., *Decision in Mississippi*, Jackson, Mississippi, 1962.

Adjutant General, Mississippi, *Annual Report* (for 1860), Jackson, Mississippi, 1861.

Orders of the Military Board of the State of Mississippi, Jackson, Mississippi, 1861.

Florida

Florida, Board of State Institutions, *Soldiers of Florida* in the Seminole Indian, Civil, and Spanish–American Wars, Live Oak, Florida, 1909.

Dickison, Col. J. J., 'Military History of Florida', *Confederate Military History*, Vol. XI, Atlanta, Georgia, 1899.

Davis, W. W., *The Civil War and Reconstruction in Florida*, New York, 1913.

Coles, David *et al*, 'The Florida Issue', *Military Images*, Vol. XIV, No. 4 (January–February 1993).

Alabama

Wheeler, Lieut. Gen. Joseph, 'Alabama', *Confederate Military History*, Vol. XI, Atlanta, Georgia, 1899.

Fleming, Walter L., *Civil War and Reconstruction in Alabama*, New York, 1905.

Owen, Thomas, M., 'The Military Forces of Alabama', *Alabama Historical Quarterly*, I (1939), 40–50.

Brooks, Ross, 'Confederate Uniforms, Part 1, Alabama', *Minie News*, September 1985.

Rodgers, Thomas, 'Uniforms of the Confederacy – Plate 79: 1st Volunteer Regiment, Alabama Militia, 1857–1861', *Journal, Confederate Historical Society*, Vol. XX, No. 1 (Spring 1992), 20–22.

Rodgers, Thomas & Field, Ron, 'Uniforms of the Confederacy – Plate 80: 2nd Volunteer Regiment, Alabama Militia, 1860–1861', *Journal, Confederate Historical Society*, Vol. XX, No. 2 (Summer 1992), 36–39.

Georgia

Derry, Joseph T., 'Georgia', *Confederate Military History*, Vol. VI, Atlanta, Georgia, 1899.

Thomas, Thomas, W., *History of the Doles-Cook Brigade, Army of Northern Virginia, C.S.A.*, Atlanta, Georgia, 1903.

Bryan, T. Conn, *Confederate Georgia*, Athens, Georgia, 1953.

Jones, Charles T., *Georgia at War, 1861–1865*, Atlanta, Georgia, 1909.

Candler, Allen D. (editor), *The Confederate Records of the State of Georgia*, 4 vols, Atlanta, Georgia, 1909–1910.

Hill, Louise B., *Joseph E. Brown and the Confederacy*, Chapel Hill, North Carolina, 1939.

Kerksis, Sydney C. (editor), 'Uniform and Dress of the Army of Georgia', *Military Collector & Historian*, XIII (1961), pp. 122–124.

Brooks, Ross, 'Confederate Uniforms, Part 4, Georgia', *Minie News*, November 1985.

Warren, Richard, 'Confederate Military Equipage: Georgia Jackets', *Journal, Confederate Historical Society*, Vol. XVII, No. 4 (Winter 1990), 94.

Louisiana

Bergeron Jr, Arthur W., *Guide to Louisiana Confederate Military Units 1861–1865*, Baton Rouge, Louisiana, 1989.

Works Project Administration, Louisiana, MS, 'Historical Militia Data on Louisiana Militia', 1851–1872 (typescript at USAMHI).

Dimitry, John, 'Louisiana', *Confederate Military History*, Vol. X, Atlanta, Georgia, 1899.

Bragg, Jefferson Davis, *Louisiana in the Confederacy*, Baton Rouge, Louisiana, 1941.

Moneyhon, Carl, & Roberts, Bobby, *Portraits of Conflict – A Photographic History of Louisiana in the Civil War*, Fayetteville, Arkansas, 1990.

Jones, Terry L., *Lee's Tigers: The Louisiana Infantry in the Army of Northern Virginia*, Baton Rouge, Louisiana, 1989.

Moore, Allison, *He Died Furious*, Baton Rouge, Louisiana, 1983.

Brooks, Ross, 'Confederate Uniforms, Part 6, 'Louisiana', *Minie News*, February 1986.

Texas

Roberts, Col. O. M., 'Texas', *Confederate Military History*, Vol. XI, Atlanta, Georgia, 1899.

Henderson, Harry M., *Texas in the Confederacy*, San Antonio, Texas, 1955.

Oates, Stephen B., *Confederate Cavalry West of the River*, Austin, Texas, 1961.

Fitzhugh, Lester N., *Texas Batteries, Battalions, Regiments, Commanders and Field Officers, Confederate States Army, 1861–1865*, Midlothian, Texas, 1959.

Wright, Marcus (compiler) and Simpson, Harold B. (editor), *Texas in the War, 1861–1865*, Hillsboro, 1965.

Virginia

Wallace, Jr Lee A., *A Guide to Virginia Military Organizations 1861–1865*, Lynchburg, Virginia, 1986 (revised edition).

Manarin, Louis H., and Wallace, Jr Lee, *Richmond Volunteers 1861–1865*, Richmond, Virginia, 1969.

Manarin, Louis H. (editor), *Richmond at War – Minutes of the City Council 1861–1865*, Chapel Hill, North Carolina, 1966.

Hotchkiss, Major Jed, 'Virginia', *Confederate Military History*, Vol. III, Atlanta, Georgia, 1899.

Wallace, Jr., Lee A., and Finke, Detmar H., 'Virginia Military Forces, 1858–1861: The Volunteers of the Second Brigade, Fourth Division', *Military Collector & Historian*, X, 61–70; 95–101; XI, 70–79.

Arkansas

Harell, Col. John M., 'Arkansas', *Confederate Military History*, Vol. X, Atlanta, Georgia, 1899.

Fletcher, John Gould, *Arkansas*, Chapel Hill, North Carolina, 1947.

Woodruff, W. E., *With the Light Guns in '61–'65 . . .*, Little Rock, Arkansas, 1903.

Wright, Marcus J., *Arkansas in the War, 1861–1865*, Batesville, Arkansas, 1963.

Moneyhon, Carl, and Roberts, Bobby, *Portraits of Conflict – A Photographic History of Arkansas in the Civil War*, Fayetteville, Arkansas, 1987.

Staff & contributors, 'Western Confederates: An album of Rebs from the Trans-Mississippi West', *Military Images*, Vol. XVI, No. 2 (September–October 1994), pp. 6–19.

Tennessee

Porter, James E., 'Tennessee', *Confederate Military History*, Vol. VIII, Atlanta, Georgia, 1899.

Lindsley, John B., *The Military Annals of Tennessee, Confederate, First Series . . .*, Nashville, Tennessee, 1886.

Wright, Marcus J., *Tennessee in the War, 1861–1865*, New York, 1908.

Civil War Centennial Commission, *Tennesseans in the Civil War*, 2 vols, Nashville, Tennessee, 1964.

Temple, Oliver P., *East Tennessee and the Civil War*, Cincinnati, Ohio, 1899.

North Carolina

Clark, Walter (editor), *Histories of the Several Regiments and Battalions from North Carolina in the Great War 1861–1865*, 5 vols, Raleigh, North Carolina, 1901.

Manarin, Louis H. (compiler), *North Carolina Troops 1861–1865: A Roster*, 13 vols, Raleigh, North Carolina, 1988 (second printing).

Mast, Greg, *State Troops and Volunteers – A Photographic Record of North Carolina's Civil War Soldiers*, Vol. 1, Raleigh, N.C., 1995.

Mast, Greg, 'Tar Heels', *Military Images*, Vol. XI, No. 2 (November–December 1989), pp. 6–31.

Warren, Richard, 'Uniforms of the Confederacy – Plate 72: North Carolina State Issue Uniforms, 1861–1865', *Journal, Confederate Historical Society*, Vol. XVIII, No. 2 (Summer 1990), pp. 45–52.

Missouri

Moore, Col. John C., 'Missouri', *Confederate Military History*, Vol. IX, Atlanta, Georgia, 1899.

Bevier, R. S., *History of the First and Second Missouri Confederate Brigades, 1861–1865*, St Louis, Missouri, 1879.

Parrish, William E., *Turbulent Partnership: Missouri and the Union, 1861–1865*, Columbia, Missouri, 1963.

Westover, John G., 'The Evolution of the Missouri Militia, 1804–1919'. MS doctoral thesis, University of Missouri.

Staff & contributors, 'Western Confederates: An Album of Rebs from the Trans-Mississippi West', *Military Images*, Vol. XVI, No. 2 (September–October 1994), pp. 6–19.

Kentucky

Johnston, Col. J. Stoddard, 'Kentucky', *Confederate Military History*, Vol. IX, Atlanta, Georgia, 1899.

Thompson, Ed. Porter, *History of the First Kentucky Brigade*, Cincinnati, Ohio, 1868.

Coulter, E. Merton, *The Civil War and Reconstruction in Kentucky*, Chapel Hill, North Carolina, 1926.

Federal Writers Project (W. P. A.), 'Military History of Kentucky, Frankfort', Kentucky, 1939.

Maryland

Johnson, Brig. Gen. Bradley T., 'Maryland', *Confederate Military History*, Vol. II, Atlanta, Georgia, 1899.

Culver, Frank B., *Historical Sketch of the Militia of Maryland*, Annapolis, Maryland, 1908.

David, Mark, 'Maryland Troops in the Confederate Army', *Military Images*, Vol. X, No. 5 (March–April 1989), pp. 4–30.

Warren, Richard, 'Confederate Military Equipage: Maryland Crosses . . .', *Journal, Confederate Historical Society*, Vol. XVII, No. 4 (Winter 1990), 94.

Confederate Quartermaster Issue

Serious research into Confederate Quartermaster issue uniforms is embryonic. The best work published to date is that of Leslie D. Jensen: 'A Survey of Confederate Central Quartermaster Issue Jackets', Parts 1 & 2, in *Military Collector & Historian*, Vol. XLI, No. 3 (Fall, 1989) and No. 4 (Winter, 1989). The TimeLife volume 'Arms and Equipment of the Confederacy' in the series *Echoes of Glory* (1991) contains photographic evidence from some of the best museum collections in the U.S. In 1987 the Museum of the Confederacy published a Catalogue of Uniforms which described many items of uniform in its collection, but provides photographs of only a few. Numerous references to the issuance of uniforms of quartermaster provenance may also be found in published memoirs, unpublished diaries and letters, and newspapers of the time.

Civil War Directory

This directory is a comprehensive guide for American Civil War re-enactors, Civil War historians, art collectors, modellers and wargamers.

American Re-enactment Groups

Big battle re-enactments in America can boast upwards of 6000 troops. At the Gettysburg anniversary re-enactment in 1988 over 14,000 men took part. Many British re-enactors travel to the United States during the summer to take part with members of American re-enactment groups. The following is a list of some of the hundreds of groups in the United States.

5th New York Volunteer Infantry, Duryee's Zouaves. Contact: PO Box 1601, Alexandria VA 22313. The 5th New York is one of the oldest re-enactment units and its captain is the noted American Civil War historian, Brian Pohanka. During the American Civil War, the original 5th New York boasted dozens of Englishmen in its ranks, some of them Crimean War veterans.

28th Massachusetts Volunteer Infantry. Contact: Guy Morin, PO Box 108, Auburn, MA 01501. Phone: 508 832 3175.

48th New York Volunteer Infantry. Contact: Lou Evans, 1321 Hammerhead Lane, Virginia Beach, VA 234646326.

111th Pennsylvania Volunteer Infantry Company I. Contact: Patrick A. Tarasovitch, 9800 Mark Road, Erie, PA 16509.

28th Pennsylvania Volunteer Infantry, Company C. Contact: Andy Waskie, G.A.R. Museum, 4278 Griscom Street, Philadelphia, PA 19124. Phone: 215 289 6484.

56th Pennsylvania Volunteer Infantry. Contact: 1st Sergeant Grehl, RR 6 Box 6394E, Stroudsburg, PA 18360.

9th New York Heavy Artillery. Contact: Frank Cutler, 6343 Kelly Road, Sodus, NY 14551. Phone: 315 483 9254.

76th Pennsylvania, Keystone Zouaves. Contact: Mike Deem, 437 Corona Drive, Morgantown, WV 26505.473.

2nd Maine Cavalry. Contact: Major Bunker, 903 Anne Street Wharf, Baltimore MD 21231. Phone: 410 276 8220.

81st Pennsylvania Volunteer Infantry, Company K. Contact: Theodore P. Dombroski, 768 McNair Street, Hazleton, PA 182021.

46th Illinois Volunteer Infantry. Contact: Andy Gelman, PO Box 1022, Highland Park, IL 60035. Phone: 708 831 2648.

119th New York Volunteer Infantry Company H. Contact: Joe Billardello. PO Box 184, Manorville, NY 11949.

1st New Jersey Artillery Battery B. Contact: Greg Putman, 18A Anbrey Street, Summit, NJ. Phone: 201 535 3745.

1st Regiment Berdan's Sharpshooters, Company B. Contact: Thomas Carton 914 782 9497 or John Caret 516 666 7348. This group is mainly based in the New York, New Jersey and Pennsylvania areas.

14th New Jersey Volunteer Infantry, Co. K. Contact: 14th NJ Volunteers PO Box 646, Dayton, NJ 08810 or phone Steve Milek on 908 521 2329.

8th Michigan Volunteer Infantry, Co C. Contact: John Milteer 914 692 5902.

46th Illinois Volunteer Infantry. Contact 46th IVI, PO Box 921, Joliet IL 604340921.

2nd New Jersey Volunteer Cavalry, Co A. Contact: Bill Anania, PO Box 673, Middletwn, NJ 07748. Phone: 908 671 1546.

9th Pennsylvania Reserves Co A. Contact: Bob Luther, 137 Fieldgate Drive, Pittsburgh PA 15241.

1st Minnesota Volunteer Infantry Co D. Contact: James D Owens, 1639 Belvedere Boulevard, Silver Spring MD 20902.

24th Michigan Volunteer Infantry. Contact: 604 Linden Street, Big Rapids, MI 49307. Phone: 616 796 0747.700.

83rd Pennsylvania Volunteer Infantry. Contact: Robert F. Frazier, 5511 Partridge Court, Harrisburg PA 17111. Phone 717 787 7111 during the day.

Co. B Tiger Rifles (Wheat's Tigers). Contact: Peter Leccese, 9137 85th Street, Woodhaven, NY 11421. Phone: 718 296 5897.

19th Virginia Volunteer Infantry. Contact: R. Mason, 14204 Radford Court, Woodbridge VA 22191.

1st Regiment Virginia Volunteers, Co D. Contact: Bob Lyons, 15 Highfields Drive, Baltimore, MD 21228. Phone: 410 747 3271.

21st Mississippi Volunteers Co H. Contact: John J. Wrona, 363 Quaker Highway, Uxbridge MA 01569. Phone: 508 278 6056.

21st Virginia Volunteers Co F. Contact: Floyd Bane, 14407 Huntgate Woods Road, Midlothian, VA 23112. Phone: 804 231 7852.

3rd Arkansas. Contact: Denis on 804 363 1903 or Terry on 717 939 3629.

1st Virginia Cavalry. Contact: Nick Nichols, HCR 3, Box 378A, Rochelle, VA 22736. Phone: 703 948 6879.

13th North Carolina Troops. Contact: Red Hovey, 9225 Surrey Road, Mint Hill, NC 28227. Phone: 704 545 9760.

21st Regiment, North Carolina Troops. Contact: Clark Fox, 410 Keating Drive, Winston Salem, NC 27104.

51st North Carolina Volunteer Infantry. Contact: Mike Murley, 910 425 6836 or Mike Carraway 910 424 4936.

19th Virginia Volunteer Infantry, Co K. Contact: Ken Thaiss, 10 Carriage Way, Freehold, NJ 07728. Phone: 908 780 4802. Fax: 908 780 4803.

30th Virginia Volunteer Infantry. Contact: Bruce Drummond, 6

Oakcrest Court, East Northport, NY 11731. Phone: 516 754 1918.

55th Virginia Volunteer Infantry. Contact: Eugene Tucceri, 38
Beverley Heights, Middletown, CT 06475. Phone: 203 347 5750.

45th Alabama Volunteer Infantry/18th Missouri Volunteer Infantry.
Contact: Mark Hubbs, 205 464 9751.

58th Virginia Infantry. Contact: Chris Loving, 703 724 0974.

1st Tennessee Volunteer Infantry, Co B. Contact: Ed Sharp, 12211
Army Dee Lane, Medway, Ohio, 45341.

7th Tennessee Volunteer Infantry. Contact: Sergeant Howard, 609
625 3233.

British Re-enactment Groups

In Britain, the two main umbrella organizations for American Civil
War re-enactment groups are the Southern Skirmish Association,
Soskan, and the American Civil War Society the A.C.W.S.

For information about joining Soskan write to: The Secretary,
Southern Skirmish Association, PO Box 485, Swindon SN2 6BF.
Soskan has the following Northern Southern units, for prospective
recruits to choose from.

2nd U.S. Artillery Battery A
2nd U.S. Sharpshooters
2nd U.S. Cavalry
18th Missouri
28th Missouri
28th Massachuseetts
42nd Pennsylvania
1st Minnesota Infantry
1st Minnesota Artillery
79th New York Veteran Reserve
6th Pennsylvania Cavalry

1st Arkansas
15th Arkansas
9th Kentucky
16th Tennessee
Palmetto Sharpshooters
4th Virginia
7th Virginia Cavalry
17th Virginia
23rd Virginia
Confederate Artillery
Virginia Medical Department

For information about the A.C.W.S. write to PO Box 52, Brighouse,
West Yorkshire, HD6 1JQ and you can be put in touch with one of
the following Northern/Southern units.

2nd US Infantry

24th Michigan
2nd Wisconsin
19th Indiana
14th Brooklyn
69th New York
2nd US Artillery Battery B

The 24th Michigan can also be contacted directly by writing to
Mark Gregory, 82 Brierly Street, Bury, Lancashire BL9 9HW. Phone:
0161 7052433.

32nd Virginia Infantry
1st Tennessee Infantry
43rd North Carolina Infantry
2nd South Carolina Infantry
13th Mississippi Infantry
4th Texas Infantry
1st Louisiana Zouaves
Washington Artillery of New Orleans
Virginia Artillery

55th Virginia
Widely acclaimed as Britain's finest American Civil War re-
enactment group, the 55th Virginia Infantry is an independent unit
and not a member of either Soskan or the A.C.W.S. The 55th is
noted for the excellence of its drill displays, authentic dress,
accoutrements, and encampments. For information write to: Richard
O'Sullivan, Flat 11, Grove Lodge, Crescent Grove, Clapham
Common, London SW4 7AE. Phone: 020 7622 4109

Civil War Re-enactment Suppliers

The growth in living history and battle re-enactments over
the past few years has led to a steady growth of specialist equipment
suppliers in Britain and the United States, who can satisfy re-
enactment requirements from a forage cap to a tent peg.

Britain's largest supplier of American Civil War re-enactment
equipment including haversacks, cap pouches, cartridge boxes,
buttons and buckles is Alan Thrower who runs The Sutler's Store, 16
Howlett Drive, Hailsham, East Sussex, BN27 1QW.

Many British American Civil War re-enactors buy their clothing
from companies in the United States. Some of the best Civil War
uniforms renowned for their correct cut and color are manufactured
by Charlie Childs. Charlie runs his company County Cloth from
13797C, Georgetown Street NE, Paris, Ohio, 44669.

The United State's oldest established American Civil War re-
enactment clothing supplier is the C & D Jarnagin Company, PO
Box 1860, Corinth, MS 38834. Phone: 601 287 1977. Fax: 601 287
6033. Apart from complete uniforms, Jarnagin also specializes in
leather gear, footwear and tinwear.

Other U.S. firms manufacturing reproduction uniforms include Confederate Yankee, PO Box 192, Guildford, CT 06437. Phone: 203 453 9900. Centennial General Store, 230 Steinwehr Avenue, Gettysburg, PA 17325. Phone: 717 334 9712.

Civil War A frame tents and shelter halves are available from Panther, 1000 PO Box 32, Normantown, WV 25267. Phone: 304 462 7718.

American Civil War Organizations

The American Civil War Round Table (UK) is Britain's leading Civil War study group and one of hundreds of American Civil War Round tables around the world. The American Civil War Round table (UK) has members all over Britain and regular meetings are held, usually in London. For further informastion contact, Tony Daly, 57 Bartlemas Road, Oxford OX4 1XU. Tel: 01865 201216.

The Military Order of the Loyal Legion of the United States is open to direct and collateral descendants of commissioned officers of the Union Army and was founded in 1865. For information contact Robert G. Carroon, 23 Thompson Road, West Hartford, CT 01072535.

Sons of Union Veterans of the Civil War is open to male descendants of Civil War soldiers. Write to S.U.V.C.W. 1310 Forest Park Avenue, Dept TC, Valparaiso, IN 46383.

Heritagepac is a national lobbying group dedicated to preserving U.S. battlefields against business concerns who want to turn battlesites into shopping malls or housing developments. For information write to PO Box 7281, Little Rock, AR 72217.

The Save Historic Antietam Foundation is aimed at preserving one of the U.S.'s most important Civil War battle sites. For information contact SHAF at PO Box 550, Sharpsburg, MD 21782. Phone: 301 432 2522.

The Bucktail Regimental Association studies and celebrates the men of Pennsylvania's famous Bucktail regiments. For information contact Major Richard Miller, 1405 Blue Mountain Parkway, Harrisburg, PA 17112. Phone: 717 545 9830.

The Fourteenth Brooklyn Regiment, New York State Militia Society of New York Inc., preserves the memory of the famous Red legged devils, one of the most outstanding regiments of the Civil War. Write to Morton Berger, 2978 Ave. 'W' Apt 2A, Brooklyn, NY 11229 for details. Mr Berger is the society's historian and curator of the 14th Brooklyn's armoury.

The Ulysses S. Grant Network promotes the study of the fabled Union general. Write for details to 238 Morse Avenue, Wyckoff, NJ 07481.

The Company of Military Historians has published many articles and plates on American Civil War regiments and its international membership boasts the cream of Civil War scholars. For details write to The Company of Military Historians, North Main Street, CT 06498A.

The Sons of Confederate Veterans is open to descendants of men who fought for the South during the Civil War. For information write to Arthur Kuydenkall Jr, 193 Clover Ridge Ct, Edgewater, Florida, 32141.

The John Pelham Historical Association celebrates the life and times of the South's finest horse artillery commander. For membership details write to Peggy Vogtsberger, 7 Carmel Terrace, Hampton, VA 23666. Phone: 804 838 3862.

The Turner Ashby Historical Society commemorates the life and times of Southern hero, Turner Ashby. Write to Patricia Walenista, 810 W. 30th Street, Richmond, VA 23255. Phone: 804 232 3406.

The Immortal 600 Memorial Fund commemorates Confederate officers who have no marked graves. For details write to The Immortal 600 Memorial Fund, PO Box 652, Sparta, GA 31087.

Museums and Battlefields

Most American battlefields have visitor centres with museums and one of the most impressive is at the Gettysburg Military Park. Many people are put off by the drive into Gettysburg because the town itself has become a tourist trap complete with a wax museum, but the uniforms, equipment and artefacts in the visitor centre more than make up for this. The battlefield itself retains all the drama of the epic three-day conflict, the largest ever fought on U.S. soil. Walking across the scene of Pickett's charge is particularly memorable.

For brooding atmosphere though, the Antietam battlefield which has been relatively unspoiled by commercialism cannot be beaten, and it also has a fine visitors' centre, with many uniforms and artefacts on display. Twenty-six miles southwest of Washington D.C. is the Manassas National Battlefield Park, encompassing both the first and second battle. The visitor centre has good exhibits concentrating on the early period of the war, including the uniform worn by Corporal Brownell of the Fire Zouaves. The park also boasts a fine monument to Confederate General Stonewall Jackson. At Fort Sumter and Fort Moultrie in Charleston Harbor you can see where the war really began when the Confederates bombarded Sumter. Both forts have been preserved very well and both have a selection of unusual artefacts.

Of the many Western battlefields, Shiloh Military Park in Tennessee comes highly recommended. The battlefield itself has almost the same atmosphere as Antietam and the well laid out visitors' centre boasts a wealth of exhibits.

A number of American museums such as the West Point museum at the academy in New York State boast an impressive collection of Civil War memorabilia. The U.S. cavalry Museum at Fort Riley, Kansas, has an impressive display of Civil War memorabilia and includes an extensive collection of saddles.

Urban areas also boast impressive museums, the Smithsonian in Washington D.C. boasts a fine collection of Civil War artefacts as does Fort Ward in Alexandria, Virginia, which was the fifth largest of the 68 forts manned to protect Washington during the Civil War.

The G.A.R. Museum at 4278 Griscom Street, Philadelphia is another museum with some fine artefacts.

The Museum of the Confederacy at 1201 Clay Street, Richmond, VA 23219, is a must for both Yankee and Confederate military enthusiasts. The many artefacts include Jeb Stuart's plumed hat, a Union Zouave's fez picked up at First Manassas, and an impressive collection of flags.

To see where the war ended, a trip to Appomattox Court House, 3 miles east of the town of Appomattox in Virginia is a must. It was here that Lee surrendered to Grant and an impressive re-enactment of the Confederate surrender was made in the village in 1989. Today, Appomatttox Court House has a brooding character all of its own.

For a flavour of American life in Britain, then a trip to the American Museum at Claverton Manor, Bath, is recommended. It's not specifically Civil War, but a large scale Civil War Battle is held behind the museum every year, in September.

Specialist tour operators run trips to American Civil War battlefields and the East Coast sites conveniently grouped together in Maryland, Pennsylvania and Virginia, are at most a day's drive from each other. Holts' Tours Ltd, Britain's oldest specialist operator runs yearly trips to a variety of battlefields. Write to Holts' Battlefields & History, Golden Key Building, 15 Market Street, Sandwich, Kent CT13 9DA for details.

Civil War Book Suppliers

More books have been written about the American Civil War than possibly World Wars I and II. Not only have many modern historians written about the American Civil War, but the era spawned numerous diaries and recollections of the conflict, as well as a steady stream of regimental histories in the years following the war. The following is a list of some leading American Civil War book suppliers.

Michael Haynes, 46 Farnaby Road, Bromley, Kent BR1 4BJ (Phone: 020 8460 1672) sells a wide variety of Civil War books, both new and secondhand. Write or call to be put on his mailing list.

Kennesaw Mountain Military Antiques, 1810 Old Highway, 41 Kennesaw, GA 30152 (Fax: 770 424 0434) offer a good range of new Civil War books and reprints including such gems as *Where Bugles Called* and *Rifles Gleamed*.

Broadfoot Publishing Company, 1907 Buena Vista Circle, Wilmington, NC 28405 (Phone: 800 537 5243; Fax: 910 686 4379) has republished both the Army Official Records and the Supplement of the Official Records, indispensable books to any American Civil War enthusiast.

Olde Soldier Books Inc., 18779 B North Frederick, Gaithersburg, MD 20879 (Phone: 301 963 2929; Fax: 301 963 9556) offers a wide selection of books, autographs, letters and documents.

First Corps Books, 42 Eastgrove Court, Columbia SC 292122404

(Phone 803 781 2709) has a large selection of new and difficult to obtain out of print books.

Richard A. La Posta 154 Robindale Drive, Kensington, CT 06037 (Phone: 203 828 0921) specializes in regimental histories and has many first editions.

The Command Post, Dept CN, PO Box 141, Convent Station, NJ 079610141 (Phone: 800 722 7344) stocks many fine books.

Longstreet House, PO Box 730, Hightstown, NJ 08520 (Phone: 609 448 1501) specializes in books about New Jersey, Gettysburg and New York Civil War history.

The J.W. Carson Company (CWN), 130 Myrtle Street, Le Roy, New York, 144821332, promises to supply important Civil War books at affordable prices, including a reprint of the 1866 edition of *Campaigns of the Army of the Potomac.*

The Morningside Bookshop, PO Box 1087, Dayton, Ohio, 45401, with a shop at 260 Oak Street, Dayton, Ohio, 45410 (Phone: 1 800 648 9710) has one of the States largest selection of Civil War books and specializes in fine reprints.

Civil War Magazines and Newspapers

One of the finest Civil War magazines on the market is *Military Images* which features excellent articles and original pictures of Civil War soldiers. For subscription details write to *Military Images*, Rt 1, Box 99A, Henryville, PA 18332.

North South Trader, PO Drawer 631, Orange VA 22960, contains many fine articles on relic collecting and uniforms.

The Civil War News, Route 1, Box 36, Tunbridge, VT 05077 (Phone: 802 889 3500. Fax: 802 889 5627) is a monthly 'bible' on American and international Civil War events. The Civil War News also features an extremely useful small ads section and book reviews pages.

The Union Times, U.A.D.F. Publications, 5330 County Road 561, Clermont, FL 34711 (Phone: 904 394 7206) covers the Civil War Seminole War and Mexican War in South Eastern America.

The Artilleryman, Rt. 1, Box 36, Tunbridge, VT 05077 (Phone: 802 889 3500) is a specialist magazine with articles on American Civil War artillery and artillery re-enactors.

America's Civil War is a glossy magazine with plenty of interest. Write to PO Box 383, Mount Morris, IL 610547947 for subscription details.

In the same league is *Civil War*, the magazine of the Civil War Society, published by Outlook Inc, PO Box 770, Berryville, VA 22611. Civil War Society membership details are also available from this address.

Artefacts

There are a number of good Civil War artefact suppliers, and even today some items can be picked up at reasonable prices.

The Union Drummer Boy, which has a correspondence address at 420 Flourtown Road, Lafayette Hill, PA 19444 and a shop at 5820 York Road, Lahaska, PA 18931, offers a selection of excavated and non excavated relics. Their phone number is 610 825 6280.

R. Stephen Dorsey, Antique Militaria, at PO Box 263, Eugene, OR 97440 (Phone: 541 937 3348) has a wide selection of guns and edged weapons.

The Powder Horn Gunshop Inc., PO Box 1001, 200 W. Washington Street, Middleburg, VA 22117 (Phone: 540 687 6628) also has a wide range of items, including original belt plates.

One of the most famous centres for American Civil War artefacts is the Horse Soldier at 777 Baltimore Street, Gettysburg PA (Phone: 717 334 0347), mailing address PO Box 184E, Cashtown, PA 17310. A wide selection of goods are on offer and a catalogue is available for overseas customers.

Lawrence Christopher Civil War Relics, 4773 Tammy Dr. N.E., Dalton, GA 30721 (Phone: 800 336 8894 or 706 226 8894) has a selection of buttons, buckles, and bullets.

Car War Videos and Art

Classic Images Productions International at PO Box 1863, Charlbury, Oxfordshire, OX7 3PD (Phone or Fax: 01608 676635) offers the entire range of Classic Images battle re-enactment videos shot at anniversary events in America and featuring thousands of re-enactors in action. They also have *Echoes of the Blue and Gray Volumes One & Two*, actual footage of Civil War veterans shot after the war with some old soldiers actually describing their experiences. *Gettysburg 75th 1863–1938 The Last Reunion of the Blue & Gray*, also has some rare color footage of the combatants at Gettysburg meeting for the last time. Classic Images productions has become Britain's largest emporium of videos, books and art and a catalogue is available.

Civil War art has become extremely collectable during the past decade and the dean of American artists is Don Troiani, whose limited edition prints are available from Historical Art Prints, PO Box 660, Drawer U, Southbury, CT 064880660 (Phone: 203 262 6680). Classic Images Productions International also hope to be stocking his work.

The Heritage Studio, 2852 Jefferson Davis Highway, Suite 10912. Stafford, VA 22554 (Phone: 540 659 1070 or 540 899 6675) stocks work by the artist Donna J. Neary, who has a particularly vigorous style.

Limited editions prints by Don Stivers are available from Stivers Publishing, PO Box 25, Waterford, VA 3800 22190.

Rick Reeves is another talented artist, whose work is available from Paramount Press Incorporated, 1 West Main Street, Panama, NY 1467 (Phone: 716 782 4626).

Dale Gallon who specializes in action scenes, often opens his studio at 777 Baltimore Street, Gettysburg, PA to the public. His prints are available from Dale Gallon Historical Art Inc., PO Box 43443, Gettysburg, PA 17325 (Phone: 717 334 0430).

Many businesses trade in Civil War art and one of the best known outlets for buying prints by Troiani and many other artists is Volar Art & Frame Ltd, 718 Caroline Street, Fredericksburg, VA 22401 (Phone: 703 372 3376).

Stan Clark Military Books, 915 Fairview Avenue (CWN), Gettysburg, PA 17325 (Phone: 717 337 1728, Fax: 717 337 1728) also has a large selection of prints by Troiani and other well known artists.

Civil War Sculpture

Limited edition Civil War Sculptures have also become very collectable. The finest exponent of limited edition bronzes is Ron Tunison, who like Don Troiani is a member of the Society of American Historical Artists. Tunison began his artistic career just modelling one-off clay figures, but there was so much demand for his work that he eventually turned to bronzes. Some of his most attractive and reasonably priced work is a series of busts of Civil War personalities, including George Armstrong Custer. For details write to Historical Sculptures, PO Box 141, Cairo, NY 12413 (Phone: 518 622 3508).

Terry Jones is another fine sculptor particularly with his recent figure of Joshua L. Chamberlain. He can be contacted at 234 Hickory Lane, Newtown Square, PA 19073 (Phone: 610 353 2210).

American Civil War Model Soldiers

Paul Clarke who runs Shenandoah Miniatures at 12 Holywood Grove, Carnegie, Victoria 3163, Australia. (Fax: 00 61 3 534 1443) produces a fine range of 54mm American Civil War Figures. Particularly impressive is his range of Zouaves and Paul is planning some speciality figures in the range. To go with his figures, Paul also has an extensive spare parts list.

Tradition of London Ltd, 33 Curzon Street, Mayfair, London W1Y 7AE. (Phone: 020 7493 7452. Fax: 020 7355 1224) has plenty of Civil War Figures in its range. Some, including a 14th Brooklyn figure were sculpted by Andrew C. Stadden. Tradition also has some sets of toy American Civil War figures, notably a set of 114th Pennsylvania Volunteer Infantry.

Chosen Men, 74 Rotherham Road, Holbrooks, Coventry, CV6 4FE. (Phone or Fax: 01203 666376) produce 120mm resin figure kits of a New Hampshire Volunteer, a Tiger Zouave and a Berdan's Sharpshooter.

Fort Duquesne Military Miniatures, 105 Tristan Drive, Pittsburgh, PA 15209 (Phone: 412 486 1823) has an extensive range of figures and busts including a kit of an 83rd Pennsylvania Volunteer and a bust of a 155th Pennsylvania Volunteer, both sculpted by Gary Dombrowski. Fort Duquesne Miniatures are available in Britain from Historex Agents, Wellington House, 157 Snargate Street, Dover, Kent CT17 9BZ.

Terry Worster Miniatures, 8529 Ablette Road, Santee, CA 92071 (Phone: 619 258 1888) has a range of exquisite portrait busts including US Grant, George Meade and Thomas Meagher. He also carries a range of Civil War artillery models manufactured by Bayardi.

Michael Roberts Ltd, 2221 Hunters Road SW, Roanoke, Virginia 24015 (Phone: 540 342 7441 or 343 2241) produces some fine figure kits, including a US Army Brigadier General.

Acknowledgments

UNIFORMS OF THE UNION ARMY BY ROBIN SMITH
The author would like to thank Richard Warren; Ron Field; David Scheinmann; Mike McAfee; Brian Pohanka; Martin Schoenfeld and Richard Sullivan whose help was invaluable in writing this book.

UNIFORMS OF THE CONFEDERATE ARMY BY RON FIELD
The author would also like to thank Richard O'Sullivan; Val Czemy of the 55th Virginia Regiment; Joseph Matheson Jr, Camden Archives; Joanna Norman, Photographic Collection, Florida State Archives; Cory Hudgins, Curator of Photographic Collections, Museum of the Confederacy; John Bigham, Curator of Education, South Carolina Confederate Relic Room and Museum; Elizabeth P. Bilderback, Assistant Manuscripts Librarian, South Caroliniana Library; Norwood A. Kerr, Archival Reference, Alabama Department of Archives and History; Gail DeLoach, Photographic Archivist, Georgia Department of Archives and History; Pat Ricci, Confederate Memorial Hall, New Orleans; Victor Bailey, Mississippi Department of Archives and History; Steve Massingill, North Carolina Division of Archives and History; Dr. Thomas Sweeney, General Sweeney's Museum of Civil War History; Claire Maxwell, Photographs Curator, Austin History Center; Anna Peebler, Photo Archivist, Rosenberg Library; Kathy Knox, Special Collections, Woodruff Library, Emory University; Adam Scher, Curator of Collections, Lynchburg Museum System; Michael J. McAfee, Curator of uniforms and history, West Point Museum; David Wynn Vaughan; Dan Snipes; Herb Peck Jr; Jim Enos; Dave Mark; Russell Hicks Jr; Steven Lister; Alan Thrower; Robin Forsey; Thomas Arliskas; Geoff Walden; David P. Hunter; Richard W. Hatcher, III; and Ross Smith, without whose assistance this book would not have been possible.

Index

Agnus, Captain Felix 37, 90
Aid Society
    Ladies Aid Society 192, 216
    Randolph County Central Committee 236
    Soldier Aid Society 202
    South Memphis Ladies' Sewing Society 242
    Union County Central Committee 236
    Aiken, Colonel D. Wyatt 267
Aiguilettes 137
Alabama
    2nd Alabama Infantry 184–5
    6th Alabama Infantry 184
    12th Alabama Infantry 185
    14th Alabama Infantry 182
    15th Alabama Infantry 184
    19th Alabama Infantry 185
    40th Alabama Infantry 181
    1st Artillery Battalion 181
    9th Volunteer Infantry 182
    Alabama Volunteer Corps 178–9, 182
    An Act for the Org. of the Army of Alabama
        179
    Republic of Alabama 178
Alabama Military Companies
    Alabama Rifles 181
    Alabama Zouaves 180
    Auburn Guards 180
    Billy Gilmer Grays 182
    Calhoun Guards 185
    Camden Rifles 181
    Cherokee Rangers 185
    Dale County Beauregards 184
    Henry Pioneers 184
    Independent Blues 192
    Mobile Rifle Guard 179
    Montgomery Mounted Rifles 179, 181
    Montgomery True Blues 181
    Perote Guards 181, 184
    Pickens Stars 181
    Pioneer Guards 181
    Raccoon Roughs 184
    Sumter Shorter Guards 185
    Tuskegee Light Infantry 180
Alabama Militia
    1st Regiment 179
    2nd Volunteer Regiment 180
    4th Regiment 185

Alabama Newspapers
    Montgomery Weekly Advertiser 185
    Alabama State Uniform 182
Albany Burgesses Corps 105, 107
Albany Zouave Cadets 93
Alexandria, Virginia 88, 93
Ambulance Corps 83
Arkansas Regiments and Battalions
    2nd Arkansas Infantry 233
    4th Arkansas Infantry 232
    11th Arkansas Infantry 233
    19th Arkansas Infantry 237
    23rd Arkansas Infantry 236
    24th Arkansas Infantry 236
    27th Arkansas Infantry 237
    1st Arkansas (Fagan's) 234, 236
    1st Arkansas Cavalry 235–6
    3rd Arkansas State Infantry 232
    5th Arkansas State Infantry 232
    Appeal Battery, Arkansas Light Artillery 237
    Arkansas Military Institute 232
    Military Board 217, 233, 235–6
    Phifer's Battalion of Cavalry 237
Arkansas Military Companies
    Belle Point Guards 232, 234
    Camden Knights 234
    Capital Guards 232
    Centerpoint Riflemen 234
    City Guard 234
    Crockett Rifles 236
    Davis Blues 232, 234
    Eldorado Sentinels 234
    Fort Smith Rifles 232–3
    Jackson Port Guards 234, 239
    Lisbon Invincibles 236
    Ouchita Grays 234
    Pulaski Battery 235
    Pulaski Lancers 232
    Southern Defenders 236
    Totten Artillery 235
Army of the Potomac 129, 131
Artillery Uniforms 70
Austrian knots 95

Bands 38
Bayonets 43
Bearskin busbies 105

Belt plates 119., 121, 125–7
Berdan, Col. Hiram 76
Berdan's Sharpshooters 34, 42–3, 76–7, 80–1
Bersaglieri 96, 108
Blankets 30–1, 64
Boots 28–9, 61, 66
Bowie knives 28, 64
Bragg's, General Braxton 10, 19
Brown, Governor Joseph E. 188, 192, 202
Brownell, Corporal Francis E. 137
Buckne, Simon Bolivar 254–5
Bucktails 31–2
Burnside, General Ambrose E. 84–5
Butler, General Benjamin 257
Butterflies, 1st U.S. Hussars 68, 70
Buttons 25, 128

Cameron Highlanders 96
Camp Quantico 212, 214
Camp Qui Vive 209
Cannon 73
Canteens 36, 62
Cap pouches 36
Carbines 42
Cartridges 36, 40
Cartridge boxes 36, 120
Cartwright Lieutenant Thomas W. 111
Cavalry uniforms 60
Chasseur uniforms 88, 95
Cincinatti Rover Guards 107
Clark, Governor Edward 211
Collis Captain H. T. 93, 126
Collis Zouaves 93
Colt pistols 42, 45
Company letters 127, 129
Confederacy 9–10, 13, 19
Confederate
    C.S. Quartermaster Department Clothing
        Bureau 230, 237
    Confederate Clothing Bureau 223, 263
    Confederate commutation system 19
    Confederate Quartermaster 19
Confederate cavalry 46, 60–1, 70
Connecticut Governor's Footguard 105
Connecticut Militia 116
Corps badges 129–31, 133, 135
Corps of Engineers 81

Cravats 44
Custer, George Armstrong 70

Davis, President Jefferson 203
DeVilliers, Charles A. 86
Dickert, D. Augustus 269
Dragoons 46, 58, 60
Dreux, Colonel Charles 206
Duncan, Colonel Blanton 255
Duryée, Col. Abram 90
Duryée's Zouaves 88, 90, 111–12

Eagle plates 126
Ellsworth Association 92
Ellsworth Avengers 93
Ellsworth, Colonel Elmer E. 86, 88, 92
Enfield rifle muskets 40, 42–3
Epaulettes 114, 124, 129–30, 133, 135–6

Facings 59–60
False vests 95
Farnham, Lieutenant Colonel Noah 14
Fatigue blouses 58
Feather plumes 30
Fezzes 87–90, 107, 112, 122, 128
Fire Zouaves 88
Field artillery 70, 73
First Bull Run 88, 96
Flintlocks 40, 42
Florida Regiments
  1st Florida Cavalry 174–5, 177
  1st Florida Infantry 174–5
  2nd Florida Infantry 175
  5th Florida Infantry 177
  6th Florida Infantry 177
  7th Florida Infantry 175
  9th Florida Infantry 177
  West Florida Seminary 174
Florida Military Companies
  Gulf Coast Rangers 175
  Leon Rifles 174–5
  Marion Light Artillery 177
  Palatka Guard 177
  Simpson Mounted Rangers 175
  Trapier Guard 177
Footwear 28–9
Forage caps 26–7, 29, 30–3, 43–4
Frock coats 25, 32, 34, 39–40

Gaiters 28, 88, 94, 107
Garibaldi, Giuseppe 184
Garibaldi Guard 96, 108
Garrard, Colonel Kenner

Georgia Regiments and Battalions
  4th Georgia Infantry 186
  5th Georgia Infantry 187
  7th Georgia Infantry 201–2
  10th Georgia Infantry 192
  17th Georgia Infantry 190
  21st Georgia Infantry 191, 202
  22nd Georgia Infantry 192
  23rd Georgia Infantry 201
  1st Regiment Georgia Regulars 189
  1st Regiment Georgia Volunteers 188
  2nd Battalion, Georgia Infantry 188
  3rd Battalion, Georgia Sharpshooters 191
  Augusta Independent Volunteer Battalion 188
  Columbus Depot 255, 268, 270
  Georgia Army 189
Georgia Military Companies
  Baldwin Blues 192
  Bartow County Yankee Killers 201
  Ben Hill Volunteers 202
  Browns Rifles 192
  Burke Guards 192
  Clinch Rifles 187, 189, 192
  Dawson Grays 192
  Floyd Rifles 188
  Franklin Volunteers 201
  Gardner Volunteers 192
  Governor's Guards 192
  Henry Pioneers 184
  Henry Volunteers 192
  Home Guard 92
  Irish Volunteers 189
  Jackson County Volunteers 172, 190
  Macon Volunteer Zouaves 192
  Quitman Grays 169
  Republican Blues 188
  Richmond Hussars 189
  Roswell Guards 202
  Silver Grays 191
  Southern Rifles 192
  Sumter Light Guards 160, 186
  Sumter Shorter Guards 185
  Thompson Guards 192
  Twigg's Volunteers 192
  Webster Confederate Guards 190
  West Point Guards 188, 201
  Wilkinson's Rifles 192
Glover, Colonel S.L. 161
Green, Brigadier General Duff C. 185
Gettysburg 36
Godillot, M. Alexis 95
Grant, General Ulysses S. 74, 78

Hanover Courthouse 66
Hardee hats 30, 45, 65, 72
Harper's Weekly 16
Harris, Governor Isham G. 238–40
Harris Zouave Cadets 238
Hatch, Colonel Lewis M. 160–1
Havelocks 31
Haversacks 33, 36
Hat cords 30
Heavy artillery 70, 73
Henry rifles 32
Homer, Winslow 66
Hood, John Bell 211, 213
Horses 46, 62, 64, 70
Hussars 46, 66, 68

Identity discs 84
Insignia 125
Irish Brigade 42

Jambieres 154
Jean cloth 61
Johnston, Gen. Joseph E. 13, 20

Kearny, General Philip 129, 131, 137–8
Kentucky Regiments
  2nd Kentucky Cavalry 255
  4th Kentucky Cavalry 255
  11th Kentucky Cavalry 255
  1st Kentucky Infantry 255
  2nd Kentucky Infantry 269
  4th Kentucky Infantry 255
  9th Kentucky Infantry 255, 268
  6th Kentucky 204
  8th Kentucky Mounted Infantry 255
  Kentucky State Guard 254–6
  Orphan Brigade 255
  Stevenson, Quartermaster V.K. 255
Kewshaw, Joseph Brevard 267
King, Roswell 192
Knights of the Golden Circle 210
Kepis 42, 44
Kidd, Colonel James H. 70
Knapsacks 31, 34, 36

Lances 66, 68
Lincoln, Abraham 6
Louisiana Regiments and Battalions
  10th Louisiana 208
  13th Louisiana Battalion 204
  13th Louisiana Infantry 206
  18th Louisiana 208–9
  1st Louisiana Infantry Battalion 206

1st Special Battalion (2nd Louisiana Inf. Batt.) 206
21st Louisiana 208
24th Louisiana 208
2nd Louisiana 206
2nd Zouave Battalion 206
5th Louisiana 205, 208
8th Louisiana 206
Confederate Guards Response Battalion 205
Coppens' Louisiana Zouaves 206
Garibaldi Legion 205
Louisiana Military Companies
5th Company, Washington Artillery 203
Belgian Guards 205
British Guard 205
Chasseurs a Pied 161, 202
Claiborne Guards 209
Confederate States Rangers 208
Crescent City Rifles 206
Donaldsonville Artillery 208
Garibaldi Guards 205
Home Sentinels 206
Hope Guard 206
Legion Française 205
Louisiana Cadets 206
Louisiana Guard 206
Louisiana Guerrillas 204
Monroe Cadets 206
Monroe Guards 208
Monroe Zouaves 206
Orleans Battalion of Artillery 203
Orleans Cadets 206
Orleans Flying Artillery 205
Orleans Rifles 205
Ouachita Fencibles 206 208
Pelican Rifles 208
Phoenix Company 206
Southern Celts 206
Tiger Rifles 204, 206
Washington Artillery of New Orleans 203
Wheat's 1st Special Battalion 208
Young Cadets 206

Marschall, Nicola 261
Maryland
1st Maryland Cavalry 260
1st Maryland Infantry 257
53rd Militia Infantry 257
Maryland Guard Battalion 257, 260
Maryland Zouaves, 1st Regiment 259
McClellan, General George B. 32, 44, 86
McDowell, Brigadier General Irvin 44
Meigs, Montgomery, Quartermaster General 95

Meagher, General Thomas Francis 42, 44, 96, 105, 135
Medals 137–8
Medics 83
Mexican War 83, 112, 119
Michigan Cavalry Brigade 66, 70
Michigan Lancers 66
Mississippi Regiments and Battalions
10th Mississippi Infantry 167–8
11th Mississippi Infantry 167–8
12th Mississippi Infantry 167, 169–70, 173
14th Mississippi Infantry 169
15th Mississippi Infantry 167, 173
1st Battalion Mississippi Cavalry 168
1st Mississippi Infantry 167
8th Mississippi Infantry 168, 172
9th Mississippi Infantry 167–8
18th Mississippi Infantry 170
Army of Mississippi 165–6, 169
Military Board 165–9
Mississippi Manufacturing Company 172
Mississippi Military Companies
Alcorn Rifles 167
Ben Bullard Rifles 167
Bolivar Troop 168
Burt Rifles 170
Choctaw Guards 167
Confederate Guards 173
James Creek Rifles 167
Jeff Davis Rifles 167
Lamar Rifles 167
Long Creek Rifles 173
Mississippi Rifles 168
Natchez Fencibles 167–9
Prairie Guards 168
Satartia Rifles 173
Shubuta Rifles 169
Smith-Quitman Rifles 170
True Confederates 168
Van Dorn Reserves 168
Water Valley Rifle Guard 167
Mississippi Militia
2nd Regiment, 1st Brigade, of the Volunteer Militia 167
Mississippi State Penitentiary 172
Missouri Regiments
1st Missouri Brigade, Volunteer Militia 250
1st Regiment, Missouri Volunteer Militia 250
2nd Regiment, Missouri Volunteer Militia 251
3rd Battery, Missouri Light Artillery, C.S.A. 250
3rd Missouri Infantry 251

Missouri Military Companies
Emmet Guard 251
Missouri Light Artillery 251
St Louis Grays 251
St Louis Artillery 250–1
Washington Blues 251
Moore, Colonel John C. 217
Moore, Governor A.B. 181–5
Moore, Henry Augustus 167
Morgan, John Hunt 255

National Lancers 46
Neckties 70
North Carolina Regiments
1st Regiment N.C. Cavalry 244
1st Regiment N.C. Volunteers 244
33rd Regiment N.C. Troops 246
36th Regiment N.C. Troops 269
58th Regiment N.C. Troops 269
6th Regiment N.C. Troops 246
14th Regiment N.C. Troops 244
North Carolina Companies
Buncombe Rangers 244
Buncombe Rifles 243
Caldwell Rough and Ready Boys 244
Charlotte Grays 243
Edgecombe Guards 243
Enfield Rifles 244
Guilford Grays 244
Iredell Blues 243
LaFayette Light Infantry 244
Lincoln Guards 244
Montgomery Grays 244
Moore's Creek Rifle Guards 244
Mountain Tigers 244
Orange Light Infantry 243
Poplar Spring Grays 244
Southern Stars 244
Thomasville Rifles 244

Oil cloth covers 31
Orange Blossoms, 124th New York Volunteer Infantry 84
Osborn & Durbec 155
Overcoats 29–30, 57, 59

Pea Ridge 250
Perry, Governor Madison S. 175
Pettus, Governor John J. 165, 172
Pill box hats 70
Pistols 64
Ponchos 29
Prim, General 90

Quartermasters Department 17–19

Regular United States Army's Regiment of
    Voltigeur 161
Republic of South Carolina 142
Rhode Island Detached Militia 124
Ringgold caps 72
Rush, Colonel 63, 66
Rush's Lancers 66, 68, 72
Russell, William H. 144
Russian shoulder knots 65, 73, 76

Sabres 64
Sack coats 24–5, 44
Saddles 62, 64
Sashes 35, 74, 83–4
Schuyllkill Arsenal 17, 19
Seminole war 43
Shakos 18, 96, 105, 119
Shell jackets 46, 48, 57–60, 64–6, 70, 72
Shenandoah Valley 70
Sherman, General William Tecumsheh 10–11, 13
Shirts 24, 27, 110
Shoulder scales 47–8, 66
Signal Corps 83
Slouch hats 33, 45
Socks 27–8
South Carolina
    17th Regiment of Infantry 142
    1st Regiment of Artillery 142
    1st Regiment of Infantry 160
    1st Regiment of Rifles 142, 144
    1st Regiment of Rifles, South Carolina
        Volunteers 162
    1st Regiment, South Carolina Artillery 159
    20th South Carolina Volunteers 162
    2nd South Carolina Volunteers (Kershaw's)
        163
    3rd Regiment., South Carolina Artillery 159
    1st South Carolina Volunteers 154, 160
    7th South Carolina Cavalry 159
    7th South Carolina Volunteers (Bacon's) 159
    Charleston Fire Department 155
    Corps of Military Engineers 159
    Dismounted Dragoon Battalion 159
    Gregg's 1st South Carolina 161
    Hagood's 1st South Carolina Volunteers 158
    Hampton Legion 159, 161
    Holcombe Legion 160
    Industrial School for Girls 160
    Regular Army of South Carolina 159
    Uniform and Dress of the Officers of the
        Volunteer 158

South Carolina Military Companies
    Ætna Guards 144, 155
    Beaufort Volunteer Artillery 155
    Brooks Grays 159
    Cadet Riflemen 144
    Carolina Light Infantry 144
    Charleston Light Dragoons 158
    Charleston Riflemen 142
    Charleston Zouave Cadets 144
    Davis Guards 159
    German Artillery 155
    Gist Riflemen 159
    Keowee Riflemen 157
    Meagher Guard 142
    Moultrie Guards 142
    Palmetto Guard 142, 155
    Pee Dee Rifles 159
    Phoenix Rifles 155
    Richland Volunteer Rifle Company 159
    Rutledge Mounted Riflemen 142
    South Carolina Zouave Volunteers 159
    Southern Guards 159
    Union Light Infantry 154–5
    Vigilant Rifles 142
    Washington Light Infantry 157, 161
    Camden Volunteers 163
    Edgefield Riflemen 160
    Edisto Rifles 159
Spangler's Spring 36
Springfield rifle musket 40, 42–3
Spurs 64
Starke, Colonel W.E. 267
State troops 113–24
Stevens, Captain C.A. 80–1
Stirrups 64
Sword knot 57, 64
Swords 60

Talmas 59, 62. 70
Taylor, General Richard 208
Tennessee
    12th Tennessee Infantry 242
    154th Regiment of Tennessee 238
    1st Company, Tennessee Artillery Corps 242
    1st Tennessee Volunteer Infantry 240
    23rd Tennessee Infantry 240
    2nd Tennesse Field Battery 242
    37th Tennessee Infantry 241
    3rd (Memphis) Tennessee Battalion 241
    3rd Tennessee Infantry 241
    45th Tennessee Infantry 240
    55th Tennessee Infantry 242
    6th Battalion Tennessee Cavalry 242

    6th Tennessee Infantry 242
    A Digest of the Militia Laws of Tennessee 240
    Military and Financial Board of the State of
        Tennessee 242
    Turney's 1st Tennessee Volunteers 238–9
Tennessee Military Companies
    Beauregards 236, 238
    Bluff City Grays 238
    Boon's Creek Minute Men 240
    Crocket Rangers 239
    Fayetteville Guard 240
    Garibaldi Guards 238
    Henry Guards 238
    Hickory Rifles 238
    Highland Guard 238
    Jackson Grays 242
    Jackson Guards 238
    Maury Grays 241
    McNairy Guards 238
    Memphis Light Guard 238
    Memphis Zouaves 238
    Rock City Guard 239–40
    Sons of Liberty 226, 238
    The Danes 242
    Tullahoma Guards 240
Texas
    12th Texas Cavalry 213
    13th Texas Cavalry 218
    14th Cavalry Battalion Partisan Rangers 218
    16th Texas Infantry 218
    18th Texas Cavalry 215, 217–8
    1st Regiment Galveston Volunteers 210
    1st Texas Infantry 212–6
    27th Texas Cavalry 213
    2nd Cavalry Regiment (Pyron's) 218
    2nd Mounted Riflemen 217
    2nd Texas Infantry 217
    3rd Texas Cavalry 211
    3rd Texas Infantry 218
    4th Texas Infantry 215
    5th Texas Cavalry 213
    8th Texas Cavalry 212
    9th Texas Cavalry 218
    Bate's Battalion (Brazoria Coast Regiment),
        Texas 218
    Committee of Public Safety 210
Texas Military Companies
    Alamo Rifles 210
    Bastrop County Rawhides 213
    Bayou City Guard 217
    Crockett Southrons 214
    Dixie Blues 217
    Galveston Artillery 210

Galveston Zouaves 210
Grimes County Grays 216
Grimes County Rangers 213
Henderson Guards 216
Texas Invincibles 214
Lane Rangers 210
Lone Star Company 210
Lone Star Defenders 211
Lone Star Rifles 210, 212
Milam County Grays 217
Milam Rifles 210
Porter Guards 216
Reagan Guards 214
Refugio Riflemen 210
Sandy Point Mounted Rifles 216
Star Rifles 210, 213, 215
Texas Polk Rifles 217
Tom Green Rifles 215–6
Tom Lubbock Rangers 212
Turner Rifles 210
Washington Light Guards 210
Wigfall Guards 210
Textile Mills
Barnett Micon & Company 185, 270
Belville Factory 192
Bonsack & Whitmore 224
Crenshaw Woollen Mill 224, 226–7
Eagle Factory, Columbus 192, 270
Eagle Manufacturing Company 185, 246
Ivy Woollen Mill 270
Kelly's Mills 229
Kelly, Tackett & Ford of Manchester 224
Kent, Paine & Co. 224
Milledgeville Manufacturing Co. 192
Phillips, Fariss & Company 270, 185
Prattville Manufacturing Company 185
Rock Island Mills 155, 159, 242, 246
Scotsville Manufacturing Company 224
Swartz Woollen Mills 224, 229
Sweetwater Factory 270
Wilkinson Manufacturing Company 172
Tilghman, Brigadier-General Floyd 173
Twiggs, General David E. 210
Tiffany & Co. 70
Tirailleurs Algeriens 95
Tombeaux 88, 90, 92, 108, 110
Trousers 24, 26, 28, 30, 36, 39, 44, 59, 64–6, 70
Turbans 87, 90, 93

Uniforms
bearskin caps 251
dress cap 217, 220–1, 231, 240, 244, 251
fatigue jacket 218, 220–1, 223

forage cap 155, 158–60, 163, 220–27, 230, 234, 236–7
frock coat 144, 154–5, 157–68, 173, 177, 179, 214–23
frock shirts 182
Georgia-pattern jacket 190
guerrilla shirt 253
Hardee hat 213, 217, 222–8, 234, 238–9, 239–40, 244, 250, 255
hunting shirt 212–13
jambiere 154
Mexican War-pattern cap 180
overshirt 212–4, 217
plastron 224, 242, 244
pompon 116, 220–3
sack coats 120, 155, 175, 189, 216–7
serouel 204
'Sicilian' cap 177, 184, 189, 192, 206
tail-coat 222–3
Tricorne hats 168, 202

U.S. Marine Corps 76

Veteran Reserve Corps 79, 83
Virginia Regiments
11th Virginia 224–6
11th Virginia Infantry 224–5, 228
13th Virginia Cavalry 227
15th Virginia Infantry 226
16th Regiment, Virginia Militia 222
179th Regiment Virginia Militia 226
18th Virginia Infantry 222
1st Regiment of Volunteers 219
21st Virginia Infantry 257
2nd Battalion of Virginia Voluteers 219
2nd Virginia Cavalry 226–8
3rd Virginia Cavalry 229
44th Virginia Infantry 226, 229
4th Virginia Cavalry 229
6th Virginia Cavalry 227
Drum Corps 223
Military Institute 232
Virginia Military Companies
Amelia Light Dragoons 227
Danville Blues 222
Drum Corps 223
Fireside Protectors 220, 226
Little Fork Rangers 229
Loudon Light Horse 227
Lynchburg Beauregards 226
Mountain Rangers 227
Old Dominion Dragoons 229
Prince William Cavalry 229

Richmond Howitzers 221
Richmond Mounted City Guard 220
Richmond Zouaves 230
Sussex Light Dragoons 227
Virginia Life Guard 226
Wise Troop 227
Coleman Guards 222
Company G 221
F Company 217
Fincastle Rifles 226
Fredericksburg Rifle Grays 222
Home Guard 224
Loudon Cavalry 227
Lynchburg Artillery 226
Lynchburg Home Guard 228
Lynchburg Rifle Grays 225, 228
Lynchburg Rifles 224–5
Montgomery Guard 220
Old Dominion Guard 223
Richmond City Guard 220
Richmond Grays 219–20, 223
Richmond Light Infantry Blues 221
Sons of Liberty 226, 239
Southern Guards 225–6
Washington Guards 222
Woodis Riflemen 222
Virginia State Line 230

Wallace, Colonel Lew 90
War Department 46, 61–2
Wayne, General Henry C. 189
West Florida Seminary 174
Wheat, Chatham Roberdeau 206, 208
Whipple hats 62, 120
Wilder's Mounted Brigade 60
Wilson's Creek 235, 250
Winslow, Captain Cleveland 44
Wolverines 70

Zarvona, Colonel Richard Thomas 259
Zouaves 86–112